CONSPIRACY FACTS:

NEOCONS UNMASKED

By **Cushman Cunningham**

ACKNOWLEDGEMENT

Reading most dedications I would question in my own mind if the person's wife or helpmate was truly as important to the completion of the publication as the author stated. In this instance there are few words that can describe the importance of **PHYLLIS JANET MARINO** to the completion of this writing. Her continuing criticism, enthusiasm, corrections, redrafting perseverance, encouragement and every imaginable secretarial skill were instrumental in bringing this book to its level of expertise. It is absolute to say that I could not have achieved this critical commentary without her help and devotion.

Publisher, Jon Larsen Shudlick

On the Cover: Original mask of Guy Fawkes from the film V for Vendetta at the Musée des miniatures et décors de cinéma in Lyon, France. By Enrique Dans from Madrid, Spain (We are legion Uploaded by SunOfErat) [CC BY 2.0 (http://creativecommons.org/licenses/by/2.0)], via Wikimedia Commons

Publisher Contact Information:

CRITICAL THINKING INSTITUTE
P.O. Box 50009
Fort Myers, FL 33994
E-Mail: shud21@comcast.net
Telephone: 239-218-4028
Cover Design and Book Layout by Linda Leppert
To order additional copies or bulk orders call: 239-218-4028
ISBN: 978-0-9909873-3-8
Library of Congress Control Number: 2016931687
This book is printed in the United States of America

The publisher, Jon Larsen Shudlick, is a former Army Chief Investigator and former five term mayor of Ocean Ridge, Florida.

PUBLISHER'S STATEMENT

The author and publisher of this critical manuscript both realize the controversial nature of these topics. Therefore, we suggest and request that you research these subjects on your own with all due diligence.

A most important aspect of education that our government educational system is remiss from emphasizing is the concept of **thinking critically** or **critical thinking**. Critical thinking means you question what you hear and read. Teaching itself should help you understand **how to think**, not what to think. Asking questions like who, what, where,when, why or how after reading a subject and then interpreting on your own, leads you to **thinking critically** or **critical thinking**. Today with vast information available at your fingertips through the Internet, Wikipedia, CD's, books, magazines, a variety of newspapers, journals and so many different points of reference there is really no reason not to be knowledgeable about any topic you wish to pursue.

Unfortunately, the present social engineering educational agenda is **unacceptable, inferior and a complete failure**. Our government educational system has plunged our country into third world status, falling from a rank of **4th** among industrialized nations to **34th!!!** My friend, author, Jim Anderson states, "Our country has become nothing more than a third world country with the bomb." If you use your own ability to **think critically** and follow up on topics important to you and your future you can be much more confident in your own ideas and attitudes. With that knowledge and self-reliance you can achieve unlimited success.

This book is dedicated to the memory of a Great Populist...

My Struggle

By **Willis A. Carto**

"Nothing is more important than true history."

Willis A. Carto

I, Willis Carto, was born in 1926 in historic Fort Wayne, Indiana, to Willis Frank Carto, 22, of Huguenot descent, and Dorothy Louise Allison Carto, 21. My paternal grandmother, Lillian Hite, was of German blood. Her parents arrived in Indiana (then considered the Wild West) in a covered wagon.

My dad, who sold paper to printers in the area, got me interested in printing, and I learned to set type by hand and to use the linotype machine. I had a job at the Ideal Printing Co. under boss Claude Bishop after school.

My whole family would listen to the radio broadcasts of Fr. Coughlin and discuss them afterward—my first contact with the so-called right wing.

I became interested in newspapers, thanks primarily to my hero Col. Robert R. McCormick, the owner and editor of the highly nationalist newspaper *The Chicago Tribune*, which at that time boasted a daily circulation of 1 million in what McCormick described as "Chicagoland." It was thrilling to visit the Trbune Tower when the presses were running and the papers were rolling off as the ground trembled.

While still in high school I started my own small paper called *The Canteen Chronicle.*

Soon after graduation I tried to join the Navy to participate in Franklin Roosevelt's war (WWII) but was rejected because of a small wart on my arm they called "muluscum contagioso," which soon disappeared of its own accord. I was drafted and was shot by a Japanese sniper but survived. Another time a Japanese soldier threw a grenade at my squad. It went off, but marvelously no one was harmed—a rare occurrence. I attained the rank of corporal and won the Purple Heart.

For a few years after World War II I traveled the country and got to know more about my fellow Americans, white and black, nationwide, while distributing free samples of soap house to house.

In 1952 I launched my political career, going to work for Aldrich Blake and an activist group he established called America Plus, which soon evolved into Liberty and Property.

On Oct. 1, 1955 I started a monthly anti-communist newsletter: *Right: The National Journal of Forward-Looking Americanism.*

Shown above is Willis Carto *(center) flanked by two people for whom he had great respect. They are (left) filmmaker Tito Howard, whose video on the attack on the USS Liberty helped break down the wall of censorship surrounding the event and (right) Phil Tourney, a survivor of the Liberty attack who has been a tireless advocate for those slain and wounded in the assault.*

By the late 1950s it was clear to me a new organization was needed to get the right wing together, and the idea of a lobby for liberty—Liberty Lobby, headquartered in Washington, D.C.—began to crystallize and became a reality.

Over the decades I have launched or continued numerous periodical publications and published more than 200 books, and I'm publishing more every year. Most important in the early days were the monthly *American Mercury* and a book publishing house, Noontide Press, both on the West Coast. In 1975, Liberty Lobby initiated a weekly tabloid newspaper called *The Spotlight*, providing the only real news in hard copy in the land. It was the first medium of note to shine a light on the secretive Bilderberg group, among many other important topics. The paper attained a circulation of 300,000-400,000. My position has been consistently America first, not Israel or any foreign country.

The Israelis literally control America's media—all except a few of us. My relatively new weekly newspaper *American Free Press (AFP)*—the successor to *The Spotlight*—and my bimonthly journal of authentic history and nationalist thought *The Barnes Review (TBR)*, and a few other patriotic, independent publications around the country are not controlled by the Israelis. They control our Congress—and I've spent most of my life fighting this, or at least making the situation known to the American people.

No man in the world is more responsible than Willis Carto *for the success of The Holocaust Revisionist movement. Here Willis is shown at a conference he organized to promote the work of some of the world's top Holocaust scholars. From left to right (front row) are pictured American execution expert Fred Leuchter, Swiss researcher Juergen Graf, Holocaust "denier" Russ Granata and Australia's Dr. Fredrick Töben. Back row, from left to right are pictured chemist and publisher Germar Rudolf, engineer Richard Krege and a beaming Willis Carto.*

We have become obsessed with a guilt complex—much of it stemming from the alleged "holocaust" or extermination of "6 million" Jews, which never happened, in National Socialist Germany. Like a metastasizing cancer, this guilt complex spreads to cover every other "victim group" under the Sun: blacks, American Indians, women or what have you. Actually, along with alert scholars such as Dr. Kevin McDonald, I consider whites the most victimized group in the country, but it has become "politically incorrect" to point this out—which is itself part of the victmization.

***This photograph** was taken of Willis Carto while emceeing one of his many free speech conferences. Willis was sharp as a tack until the day he died, his mind constantly focused on getting more subscribers for **AFP** and his history magazine **The Barnes Review**. As one much younger employee once remarked: "Even at his age, Willis can still out-run me up the stairs." Father Time, however, caught up with the hard-driving Carto. He passed away on October 26, 2015.*

For several years, my allies and I had a revived national Populist Party going, but it was an uphill battle, with many right wingers being neutralized by pseudoconservatives like President Ronald Reagan.

There was also the problem of hostile infiltrators in the Populist Party, and in the Institute for Historical Review (IHR). The IHR was an outfit I founded in 1978, designed to promote authentic history and debunk establishment lies about our past.

The IHR published a periodical, *The Journal of Historical Review (JHR)*, but because of subversion the IHR and JHR fizzled out. Since the JHR was being destroyed by these dubious characters, I started TBR to carry on its good work. Nothing is more important than true history.

After a few years, the destruction extended to Liberty Lobby and its publication *The Spotlight*, so I started a new weekly newspaper, *American Free Press*, also in tabloid format to take its place. AFP has proved a great success.

At one point, by 1995, TBR achieved a circulation of 11,000.

AFP and TBR have continued publishing right up to the present day, and hopefully will continue for many years to come, although it is hard slogging, bucking the establishment. The editors of the two publications are: myself of course, Paul Angel (AFP & TBR), John Tiffany (both), Pete Papaherakles (both), Chris Petherick (AFP) and Ron Ray (both), with key office assistance from Julia Foster, Jeanette Kimble and others. We have had many exciting years exposing authentic history (I like to call it Revisionism) and the real news, as well as giving our readers great information about good health, and we look forward to many yet to come, although we are currently feeling quite a pinch from the continuing depression caused by the privately owned "Federal" Reserve Bank.

I also have established an Internet presence, and an Internet radio program called "Hot Button Debates," hosted by David Gahary, where no holds are barred.

In sum, I hope that I have been influential in the populist movement nationwide and even abroad. I only wish I could do even more to save Western civilization, Christianity and the white race.

***Willis trudges through** two and a half feet of snow in front of the old American Free Press Headquarters on Capitol Hill to make it to a Jim Traficant town hall meeting in Washington, D.C. When informed of Traficant's death last November, Carto commented: "There goes one of the few honest politicians I've ever met. We'll never see the likes of him again." And the same can be said of Carto, himself, who was most assuredly one of a kind.*

STATEMENT OF AUTHENTICITY

Included in this volume are several stories, articles and blogs I feel you as the reader will find stunningly important in your personal search for truth. Each of these writers have spent considerable time researching, editing and proofing their material. Without their conscientious and meticulous searching for the truth the information which they present here would not appear in this publication.

As the publisher, my hope is that inserting the many visuals such as maps, graphs, photos and captions will further educate the readers. Graphics and formatting of photos, maps, etc. were inserted by Linda Leppert.

Ground your intellect in truth.

FAIL, LEARN, GROW, REPEAT

Honor is a gift man gives himself.

Jon Larsen Shudlick, biographer, publisher, author

CONTENTS

The core of this book is an exposé of the Secret Empire—a two-tiered beast, with a Khazarian base and a small Black Nobility elite at the top. The Khazarians launched a massive invasion of the United States from their home base in Eastern Europe beginning about 1880. This invasion is recounted very well by Colonel John Beatty in his classic The Iron Curtain Over America. A segment of the Black Nobility have been in North America even before there was a United States, and they have been plotting the demise of the Republic since day one.

The Secret Empire is the world's foremost problem. It has almost limitless wealth but no morals. It is composed of absolute Machiavellian criminals who are hellbent on imposing a global dictatorship, with them—the Chosen People—running the show. They are the ones behind the murders of President Kennedy, Robert Kennedy, John Kennedy, Jr., Martin Luther King., Jr., 34 sailors aboard the U.S.S. Liberty, and 3,000 people in the false flag attacks of 9-11. They are also orchestrating the relentless spate of mass shootings in a desperate attempt to create a pretext for the total disarmament of the American people. If that were to happen, then the already prepared concentration camps would start to fill up. By their fruits you shall know them! This book is a wake up call to all Americans who wish to preserve our priceless heritage of freedom.

George D. Larson, PhD, History
January 25, 2016

Introduction

IGNORANCE DESTROYED

Who controls the media?

By **Jon Larsen Shudlick**

It is important for us to realize there are only six major corporations that control 85% of the media information. These include all news, headlines, sports, National Geographic, TruTV, BET, CMT, Speed Channel, NFL, FOX Sports, Mapquest and Syfy to name just a few. The major news networks produce mostly all the same stories on any given night. The only difference is possibly the sequence of those news reports.

Now, how do we find out what else actually is happening in the world?

If you are reading this paragraph you are certainly intelligent enough to make your own decisions in life. I submit that if you are shown the truth about major events you can make much better decisions. It is rough sometimes as an individual to get over the deep personal prejudices, which we all have, and look outside the box of the Controlled Major Mass Media (CMMM) which propagandizes their self-serving agenda 24/7. **The only real TRUTH, in my opinion, comes from the free Internet.** Nevertheless, there has to be a combination of information sources if people want to know the truth. We all have access to thousands of different apps. I prefer to receive most of my information from several alternate sources because I do not believe that any one app has a monopoly on the truth. The Drudge Report, Veterans Today, infowars.com, Popular Liberty, Lew Rockwell and shadowstats.com are a few of the many apps that are available for truth seekers. Any eight year old who searches the Internet on a variety of topics knows more truth or at least will come across more truth than one will ever find on the Controlled Major Mass Media (CMMM).

The amazing point which all must understand is that you as an individual are not stupid and therefore you do not have to be ignorant.

Ignorance is just lack of knowledge. The majority of people today who follow the Controlled Major Mass Media (CMMM) are truly ignorant. **"You don't *know* what you don't know."** If your talking points only come from the national leaders of the political parties that are strictly agenda driven you won't know anything more than what they want you to profess. That is why your creative thoughts and your personal intelligence building will only expand by using a free Internet. Sir Timothy John Berners-Lee gave us the World Wide Web. He could have kept it for his own financial benefit however, he gave it away to every single human being on this planet so we all could help eradicate ignorance. You must do your part!

Let's take the challenge!

I double-dare you to be a better thinker than you are now, less ignorant than you are now and more knowledgeable than you are now. I challenge you for one month to follow some of the apps that I have mentioned above or those that you find for yourself on any topic of interest to you, just to see how much new information you can learn. True knowledge is the **power of one** individual. God gave you a human brain. He gave you that intelligence so you can use it like in Luke 19: 12-27 where God wants you to multiply you talents. Under no circumstances are you to blame your environment, your parents, your friends or your teachers if you cannot improve your knowledge with the multitude of apps that are available to you. The challenge is there. I really have no concern as to where you stand politically whether it is to the left or to the right on the political spectrum. A more knowledgeable and intelligent acting country is of benefit to all its citizens.

God bless America!

Who Owns The Media?
The 6 Monolithic Corporations That Control Almost Everything We Watch, Hear And Read

By Michael Snyder – October 23, 2014

GE	**NEWS-CORP**	**DISNEY**	**VIACOM**	**TIME WARNER**	**CBS**
Notable Properties:	Notable Properties:	Notable Properties:	Notable Properties:	Notable Properties:	Notable Properties:
Comcast	FOX	ABC	MTV	CNN	Showtime
NBC	Wall Street Journal	ESPN	Nick Jr	HBO	Smithsonian Channel
Universal Pictures	New York Post	Pixar	BET	Time	NFL.com
Focus Features		Miramax	CMT	Warner Bros	Jeopardy
		Marvel Studios	Paramount Pictures		60 Minutes

Back in 1983, approximately 50 corporations controlled the vast majority of all news media in the United States. Today, ownership of the news media has been concentrated in the hands of just six incredibly powerful media corporations. These corporate behemoths control most of what we watch, hear and read every single day. They own television networks, cable channels, movie studios, newspapers, magazines, publishing houses, music labels and even many of our favorite websites. Sadly, most Americans don't even stop to think about who is feeding them the endless hours of news and entertainment that they constantly ingest. Most Americans don't really seem to care about who owns the media. But they should. The truth is that each of us is **deeply** influenced by the messages that are constantly being pounded into our heads by the mainstream media. The average American watches 153 hours of television a month. In fact, most Americans begin to feel physically uncomfortable if they go too long without watching or listening to something. Sadly, most Americans have become absolutely addicted to news and entertainment and the ownership of all that news and entertainment that we crave is being concentrated in fewer and fewer hands each year.

The six corporations that collectively control U.S. media today are Time Warner, Walt Disney, Viacom, Rupert Murdoch's News Corp., CBS Corporation and NBC Universal. Together, the "big six" absolutely dominate news and entertainment in the United States. But even those areas of the media that the "big six" do not completely control are becoming increasingly concentrated. For example, Clear Channel now owns over 1000 radio stations across the United States. Companies like Google, Yahoo and Microsoft are increasingly dominating the Internet.

But it is the "big six" that are the biggest concerns. When you control what Americans watch, hear and read you gain a great deal of control over what they think. They don't call it "programming" for nothing.

Back in 1983 it was bad enough that about 50 corporations dominated U.S. media. But since that time, power over the media has rapidly become concentrated in the hands of fewer and fewer people …

> **In 1983, fifty corporations dominated most of every mass medium and the biggest media merger in history was a $340 million deal. … [I]n 1987, the fifty companies had shrunk to twenty-nine. … [I]n 1990, the twenty-nine had shrunk to twenty three. … [I]n 1997, the biggest firms numbered ten and involved the $19 billion Disney-ABC deal, at the time the biggest media merger ever. … [In 2000] AOL Time Warner's $350 billion merged corporation [was] more than 1,000 times larger [than the biggest deal of 1983].**
>
> – **Ben H. Bagdikian,** The Media Monopoly, Sixth Edition, (Beacon Press, 2000), pp. xx—xxi

Today, six colossal media giants tower over all the rest. Much of the information in the chart below comes from mediaowners.com. The chart below reveals only a small fraction of the media outlets that these six behemoths actually own …

TIME WARNER

Home Box Office (HBO)
Time Inc.
Turner Broadcasting System, Inc.
Warner Bros. Entertainment Inc.
CW Network (partial ownership)
TMZ
New Line Cinema
Time Warner Cable
Cinemax
Cartoon Network
TBS
TNT
America Online
MapQuest
Moviefone
Castle Rock
Sports Illustrated
Fortune
Marie Claire
People Magazine

WALT DISNEY

ABC Television Network
Disney Publishing
ESPN Inc.
Disney Channel
SOAPnet
A&E
Lifetime
Buena Vista Home Entertainment
Buena Vista Theatrical Productions
Buena Vista Records
Disney Records
Hollywood Records
Miramax Films
Touchstone Pictures
Walt Disney Pictures
Pixar Animation Studios
Buena Vista Games
Hyperion Books

VIACOM

Paramount Pictures
Paramount Home Entertainment
Black Entertainment Television (BET)
Comedy Central
Country Music Television (CMT)
Logo
MTV
MTV Canada
MTV2
Nick Magazine
Nick at Nite
Nick Jr.
Nickelodeon
Noggin
Spike TV
The Movie Channel
TV Land
VH1

NEWS CORPORATION

Dow Jones & Company, Inc.
Fox Television Stations
The New York Post
Fox Searchlight Pictures
Beliefnet
Fox Business Network
Fox Kids Europe
Fox News Channel
Fox Sports Net
Fox Television Network
FX
My Network TV
MySpace
News Limited News
Phoenix InfoNews Channel
Phoenix Movies Channel
Sky PerfecTV
Speed Channel
STAR TV India
STAR TV Taiwan
STAR World
Times Higher Education Supplement Magazine
Times Literary Supplement Magazine
Times of London
20th Century Fox Home Entertainment
20th Century Fox International
20th Century Fox Studios
20th Century Fox Television
BSkyB
DIRECTV
The Wall Street Journal
Fox Broadcasting Company
Fox Interactive Media
FOXTEL
HarperCollins Publishers
The National Geographic Channel
National Rugby League
News Interactive
News Outdoor
Radio Veronica
ReganBooks
Sky Italia
Sky Radio Denmark
Sky Radio Germany
Sky Radio Netherlands
STAR
Zondervan

CBS CORPORATION

CBS News
CBS Sports
CBS Television Network
CNET
Showtime
TV.com
CBS Radio Inc. (130 stations)
CBS Consumer Products
CBS Outdoor
CW Network (50% ownership)
Infinity Broadcasting
Simon & Schuster (Pocket Books, Scribner)
Westwood One Radio Network

NBC UNIVERSAL

Bravo
CNBC
NBC News
MSNBC
NBC Sports
NBC Television Network
Oxygen
SciFi Magazine
Syfy (Sci Fi Channel)
Telemundo
USA Network
Weather Channel
Focus Features
NBC Universal Television Distribution
NBC Universal Television Studio
Paxson Communications (partial ownership)
Trio
Universal Parks & Resorts
Universal Pictures
Universal Studio Home Video

These gigantic media corporations do not exist to objectively tell the truth to the American people. Rather, the primary purpose of their existence is to make money.

These gigantic media corporations are not going to do anything to threaten their relationships with their biggest advertisers (such as the largest pharmaceutical companies that literally spend billions on advertising), and one way or another these gigantic media corporations are always going to express the ideological viewpoints of their owners.

Fortunately, an increasing number of Americans are starting to wake up and are realizing that the mainstream media should not be trusted. According to a new poll just released by Gallup, the number of Americans that have little to no trust in the mainstream media (57%) is at an all-time high.

That is one reason why we have seen the alternative media experience such rapid growth over the past few years. The mainstream media has been losing credibility at a staggering rate, and Americans are starting to look elsewhere for the truth about what is really going on.

Do you think that anyone in the mainstream news would actually tell you that the Federal Reserve is bad for America or that we are facing a horrific derivatives bubble that could destroy the entire world financial system? Do you think that anyone in the mainstream media would actually tell you the truth about the deindustrialization of America or the truth about the voracious greed of Goldman Sachs?

Sure there are a few courageous reporters in the mainstream media that manage to slip a few stories past their corporate bosses from time to time, but in general there is a very clear understanding that there are simply certain things that you just do not say in the mainstream news.

But Americans are becoming increasingly hungry for the truth, and they are becoming increasingly dissatisfied with the dumbed down pablum that is passing as "hard hitting news" these days.

"In regard to propaganda the early advocates of universal literacy and a free press envisioned only two possibilities: the propaganda might be true or it might be false. They did not foresee what in fact has happened, above all in our western capitalist democracies-the development of a vast communications industry, concerned in the main with neither the true nor the false, but with the unreal, the more or less irrelevant. In a word, they failed to take into account man's almost infinite appetite for distractions."

ALDOUS HUXLEY, 1958, IN THE ARTICLE THE CAPITALIST FREE PRESS

Michael Snyder | Editor
The Economic Collapse Blog

Michael originally published this article in 2010, but it is such an important message that I decided to reprint it. In the four years that have since passed there has been no progress worth speaking of. Please note that the graphic above the article does not quite match Michael's list. General Electric has sold it's stake in NBC. Even though things change, they somehow remain the same. General Electric sold its interest in NBCUniversal to Comcast last year. GE is the former majority shareholder in Comcast so the control continues to remain in the hands of the same big dysfunctional family.

TRUTH

READ THE TRUTH

HEAR THE TRUTH

SEE THE TRUTH

LEARN THE TRUTH

Truth Is Our Country

By **Paul Craig Roberts**

PaulCraigRoberts.org

March 17, 2015

Press Club of Mexico Awards PCR International Medal for Journalism Excellence

Last week in Mexico at the annual awards conference of the Club De Periodistas De Mexico I was given the International Award For Excellence In Journalism. In my speech I emphasized that Truth is the country of real journalists. Unlike presstitutes, the loyalty of real journalists is to Truth, not to a government or corporate advertiser. Once a journalist sacrifices Truth to loyalty to a government, he ceases to be a journalist and becomes a propagandist.

The speech is published in English and Spanish here: http://vocesdelperiodista.mx/nacional/discurso-completo-del-doctor-paul-craig-roberts-ingles-y-espanol/

The translators missed a few bits. Here is the intact speech:

Colleagues,

Thank you for this recognition, for this honor. As Jesus told the people of Nazareth, a prophet is without honor in his own country. In the United States, this is also true of journalists.

In the United States journalists receive awards for lying for the government and for the corporations. Anyone who tells the truth, whether journalist or whistleblower, is fired or prosecuted or has to hide out in the Ecuadoran Embassy in London, like Julian Assange, or in Moscow, like Edward Snowden, or is tortured and imprisoned, like Bradley Manning.

Mexican journalists pay an even higher price. Those who report on government corruption and on the drug cartels pay with their lives. The Internet encyclopedia, Wikipedia, has as an entry a list by name of journalists murdered in Mexico. This is the List of Honor. Wikipedia reports than more than 100 Mexican journalists have been killed or disappeared in the 21st century.

Despite intimidation the Mexican press has not abandoned its job. Because of your courage, I regard this award bestowed on me as the greatest of honors.

In the United States real journalists are scarce and are becoming more scarce. Journalists have morphed into a new creature. Gerald Celente calls US journalists "presstitutes," a word formed from press prostitute. In other words, journalists in the United States are whores for the government and for the corporations.

The few real journalists that remain are resigning. Last year Sharyl Attkisson, a 21-year veteran reporter with CBS resigned on the grounds that it had become too much of a fight to get truth reported. She was frustrated that CBS saw its purpose to be a protector of the powerful, not a critic.

Recently Peter Oborne, the UK Telegraph's chief political commentator, explained why he resigned. His stories about the wrongdoings of the banking giant, HSBC, were spiked, because HSBC is an important advertiser for the Telegraph. Osborne says: "The coverage of HSBC in Britain's Telegraph is a fraud on its readers. If major newspapers allow corporations to influence their content for fear of losing advertising revenue, democracy itself is in peril." http://www.globalresearch.ca/why-i-have-resigned-from-the-telegraph/5432659

Last summer former New York Times editor Jill Abramson in a speech at the Chautauqua Institution said that the New York Times withheld information at the request of the White House. She said that for a number of years the press in general did not publish any stories that upset the White House. She justified this complete failure of journalism on the grounds that "journalists are Americans, too. I consider myself to be a patriot."

So in the United States journalists lie for the government

because they are patriotic, and their readers and listeners believe the lies because they are patriotic.

Our view differs from the view of the New York Times editor. The view of those of us here today is that our country is not the United States, it is not Mexico, our country is Truth. Once a journalist sacrifices Truth to loyalty to a government, he ceases to be a journalist and becomes a propagandist.

Recently, Brian Williams, the television news anchor at NBC, destroyed his career because he mis-remembered an episode of more than a decade ago when he was covering the Iraq War. He told his audience that a helicopter in which he was with troops in a war zone as a war correspondent was hit by ground fire and had to land.

But the helicopter had not been hit by ground fire. His fellow journalists turned on him, accusing him of lying in order to enhance his status as a war correspondent.

On February 10, NBC suspended Brian Williams for 6 months from his job as Managing Editor and Anchor of NBC Nightly News.

Think about this for a moment. It makes no difference whatsoever whether the helicopter had to land because it had been hit by gun fire or for some other reason or whether it had to land at all. If it was an intentional lie, it was one of no consequence. If it was a mistake, an episode of "false memory," why the excessive reaction? Psychologists say that false memories are common.

The same NBC that suspended Brian Williams and the journalists who accused him of lying are all guilty of telling massive lies for the entirety of the 21st century that have had vast consequences. The United States government has been, and still is, invading, bombing, and droning seven or eight countries on the basis of lies told by Washington and endlessly repeated by the media. Millions of people have been killed, maimed, and displaced by violence based entirely on lies spewing out of the mouths of Washington and its presstitutes.

We know what these lies are: Saddam Hussein's weapons of mass destruction. Assad of Syria's use of chemical weapons. Iranian nukes. Pakistani and Yemeni terrorists. Terrorists in

Somalia. The endless lies about Gaddafi in Libya, about the Taliban in Afghanistan. And now the alleged Russian invasion and annexation of Ukraine.

All of these transparent lies are repeated endlessly, and no one is held accountable. But one journalist mis-remembers one insignificant detail about a helicopter ride and his career is destroyed.

We can safely conclude that the only honest journalism that exists in the United States is provided by alternative media on the Internet.

Consequently, the Internet is now under US government attack. "Truth is the enemy of the state," and Washington intends to shut down truth everywhere.

Washington has appointed Andrew Lack, the former president of NBC News, to be the chief executive of the Broadcasting Board of Governors. His first official statement compared RT, Russia Today, the Russian-based news agency, with the Islamic State and Boko Haram. In other words, Mr. Lack brands RT as a terrorist organization.

The purpose of Andrew Lack's absurd comparison is to strike fear at RT that the news organization will be expelled from US media markets. Andrew Lack's message to RT is: "lie for us or we are going to expel you from our air waves."

The British already did this to Iran's Press TV.

In the United States the attack on Internet independent media is proceeding on several fronts. One is known as the issue of "net neutrality." There is an effort by Washington, joined by Internet providers, to charge sites for speedy access. Bandwidth would be sold for fees. Large media corporations, such as CNN and the New York Times, would be able to pay the prices for a quickly opening website. Smaller independent sites such as mine would be hampered with the slowness of the old "dial-up" type bandwidth. Click on CNN and the site immediately opens. Click on paulcraigroberts.org and wait five minutes.

You get the picture. This is Washington's plan and the corporations' plan for the Internet.

But it gets worse. The Electronic Frontier Foundation, which attempts to defend our digital rights, reports that so-called "free trade agreements," such as the Trans Pacific Partnership (and the Trans Atlantic Partnership) impose prison sentences, massive fines, and property seizures on Internet users who innocently violate vague language in the so-called trade agreements.

Recently, a young American, Barrett Brown, was sentenced to 5 years in prison and a fine of $890,000 for linking to allegedly hacked documents posted on the Internet. Barrett Brown did not hack the documents. He merely linked to an Internet posting, and he has no prospect of earning $890,000 over the course of his life.

The purpose of the US government's prosecution, indeed, persecution, of this young person is to establish the precedent that anyone who uses Internet information in ways that Washington disapproves, or for purposes that Washington disapproves, is a criminal whose life will be ruined. The purpose of Barrett Brown's show trial is to intimidate. It is Washington's equivalent to the murder of Mexican journalists.

But this is prologue. Now we turn to the challenge that Washington presents to the entire world.

It is the nature of government and of technology to establish control. People everywhere face the threat of control by government and technology. But the threat from Washington is much greater. Washington is not content with only controlling the citizens of the United States. Washington intends to control the world.

Michael Gorbachev is correct when he says that the collapse of the Soviet Union was the worst thing that has happened to humanity, because the Soviet collapse removed the only constraint on Washington's power.

The Soviet collapse released a terrible evil upon the world. The neoconservatives in Washington concluded that the failure of communism meant that History has chosen American "democratic capitalism," which is neither democratic nor capitalist, to rule the world. The Soviet collapse signaled "the End of History," by which is meant the end of competition between social, political and economic systems.

The choice made by History elevated the United States

to the pre-eminent position of being the "indispensable and exceptional" country, a claim of superiority. If the United States is "indispensable," then others are dispensable. If the United States is exceptional, then others are unexceptional. We have seen the consequences of Washington's ideology in Washington's destruction of life and stability in the Middle East.

Washington's drive for World Hegemony, based as it is on a lie, makes necessary the obliteration of Truth. As Washington's agenda of supremacy is all encompassing, Washington regards truth as a greater enemy than Russians, Muslim terrorists, and the Islamic State.

As truth is Washington's worst enemy, everyone associated with the truth is Washington's enemy.

Latin America can have no illusions about Washington. The first act of the Obama Regime was to overthrow the democratic reformist government of Honduras. Currently, the Obama Regime is trying to overthrow the governments of Venezuela, Ecuador, Bolivia, and Argentina.

As Mexicans know, in the 19th century Washington stole half of Mexico. Today Washington is stealing the rest of Mexico. The United States is stealing Mexico via financial imperialism, by subordinating Mexican agriculture and self-sustaining peasant agricultural communities to foreign-owned monoculture, by infecting Mexico with Monsanto's GMO's, genetically modified organisms, seeds that do not reproduce, chemicals that destroy the soil and nature's nutrients, seeds that leave Mexico dependent on Monsanto for food crops with reduced nutritional value.

It is easy for governments to sell out their countries to Washington and the North American corporations. Washington and US corporations pay high prices for subservience to their control. It is difficult for countries, small in economic and political influence, to stand against such power. All sorts of masks are used behind which Washington hides US exploitation–globalism, free trade treaties . . .

But the world is changing. Putin has revived Russia, and Russia has proved its ability to stand up to Washington.

On a purchasing power basis, China now has the largest

economy in the world.

As China and Russia are now strategic allies, Washington cannot act against one without acting against the other. The two combined exceed Washington's capabilities.

The United States government has proven to the entire world that it is lawless. A country that flaunts its disrespect of law cannot provide trusted leadership.

My conclusion is that Washington's power has peaked.

Another reason Washington's power has peaked is that Washington has used its power to serve only itself and US corporations. The Rest of the World is dispensable and has been left out.

Washington's power grew out of World War 2. All other economies and currencies were devastated. This allowed Washington to seize the world reserve currency role from Great Britain.

The advantage of being the world reserve currency is that you can pay your bills by printing money. In other words, you can't go broke as long as other countries are willing to hold your fiat currency as their reserves.

But if other countries were to decide not to hold US currency as reserves, the US could go broke suddenly.

Since 2008 the supply of US dollars has increased dramatically in relation to the ability of the real economy to produce goods and services. Whenever the growth of money outpaces the growth of real output, trouble lies ahead. Moreover, Washington's policy of imposing sanctions in an effort to force other countries to do its will is causing a large part of the world known as the BRICS to develop an alternative international payments system.

Washington's arrogance and hubris have caused Washington to ignore the interests of other countries, including those of its allies. Even Washington's European vassal states show signs of developing an independent foreign policy in their approach to Russia and Ukraine. Opportunities will arise for governments to escape from Washington's control and to pursue the interests of their own peoples.

The US media has never performed the function assigned to

it by the Founding Fathers. The media is supposed to be diverse and independent. It is supposed to confront both government and private interest groups with the facts and the truth. At times the US media partially fulfilled this role, but not since the final years of the Clinton Regime when the government allowed six mega-media companies to consolidate 90% of the media in their hands.

The mega-media companies that control the US media are GE, News Corp, Disney, Viacom, Time Warner, and CBS. (GE owns NBC, formerly an independent network. News Corp owns Fox News, the Wall Street Journal, and British newspapers. Disney owns ABC. Time Warner owns CNN.)

The US media is no longer run by journalists. It is run by former government officials and corporate advertising executives. The values of the mega-media companies depend on their federal broadcast licenses. If the companies go against the government, the companies take a risk that their licenses will not be renewed and, thus, the multi-billion dollar values of the companies fall to zero. If media organizations investigate wrongful activities by corporations, they risk the loss of advertising revenues and become less viable.

Ninety percent control of the media gives government a Ministry of Propaganda, and that is what exists in the United States. Nothing reported in the print or TV media can be trusted.

Today there is a massive propaganda campaign against the Russian government. The incessant flow of disinformation from Washington and the media has destroyed the trust between nuclear powers that President Reagan and President Gorbachev worked so hard to create. According to polls, 62% of the US population now regards Russia as the main threat.

I conclude my remarks with the observation that there can be no greater media failure than to bring back the specter of nuclear war. And that is what the US media has achieved.

NEW
NEWS
NOW

"Why a no fly zone? The Caliphate does not have one airplane and zero pilots—please explain the reason for a no fly zone!"

Dr. Adrian H. Krieg

HOT NEWS!

November 27, 2015 Controlled Major Mass Media (CMMM) BLACK OUT!

Israeli Colonel Caught With IS Pants Down

IDF and Mossad just got caught with their hands in a very dirty cookie jar in Syria

By **F. William Engdahl**
New Eastern Outlook
November 27, 2015

This was definitely not supposed to happen. It seems that an Israeli military man with the rank of colonel was "caught with IS pants down." By that I mean he was captured amid a gaggle of so-called IS–or Islamic State or ISIS or DAESH depending on your preference–terrorists, by soldiers of the Iraqi army. Under interrogation by the Iraqi intelligence he apparently said a lot regarding the role of Netanyahu's IDF in supporting IS.

Israeli Colonel Yusi Oulen Shahak

In late October an Iranian news agency, quoting a senior Iraqi intelligence officer, reported the capture of an Israeli army colonel,

Fighters from the Islamic State of Iraq and the Levant (ISIL) marching in Raqqa, Syria.

named Yusi Oulen Shahak, reportedly related to the ISIS Golani Battalion operating in Iraq in the Salahuddin front. In a statement to Iran's semi-official Fars News Agency a Commander of the Iraqi Army stated, "The security and popular forces have held captive an Israeli colonel." He added that the IDF colonel "had participated in the Takfiri ISIL group's terrorist operations." He said the colonel was arrested together with a number of ISIL or IS terrorists, giving the details: "The Israeli colonel's name is Yusi Oulen Shahak and is ranked colonel in Golani Brigade … with the security and military code of Re34356578765az231434."

Why Israel?

Ever since the beginning of Russia's very effective IS bombing of select targets in Syria on September 30, details of the very dirty role of not only Washington, but also NATO member Turkey under President Erdogan, Qatar and other states has come into the sunlight for the first time.

Recep Tayyip Erdoğan, President of Turkey

It's becoming increasingly clear that at least a faction in the Obama Administration has played a very dirty behind-the-scenes role in supporting IS in order to advance the removal of Syrian President Bashar al Assad and pave

Bashar al Assad

the way for what inevitably would be a Libya-style chaos and destruction which would make the present Syrian refugee crisis in Europe a mere warmup by comparison.

The "pro-IS faction" in Washington includes the so-called neo-conservatives centered around disgraced former CIA head and executioner of the Iraqi "surge" General David Petraeus. It also includes US General John R. Allen, who since September 2014 had served as President Obama's Special Presidential Envoy for the Global Coalition to Counter ISIL (Islamic State of Iraq and the Levant) and, until she resigned in February 2013, it included Secretary of State Hillary Clinton.

Gen. David Petraeus

Gen. John R. Allen

Hillary Clinton

Significantly, General John Allen, an unceasing advocate of a US-led "No Fly Zone" inside Syria along the border to Turkey, something President Obama refused, was relieved of his post on 23 October, 2015. That was shortly after launch of the highly-effective Russian strikes on Syrian IS and Al Qaeda's Al Nusra Front terrorist sites changed the entire situation in the geopolitical picture of Syria and the entire Middle East.

UN Reports cites Israel

הליכוד

That Netanyahu's Likud and the Israeli military work closely with Washington's neo-conservative war-hawks is well-established, as is the vehement opposition of Prime Minister Benjamin Netanyahu to Obama's nuclear deal with Iran. Israel regards the Iranian-backed

Shi'a Islamist militant group, Hezbollah, based in Lebanon, as arch foe. Hezbollah has been actively fighting alongside the Syrian Army against ISIS in Syria. General Allen's strategy of "bombings of ISIS" since he was placed in charge of the operation in September 2014, as Russia's Putin and Foreign Minister Lavrov have repeatedly pointed out, far from destroying ISIS in Syria, had vastly expanded their territorial control of the country. Now it becomes clear that that was precisely the intent of Allen and the Washington war faction.

President of Russia Vladimir Putin

Russian Foreign Minister Sergei Lavrov

Since at least 2013 Israeli military have also openly bombed what they claim were Hezbollah targets inside Syria. Investigation revealed that in fact Israel was hitting Syrian military and Hezbollah targets who are valiantly fighting against ISIS and other terrorists. De facto thereby Israel was actually helping ISIS, like General John Allen's year-long "anti-ISIS" bombings.

That a faction in the Pentagon has secretly worked behind-the-scenes to train, arm and finance what today is called ISIS or IS in Syria is now a matter of open record. In August 2012, a Pentagon document classified "Secret," later declassified under pressure of the US NGO Judicial Watch, detailed precisely the emergence of what became the Islamic State or ISIS emerging from the Islamic State in Iraq, then an Al Qaeda affiliate.

The Pentagon document stated, "... there is the possibility of establishing a declared or undeclared Salafist Principality in eastern Syria (Hasaka and Der Zor), and this is exactly what the supporting powers to the opposition [to Assad-w.e.] want, in order to isolate the Syrian regime, which is considered the strategic depth of the Shia expansion (Iraq and Iran)." The supporting powers to the opposition in 2012 then included Qatar, Turkey, Saudi Arabia, the USA and behind-the-scenes, Netanyahu's Israel.

Precisely this creation of a "Salafist Principality in eastern Syria," today's territory of ISIL or IS, was the agenda of Petraeus, General Allen and others in Washington to destroy Assad. It's what put the Obama Administration at loggerhead with Russia, China and Iran over the bizarre US demand Assad must first go before ISIS can be destroyed. Now the game is in the open for the world to see Washington's duplicity in backing what the Russian's accurately call "moderate terrorists" against a duly-elected Assad. That Israel is also in the midst of this rats' nest of opposition terrorist forces in Syria was confirmed in a recent UN report.

What the report did not mention was why Israeli IDF military would have such a passionate interest in Syria, especially Syria's Golan Heights.

Why Israel wants Assad Out

In December, 2014 the Jerusalem Post in Israel reported the findings of a largely ignored, and politically explosive report detailing UN sightings of Israeli military together with ISIS terrorist combatants. The UN peacekeeping force, UN Disengagement Observer Force (UNDOF), stationed since 1974 along the Golan Heights border between Syria and Israel, revealed that Israel had been working closely with Syrian opposition terrorists, including Al Qaeda's Al Nusra Front and IS in the Golan Heights, and "kept close contact over the past 18 months." The report was submitted to the UN

Security Council. Mainstream media in the US and West buried the explosive findings.

The UN documents showed that the Israeli Defense Forces (IDF) were maintaining regular contact with members of the so-called Islamic State since May of 2013. The IDF stated that this was only for medical care for civilians, but the deception was broken when the UNDOF observers identified direct contact between IDF forces and ISIS soldiers, including giving medical care to ISIS fighters. Observations even included the transfer of two crates from the IDF to ISIS forces, the contents of which have not been confirmed. Further the UN report identified what the Syrians label a "crossing point of forces between Israel and ISIS," a point of concern UNDOF brought before the UN Security Council.

The UNDOF was created by a May, 1974 UN Security Council Resolution No. 350 in the wake of tensions from the October 1973 Yom Kippur War between Syria and Israel. It established a buffer zone between Israel and Syria's Golan Heights according to the 1974 Disengagement of Forces Agreement, to be governed and policed by the Syrian authorities. No military forces other than UNDOF are permitted within it. Today it has 1,200 observers.

Hezbollah bandana. | GETTY IMAGES

Since 2013 and the escalation of Israeli attacks on Syria along the Golan Heights, claiming pursuit of "Hezbollah terrorists," the UNDOF itself has been subject to massive attacks by ISIS or Al Qaeda's Al Nusra Front terrorists in the Golan Heights for the first time since 1974, of kidnappings, of killings, of theft of UN weapons and ammunition, vehicles and other assets, and the looting and destruction of facilities. Someone obviously does not want UNDOF to remain policing the Golan Heights.

Israel and Golan Heights Oil

In his November 9 White House meeting with US President

U.S. President Barack Obama and Israeli Prime Minister Benjamin Netanyahu shake hands during their meeting in the Oval Office of the White House in Washington November 9, 2015. | REUTERS/KEVIN LAMARQUE

Obama, Israeli Prime Minister Netanyahu asked Washington to reconsider the fact that since the 1967 Six-Days' War between Israel and the Arab countries, Israel has illegally occupied a significant part of the Golan Heights. In their meeting, Netanyahu, apparently without success, called on Obama to back formal Israeli annexation of the illegally-occupied Golan Heights, claiming that the absence of a functioning Syrian government "allows for different thinking" concerning the future status of the strategically important area.

Of course Netanyahu did not address in any honest way how Israeli IDF and other forces had been responsible for the absence of a functioning Syrian government by their support for ISIS and Al Nusra Front of Al Qaeda.

In 2013, when UNDOF began to document increasing contact between Israeli military and IS and Al Qaeda along the Golan Heights, a little-known Newark, New Jersey oil company, Genie Energy, with an Israeli daughter company, Afek Oil & Gas, began also moving into Golan Heights with permission of the Netanyahu government to explore for oil. That same year Israeli military engineers overhauled the forty-five mile border fence with Syria, replacing it with a steel barricade that included barbed wire, touch sensors, motion detectors, infrared cameras, and ground radar, putting it on par with the Wall Israel has constructed in the West Bank.

Interestingly enough, on October 8, Yuval Bartov, chief geologist from Genie Energy's Israeli subsidiary, Afek Oil & Gas, told Israel's Channel 2 TV that his company had found a major oil reservoir on the Golan Heights: "We've found an oil stratum 350 meters thick in the southern Golan Heights. On average worldwide, strata are 20 to 30 meters thick, and this is 10 times as large as that, so we are talking about significant quantities." As I noted in an earlier article, the International Advisory Board of Genie Energy includes such notorious names as Dick Cheney, former CIA head and infamous neo-con James Woolsey, Jacob Lord Rothschild and others.

Dick Cheney **James Woolsey** **Jacob Lord Rothschild**

Of course no reasonable person in their right mind would suggest there might be a link between Israeli military dealings with the ISIS and other anti-Assad terrorists in Syria, especially in the Golan Heights, and the oil find of Genie Energy in the same place, and with Netanyahu's latest Golan Heights "rethink" appeal to Obama. That would smell too much like "conspiracy theory" and all reasonable people know conspiracies don't exist, only coincidences. Or? In fact, to paraphrase the immortal words of Brad Pitt in the role of West Virginia First Lieutenant Aldo Raine in the final scene of Tarantino's brilliant film, Inglorious Basterds, it seems that 'Ol Netanyahu and his pecker-suckin pals in the IDF and Mossad just got caught with their hands in a very dirty cookie jar in Syria.

Commander Major General Soleimani

Breaking: Russian Pilot Rescued by Iran's General Soleimani

By **GPD** on November 26, 2015

Famed Iranian general was recently targeted by US Navy SEAL team operating inside Syria - confirmed sources

TEHRAN (FNA) – **Russian sources revealed** on Thursday that the co-pilot of the Russian SU-24 jet that was shot down by Turkey over the Syrian airspace on Tuesday was rescued in an operation by Iran's globally renowned IRGC Qods Force Commander Major General Soleimani.

Co-Pilot Captain Konstantin Murahtin

On Tuesday, a Russian Su-24 bomber jet crashed in Syria. Russian President Vladimir Putin said that the plane was downed by an air-to-air missile launched by a Turkish F-16 jet over Syrian territory, falling 4 kilometers (2.5 miles) from the Turkish border.

The crew of the plane ejected and one pilot was killed by fire from the ground, according

An Su-24 in flight.

to the Russian General Staff. The co-pilot Captain Konstantin Murahtin survived. But the story of how he survived in a land surrounded by various types of terrorist groups for tens of kilometers was unknown until today.

SPUTNIK

Emad Abshenas, a reporter for Russia's state-run Sputnik news agency, wrote a piece in the Persian-language website of the Russian agency quoting the entire story from a senior Syrian officer.

"I contacted one of the Syrian officers who is my old friend and is stationed in Lattakia and asked him to tell me the story, and here is what he said," Abshenas mentioned.

After the downing of the Russian fighter jet, the Russian helicopters took off immediately to save the co-pilot but they faced the heavy fire power of FSA (or the so-called moderate opposition, the Free Syrian Army, supported by the West) and the Turkey-backed Turkmens who targeted the helicopter with missiles and advanced weapons that they have gained recently. During the operations one Russian aid worker was killed.

Credible information was obtained that a number of special Turkish units had been sent to the scene to take the Russian co-pilot captive to blackmail Russia later. While the Russians were

Lebanese Hezbollah

Syrian Special Forces

planning for an operation to free the co-pilot immediately, General Soleimani contacted them and proposed to them that a special task force unit be formed of Hezbollah's special forces and Syrian commandos who had been trained by Iran and are fully familiar with the geographical situation of the region. The special taskforce would be responsible for the ground operation and Russia would provide them with air cover and satellite intelligence.

Soleimani promised them to return the Russian co-pilot safe and sound; a promise that was kept..

After tracing the location of the Russian co-pilot using his GPS, it was revealed that the pilot was being kept in an area 6km behind the frontline of the clashes between the Syrian army and the opposition.

Six fighters of Hezbollah's special operation unit and 18 Syrian commandos approached the frontline to carry out the ground operations. The Russian air force and helicopters concurrently created a hellfire in the region and destroyed the terrorists' headquarters. As a result most of the enemy forces deployed in the region fled the scene and the ground was paved for the special unit's advance.

The Syrian officer added that every move of the special units was monitored and covered precisely by the Russian satellites in a way that the slightest moves made 100 meters away from the area of operation was reported to them and every moment of the operation was reported to a very high-raking official in the Kremlin (that he thinks was president Putin) and it was clear that he was monitoring the entire operations through satellites from Moscow.

According to the officer who called for anonymity, the operation later turned into a hunt for the terrorists in the operation zone by the Russian air force from the sky and by Brigadier General Soleimani's operations units on the ground.

"We did not think we could receive a strike from a party that we thought to be our partner.

"If we thought of this before, we would have established the systems capable to protect our aircraft.

Vladimir Putin rails against Turkey at a press conference at the Kremlin.

"The reason we didn't do this is because we thought Turkey to be a friendly country."

The Syrian officer believed that the Russians also launched strong electronic warfare immediately to blind all enemy satellites and communication equipment in areas several kilometers away from the operational zone and when the enemies came to realize something was underway, the operations had ended. The electronic warfare was launched because the Russians were concerned that the western satellites would leak the operation to the terrorists.

Finally, the special unit saved the pilot after infiltrating 6km behind the enemy lines, killing the terrorists operating there and destroying their hi-tech equipment.

The most interesting point is that all 24 members of the special units along with the co-pilot returned to their base without even one injury after fulfilling the dangerous mission.

According to the senior Syrian officer, one of the reasons for the success of these operations was the difference between Turkey and the terrorists over the fate of the Russian pilot as the Turks wanted him alive to use him for political blackmailing against the Russians. On the other hand, the terrorists stationed in the region intended to burn the captured pilot alive. This is what they had done to the Jordanian pilot. They wanted to fill the hearts of other Russian pilots with fear.

The rift paved the way for a few golden hours for rescue operations. The opposition never imagined that such a rapid planning and action by the rescue squads would be possible, given the complicated nature of such operations.

The Syrian officer said that General Soleimani insisted on supervising the details of the operation and stayed in the the operations room commanding his forces on the ground until he was assured that his planning was a success.

6 fighters of Hezbollah's special operations unit

+ 18 Syrian commandoes

+ one famed Iranian general

+ Russian electronic warfare

= a perfect rescue mission

Sputnik reporter, Emad Abshenas states a number of interesting points evolved from this report:

1. **General Soleimani is healthy and is actively commanding operations in the front line of the war against terror. His response is with action and not by words and slogans.**
2. **There is no so called extremist or moderate opposition groups in Syria; they are all terrorists appearing in public in different clothes with different masks.**
3. **The group 4+1 can not trust other countries in the field and they should rely on themselves only to eliminate the terrorists in the region based on their own specified plans.**
4. **Iran and Russia's operational coordination in Syria is highly integrated and effective.**
5. **Most of the FSA's Syrian members had withdrawn from the region after they came under Russia's airstrikes. The commandos fought non-Syrian forces who were using classic military tactics and not guerilla warfare. Therefore, they could well be Turkish military or army forces of other countries. The commandos, of course, had no choice but to kill them given the importance of rapid action in the operation.**
6. **The terrorists present in the region possessed very modern and advanced military equipment for ground-to-ground and ground-to-air warfare that had not even been supplied to a large number of countries which are Washington's NATO allies.**
7. **Wireless contacts between the opposition forces indicate that Arabic, Turkish, Russian and French are respectively the most frequently used languages by the terrorists. This shows that Russia has to fight the terrorists until there is victory over the terrorists in Syria to safeguard its own national security.**

Declassified CIA Manual Shows How US Uses Bureaucracy To Destabilize Governments

The World War II-era document outlines ways in which operatives can disrupt and demoralize enemy administrators and police forces

By **Jake Anderson** | The Anti Media
December 8, 2015

When most people think of CIA sabotage, they think of coups, assassinations, proxy wars, armed rebel groups, and even false flags — not strategic stupidity and purposeful bureaucratic ineptitude. However, according to a declassified document from 1944, the Office of Strategic Services (OSS), which later became the CIA, used and trained a curious breed of "citizen-saboteurs" in occupied nations like Norway and France.

The World War II-era document, called Simple Sabotage Field Manual, outlines ways in which operatives can disrupt and demoralize enemy administrators and police forces. The first section of the document, which can be read in its entirety here, addresses "Organizations and Conferences" — and how to turn them into a "dysfunctional mess":

- Insist on doing everything through "channels." Never permit short-cuts to be taken in order to expedite decisions.
- Make "speeches." Talk as frequently as possible and at great length. Illustrate your "points" by long anecdotes and accounts of personal experiences.
- When possible, refer all matters to committees, for "further study and consideration." Attempt to make the committee as large as possible — never less than five.
- Bring up irrelevant issues as frequently as possible.
- Haggle over precise wordings of communications, minutes, resolutions.
- Refer back to matters decided upon at the last meeting and attempt to re-open the question of the advisability of that decision.

- Advocate "caution." Be "reasonable" and urge your fellow-conferees to be "reasonable" and avoid haste which might result in embarrassments or difficulties later on.

On its official webpage, the CIA boasts about finding innovative ways to bring about sabotage, calling their tactics for destabilization "surprisingly relevant." While they admit that some of the ideas may seem a bit outdated, they claim that "Together they are a reminder of how easily productivity and order can be undermined."

In a second section targeted at manager-saboteurs, the guide lists the following tactical moves:

- In making work assignments, always sign out the unimportant jobs first. See that important jobs are assigned to inefficient workers.
- Insist on perfect work in relatively unimportant products; send back for refinishing those which have the least flaw.
- To lower morale and with it, production, be pleasant to inefficient workers; give them undeserved promotions.
- Hold conferences when there is more critical work to be done.
- Multiply the procedures and clearances involved in issuing instructions, paychecks, and so on. See that three people have to approve everything where one would do.

Finally, the guide presents protocol for how saboteur-employees can disrupt enemy operations, too:

- Work slowly.
- Contrive as many interruptions to your work as you can.
- Do your work poorly and blame it on bad tools, machinery, or equipment. Complain that these things are preventing you from doing your job right.
- Never pass on your skill and experience to a new or less skillful worker.

The CIA is proud of its Kafkaesque field manual and evidently still views it as an unorthodox but effective form of destabilizing enemy operations around the world. Of course, so too might an anarchist or revolutionary look at such tactics and view them in the context of disrupting certain domestic power structures, many of which are already built like a bureaucratic house of cards.

It seems if any country should refrain from showcasing how easy it is to disrupt inefficient federal agencies, however, it would be the United States.

"National security is the largest institution in the world and also the most corrupt institution in the world in the sheer volume of plunder of America's financial assets."

Jake Anderson | Journalist

Born on the second of June in 1982, Anderson currently resides in Escondido, California. With an educational background in film and digital media, he finds interest in social justice, science, corporatocracy, dystopian science fiction. Anderson joined Anti-Media's team in April of 2015 as an independent journalist.

When asked about to write a description about himself, he responded in the third person:

> *Jake Anderson is a writer/journalist/filmmaker with a passion for subversive themes, fringe ideas, and social justice. He is in pre-production on several films, including a documentary about the effects of advertising on society. He also runs the popular fringe horror blog theghostdiaries.com as well as the corporate watchdog site EvilCorps.com. Jake's other passions include Burning Man, Youtopia, yoga, meditation, and imagining the distances between galaxies.*

HTTP://THEANTIMEDIA.ORG/TEAM/JAKE/

Donald Trump, US Republican Presidental Candidate, is twisting the reality on 9/11 by saying that it was "Muslims" who cheered the attacks, American scholar Kevin Barrett says.

Hey Trump! ISRAELIS cheered 9/11 attacks, not Muslims

By Kevin Barrett

November 30, 2015

Everywhere Trump goes, we need to interrupt his speeches with this information

US presidential candidate Donald Trump's recent accusation against Muslims, saying that they cheered for the September 11, 2001 attacks, is a "mangled" version of what really took place on that day, American scholar and Veterans Today Editor Kevin Barrett says.

The Republican presidential frontrunner said on Saturday that not only Arab Muslims in New Jersey cheered the 9/11 attacks, but Muslims across the world celebrated the fall of the Twin Towers of the World Trade Center.

"Donald Trump is conveying interesting versions of urban legends and some actual facts about what followed the terrorist attacks of September 11, 2001," Barrett told Press TV on Sunday.

"Israeli intelligence agents were caught wildly celebrating the airplane crashes and then the explosive destructions of the Twin Towers," Barrett said, adding that the agents were working in coordination with people already placed on the Federal Bureau of Investigation (FBI)'s terror watch list.

Omer Marmari

Oded Ellner

Yaron Shmuel

Paul Kurzberg

Sivan Kurzberg

"These dancing Israelis were cheering wildly, flicking cigarette lighters in front of the burning and then exploding Twin Towers and they were then arrested, they were found with thousands of dollars in cash stuffed in their socks," he added.

After failing lie detector tests, Barrett said, the agents flew back to Israel, where they appeared on TV and boasted that they were sent to New York to "**document the event**."

"**That is an official admission from Israeli intelligence agents that they had foreknowledge of the destruction of the World Trade Center**," Barrett added. "**So Trump mangled this story**."

"Well, that set off a chain of controversy in the American media because there were no Muslims who were celebrating anything in New Jersey," the analyst stated.

Netanyahu also cheered 9/11 attacks

Elsewhere in his remarks, Barrett said that even Israeli Prime Minister Benjamin Netanyahu was among those who were heartened by the attacks.

Benjamin Netanyahu

"His first reaction was he said 'it is very good!' but none of this will ever be reported in the Western Zionist-controlled mainstream media," he added.

Professor Barrett dismissed allegations by Western media that people in Palestine were cheering the attacks, accusing them of passing off older videos as evidence.

Prof. Kevin Barrett

"In one case a Zionist news crew managed to convince some Palestinian children to cheer and seem to be celebrating in return for candy," he noted.

Although Osama bin Laden repeatedly denied any connection to the attacks, Israel and the US designed them and tried to convince the world that al-Qaeda was behind the vicious act, Barrett said. Osama bin Laden had been on the CIA payroll for many years and his asset name was Tim Osman.

Tim Osman aka Osama bin Laden

"Palestinians Cheering the 9/11 Attacks"
Here are the propaganda videos that were quickly aired across mainstream media of Palestinians cheering the attacks in the streets of West Bank. However, it turns out they were not cheering the 9/11 attacks but they were bribed with cake to celebrate. The lady claims she did not know about the attacks at that point.

"So once again Donald Trump's words are pointing towards a true story but in both cases the story is pointing towards the real authors of the massacre of September 11, 2001, and that is the Israeli Zionists," the scholar concluded.

Trump has come under fire for proposing a plan to establish IDs and a database to track American Muslims.

However, Trump is not backing down from his controversial claim that Muslims cheered as the Twin Towers fell on 9/11.

He has told NBC News that he has "the world's greatest memory" and everybody knows about this, insisting that his claims were valid and flaunted the support he said he received on his Twitter page.

Trump also demanded apologies from those people who dared to doubt his recollection of the 9/11 attacks. "I want an apology," he tweeted. "Many people have tweeted that I am right."

THE TRIUMVIRATE

Coup d'état From Wikipedia, the free encyclopedia

A ***coup d'état*** (/ˌkuː deɪˈtɑː/); French: [ku deta], literally "blow of state"; plural: *coups d'état*, pronounced like the singular form), also known simply as a **coup** (/ˌkuː/), or an **overthrow**, is the sudden and illegal seizure of a state, usually instigated by a small group of the existing government establishment to depose the established regime and replace it with a new ruling body. A coup d'état is considered successful when the usurpers establish their dominance. If a coup fails, a civil war may ensue.

A coup d'état typically uses the extant government's power to assume political control of a country. In Coup d'État: A Practical Handbook, military historian Edward Luttwak states that a coup "consists of the infiltration of a small, but critical, segment of the state apparatus, which is then used to displace the government from its control of the remainder". The armed forces, whether military or paramilitary, can be a defining factor of a coup d'état.

MUAMMAR GADDAFI

Good Example

By **Jon Larsen Shudlick**
April 2011

Socialist People's Libyan Arab Jamahiriya government stamp.

"I have created a Utopia here in Libya. Not an imaginary one that people write about in books, but a concrete Utopia."

Muammar Gaddafi

The coup d'etat led by Colonel Muammar Gadaffi on 1 September 1969 (oil was discovered in Libya in 1959) had country wide support. King Idris of the Senussi Tribe had allowed most of the oil profits to be siphoned off by the big oil companies while he lived lavishly.

King Idris on the cover of the Libyan Al Iza'a *magazine, 15 August 1965*

Even though previous attempts for tribal unification by both the Turks (1855-1911) and Italian colonial rulers (1911-1943) failed, the country was split in two for administrative purposes. Libya consists of over 150 tribes and after Gadiffi's victory he adroitly married a woman from the Royal Barqa Tribe and unified the nation.

Gaddafi with his wife Safia during a wedding party, found in a family album at his compound in Tripoli.
PHOTOGRAPH: AFP/GETTY IMAGES

Let's look at some amazing facts on why Gadaffi was able to stay in power after having governed for over forty years, and is still loved by so many of his countrymen.

1. There is no unemployment in Libya.
2. Libya had the highest GDP (Gross Domestic Product) in Africa.
3. Less than 5% of the population is classified as poor.
4. Life expectancy in Libya is 75 years of age, highest in Africa, and 10% above the world average.
5. Libya has a literacy rate of 82%.
6. There is free health care in Libya.
7. There is free education in Libya.
8. Most Libyan families possess a house and a car except the Nomadic, Bedouin, and Tuareg Tribes.
9. Riba (usury) is not permitted. The Central Bank of Libya is wholly owned by the Libyan government and is run as a state bank with their own Libyan currency. There is no usury because there is no interest.

My credit cards range from about 7-8% at the Suncoast Credit Union to 23% at HSBC. This interest/usury system is Biblically forbidden. The fractional reserve banking scheme of the West engineered by the privately owned Federal Reserve is partly why Cape Coral and Lee County have ranked at the top of most foreclosure lists from 2008-2010. Everything that Muammar Gadaffi has done for his people I now believe almost every American would like to have happen in their own country.

Unfortunately, those moneyed elitists and war mongering Neo-cons in control in Washington, D.C. do not want a strong country anywhere. Their lust for other countries wealth and natural resources is what drives their evil souls.

At Fort Hood Texas, just outside of San Antonio (it's ironic, that is where Jim Bowie, Colonel William Travis, and former Congressman Davie Crockett perished while defending their country from foreign invaders at the Alamo) the U.S. Army is building the largest military hospital in the world. This hospital has already been under construction for over three years and will be used to care for those injured soldiers, sailors, and Marines from our dastardly invasions of Iraq and Afghanistan.

This is an obscene gesture to old men's wars (the military industrial complex along with the Bush/Cheney Halliburton no bid contracts).

The VA budget has jumped from under 9 billion to over 50 billion dollars a year. Yet gullible Americans keep on their merry way hiding under their false red, white, and blue bravado as our country sinks 15 trillion dollars in debt and Wall Street CEO's wallow in their multi-million dollar bonuses while companies like GE pay no taxes. In my opinion there are only two things red blooded Americans should ever fight for; your fellow countrymen when you are being invaded, and the Bill of Rights.

Alex D. Tocqueville stated after visiting America from France after the American Revolution, "America will be great as long as America is good." Maybe we should ask ourselves, has America ceased to be good?

And one final thing,

TO HELL WITH THE NEW WORLD ORDER!!!

“Ever since the Bush government purged the US military’s top Generals (and Colonels) in late 2001 and early 2002 because of their opposition to the wars in Afghanistan and Iraq, the US military have slavishly obeyed the will of the Neo-Cons and the Israeli Lobby.”

Cushman Cunningham

George W. Bush delivering a speech to crew aboard the aircraft carrier USS Abraham Lincoln, as the carrier steamed toward San Diego, California on May 1, 2003. REUTERS/LARRY DOWNING/FILE

Saddam Hussein

The George W. Bush (43) administration sold to the American public the idea that the 5th President of Iraq, Saddam Hussein, had weapons of mass destruction (WMD's) and intended to use them. The Zionist, Neo-con warmongering members of the George W. Bush administration convinced "W" to go to war, first with Afghanistan and then with Iraq. This demonic lie that Iraq had WMD's perpetuated by Zionist influence for the benefit of "Eretz Israel" cost the United States of America dearly in blood and treasure.

Saddam Hussein

"Shock and Awe" – 2003 Bombing of Iraq

"My belief is we will, in fact, be greeted as liberators."

VICE PRESIDENT DICK CHENEY
MEET THE PRESS
SUNDAY, SEPT. 14, 2003

The Wikipedia information states that the total U.S. casualties from the War on Terror are 66,077+ with total Americans killed (military and civilian) 9,655+. The financial cost according to Wikipedia, covering spending related to the war as of 2011 is $2.7 trillion with the estimated long term spending at $5.4 trillion including interest. Additionally, the Department of Defense funded with more than $500 million from the American Recovery and Reinvestment Act, is building the largest medical facility project in the DOD to date (the Carl R. Darnell Medical Center Replacement at Fort Hood/San Antonio, Texas). The new 947,000 square foot facility, due to open in 2015, will help facilitate treatment for amputees and the 256,820 veterans who were seen for potential post-traumatic stress disorder (PTSD) following their return from Iraq or Afghanistan. Another insufferable lie was that Osama Bin Laden (former U.S. ally who was on the payroll of the CIA) and Saddam Hussein somehow acted in tandem to plot the 9/11 terrorist attack. Nothing could be further from the truth. Go to: www.ae911truth.org Read: War Is A Racket by Major General Smedley D. Butler.

New Carl R. Darnall Army Medical Center set to open spring 2016

Downing Street memo from Wikipedia

The **"Downing Street memo"** (or the **"Downing Street Minutes"**), sometimes described by critics of the Iraq War as the **"smoking gun memo"**, is the note of a secret 23 July 2002 meeting of senior British Labour government, defence and intelligence figures discussing the build-up to the war, which included direct reference to classified United States policy of the time. The name refers to 10 Downing Street, the residence of the British prime minister.

The memo recorded the head of the Secret Intelligence Service (MI6) as expressing the view following his recent visit to Washington that **"[George W.] Bush wanted to remove Saddam Hussein, through military action, justified by the conjunction of terrorism and WMD. But the intelligence and facts were being fixed around the policy."**

It quoted Foreign Secretary Jack Straw as saying it was clear that Bush had "made up his mind" to take military action but that **"the case was thin."**

Straw also noted that Iraq retained "WMD capability" and that "Saddam would continue to play hard-ball with the UN."

The military asked about the consequences "if Saddam used WMD on day one," posing Kuwait or Israel as potential targets.

Attorney-General Lord Goldsmith warned that justifying the invasion on legal grounds would be difficult. However, the meeting took place several months before the adoption of United Nations Security Council Resolution 1441, the resolution eventually used as the legal basis for the invasion of Iraq. **UNR687 also provided a pre-existing basis, as it required Iraq to divest itself of "100%" of all WMD capacity, which the Memo agreed it had not.**

A copy of the memo was obtained by British journalist Michael Smith and published in the *The Sunday Times* in May 2005, on the eve of British elections. Smith stated that the memo was equivalent to the Pentagon Papers which exposed American intentions in the Vietnam War and alleged the American media did not report more about it do due a perceived bias towards support for the war. Though its authenticity has never been seriously challenged, the British and American governments have stated that the contents do not accurately reflect their official policy positions at the time.

Introduction

The memo was first published in *The Sunday Times* on 1 May 2005, during the last days of the UK general election campaign.

It went largely unremarked in the U.S. press at first, but was heavily covered in progressive blogs such as those on Daily Kos, because of a remark attributed to Richard Dearlove (then MI6 head) that **"the intelligence and facts were being fixed [by the U.S.] around the policy" of removing Saddam Hussein from power, which was interpreted to show that US intelligence on Iraq prior to the war was deliberately falsified, rather than simply mistaken.**

As this issue began to be covered by American media (*Los Angeles Times* on 12 May 2005, *Washington Post* on 13 May 2005, two other main allegations stemming from the memo arose: that the UN weapons inspection process was manipulated to provide a legal pretext for the war, and that pre-war air strikes were deliberately ramped up in order to soften Iraqi infrastructure in preparation for war, prior to the October U.S. Senate vote permitting the invasion.

Some elements of the U.S. media have portrayed the document as faked or fraudulent, and Dana Perino referred in her daily White House press briefing on 4 December 2008 to the fact that the Bush administration has "debunked" the document previously. The British have tacitly validated its authenticity (as when Tony Blair replied to a press conference question by saying "that memorandum was written before we then went to the United Nations.")

A group of 131 members of Congress led by John Conyers, repeatedly requested that President George W. Bush respond to the contents of the document. A resolution of inquiry was filed by Representative Barbara Lee, which would request that the President and the State Department turn over all relevant information with regard to US policy towards Iraq. The resolution had 70 co-sponsors.

$1 Trillion Dollars

$1,000,000,000,000

If you spent $1 million a day since Jesus was born, you would not have spent $1 trillion by now.

Smedley Darlington Butler *(July 30, 1881 – June 21, 1940) was a United States Marine Corps major general, the highest rank authorized at that time, and at the time of his death the most decorated Marine in U.S. history.*

War Is a Racket *is the title of two works, a speech and a booklet, by the retired major general and two time Medal of Honor recipient. In them, Butler frankly discusses from his experience as a career military officer how business interests commercially benefit (including war profiteering) from warfare.*

Smedley Butler on Interventionism

Excerpt from a speech delivered in 1933, by
Major General Smedley Butler, USMC

War is just a racket. A racket is best described, I believe, as something that is not what it seems to the majority of people. Only a small inside group knows what it is about. It is conducted for the benefit of the very few at the expense of the masses.

I believe in adequate defense at the coastline and nothing else. If a nation comes over here to fight, then we'll fight. The trouble with America is that when the dollar only earns 6 percent over here, then it gets restless and goes overseas to get 100 percent. Then the flag follows the dollar and the soldiers follow the flag.

I wouldn't go to war again as I have done to protect some lousy investment of the bankers. There are only two things we should fight for. One is the defense of our homes and the other is the Bill of Rights. War for any other reason is simply a racket.

There isn't a trick in the racketeering bag that the military gang is blind to. It has its "finger men" to point out enemies, its "muscle men" to destroy enemies, its "brain men" to plan war preparations, and a "Big Boss" Super-Nationalistic-Capitalism.

Major Smedley D. Butler in USMC uniform, c1910.

It may seem odd for me, a military man to adopt such a comparison. Truthfulness compels me to. I spent thirty-three years and four months in active military service as a member of this country's most agile military force, the Marine Corps. I served in all commissioned ranks from Second Lieutenant to Major-General. And during that period, I spent most of my time being a high class muscle- man for Big Business, for Wall Street and for the Bankers. In short, I was a racketeer, a gangster for capitalism.

I suspected I was just part of a racket at the time.

Now I am sure of it. Like all the members of the military profession, I never had a thought of my own until I left the service. My mental faculties remained in suspended animation while I obeyed the orders of higher-ups. This is typical with everyone in the military service.

I helped make Mexico, especially Tampico, safe for American oil interests in 1914. I helped make Haiti and Cuba a decent place for the National City Bank boys to collect revenues in. I helped in the raping of half a dozen Central American republics for the benefits of Wall Street. The record of racketeering is long. I helped purify Nicaragua for the international banking house of Brown Brothers in 1909-1912 (where have I heard that name before?). I brought light to the Dominican Republic for American sugar interests in 1916. In China I helped to see to it that Standard Oil went its way unmolested.

Butler (second from right) in Veracruz, Mexico - 1914

During those years, I had, as the boys in the back room would say, a swell racket. Looking back on it, I feel that I could have given Al Capone a few hints. The best he could do was to operate his racket in three districts. I operated on three continents.

Wendell Neville and Smedley Butler Review Marines, 31 October 1929

Bashar Assad wins Syria presidential election with 88.7% of vote

In a photo released on the Syrian Presidency's Facebook page, Syrian President Bashar Assad casts his vote on Tuesday, June 3, 2014 with his wife, Asma, at his side. Bashar al-Assad won 88.7 percent of the vote in Syria's presidential election, securing a third term in office despite a raging civil war which grew out of protests against his rule.

Embattled Syrian president Bashar Al-Assad received Moran Ignatius Aphrem II Karim, the elected patriarch of the Syriac Orthodox Church, at the presidential palace in Damascus.

Karim expressed his hope that security and peace would soon prevail in Syria, whose people he said were a shining example of national unity. He further asserted that the Syriac Orthodox Patriarchate supports the Syrian people's struggle against terrorism and their right to self-determination away from the interference of any foreign side.

The patriarch also stressed that the followers of the Syriac Church are determined to remain steadfast in their homeland and defend it with all their capacities and expressed his happiness to return to Damascus, the capital of Syria and the Syriac Church.

Putin Destroys 40% of ISIL's Infrastructure in One Week

By **Stuart Hooper**
October 9, 2015

21st Century Wire says...

The Russians are taking no prisoners and are certainly not waiting for the West's help.

Syria's Ambassador to Russia, Riad Haddad, has confirmed that Russian airstrikes have managed to destroy around 40% of the Islamic State's infrastructure in just one week.

Haddad said that, "according to our data, about 40 percent was destroyed. In addition, a lot of terrorists have been killed. Now, they are retreating toward the Turkish border, as this country has traditionally provided them with protection."

The Su-34 – an effective force for eradicating terrorism. (PHOTO CREDIT: ALEX BELTYUKOV)

Many reports emerged just 72 hours after the start of the Russian campaign that many terrorists were already on the run and in complete disarray. Russia has been unafraid to pursue a policy of eradication when it comes to dealing with the destabilizing terroristic forces in Syria, and cruise missiles have quite literally caused a terror exodus.

For a year the West claimed to be fighting ISIS and many Western leaders have denounced the group's activities. Yet, that rhetoric has not been backed up with any substantial action. The year-long Western bombing campaign has been totally ineffective at doing anything other than lining the pockets of executives in the military industrial complex.

Russia has now even openly denounced Western refusals to assist their campaign, asking whose side is the West really on?

Perhaps, the West truly does not have any intel on ISIS because they have been too busy trying to remove Assad.

Russia's President Vladimir Putin (right) and Patriarch of Moscow and All Russia Kirill attend a meeting with Russian Orthodox church bishops in Moscow in this Feb. 1, 2013 file photo provided by Ria Novosti. | REUTERS

Russian Orthodox Church supports Putin's 'holy war' in Syria to protect Christians

By **Hazel Torres**
October 2, 2015

Russia is waging a "holy war" in Syria to protect innocent Christians against the "tyranny of terrorism," the powerful Russian Orthodox Church declared in a statement on Wednesday as Russian warplanes began pounding targets in Syria.

"Russia took a responsible decision to use military forces to protect the Syrian people from the woes brought on by the tyranny of terrorists," Russian Orthodox Church's Patriarch Kirill said in an official statement.

The Patriarch said Russia's armed intervention became necessary since "the political process has not led to any noticeable improvement in the lives of innocent people, and they need military protection."

Archpriest Vsevolod Chaplin, a spokesman for the Russian Orthodox Church, which has 150 million members worldwide, pointed out that President Vladimir Putin's decision to send Russian forces to Syria has the approval of parliament and is "consistent with international law, the mentality of our people and the role that our country has always played in the Middle East," the Interfax news agency said as reported by the International Business Times.

Chaplin said Russia cannot turn its back on Christians and other minority groups being wiped out by Islamic State militants and other extremist forces.

"The fight against terrorism is a holy struggle and today our country is perhaps the most active force in the world to combat terrorism," the Russian Orthodox Church spokesman said.

A senior Muslim cleric has also expressed his support for the Russian military intervention in Syria, saying Syrians are "practically our neighbours."

"We fully back the use of a contingent of Russian armed forces in the battle against international terrorism," said Talgat Tadzhuddin, head of the Central Spiritual Administration of Muslims of Russia, as reported by the RIA Novosti state news agency.

Chaplin said a council representing Russia's other major religions — Orthodox Christianity, Islam, Judaism and Buddhism — will release a joint statement shortly expressing its support for "the decision taken by our government."

Speaking on Russian television, Putin defended his country's military incursion in Syria, Russia's lone ally in the Middle East.

"The only correct way to fight international terrorism ... is to act preemptively, to battle and destroy fighters and terrorists on the territories they have already seized, not to wait for them to come to us," Putin said.

Kremlin Chief of Staff Sergei Ivanov said Russian forces

will be targeting ISIS militants in Syria at the request of President Bashar al-Assad.

Earlier on Monday, Putin delivered a speech before the United Nations where he urged the world to support Assad. "We believe it's a huge mistake to refuse to cooperate with the Syrian authorities, with the government forces, those who are bravely fighting terror face-to-face," Putin said.

Russian President Vladimir Putin addresses attendees during the 70th session of the United Nations General Assembly at the U.N. Headquarters in New York, September 28.

READ: THE FULL TRANSCRIPT OF RUSSIAN PRESIDENT VLADIMIR PUTIN'S SPEECH AT THE UNITED NATIONS GENERAL ASSEMBLY

http://www.newsweek.com/transcript-putin-speech-united-nations-377586

Henry Wallace, Vice-President of the USA said concerning the third World War:

Henry Agard Wallace
33rd Vice President
of the United States

"We shall decide sometime in 1943 or 1944 whether to plant the seeds of World War number three. That war will be probable in case we double cross Russia. That war will be probable if we fail to demonstrate that we can furnish full employment after this war comes to an end and if Fascist interests motivated largely by anti-Russian bias get control of our government. Unless the western democracies and Russia come to a satisfactory understanding before the war ends, I very much fear that World War number three is inevitable. Without a close trust and understanding between Russia and the United States, there is a grave possibility of Russia and Germany sooner or later making common cause."

"Of course, the ground for World War number three can be laid by actions of other powers even though we, the United States, follow a constructive course. For example, such a war would be inevitable if Russia should again embrace Trotzkyism, ferment a worldwide revolution or if British interests should again be sympathetic to anti-Russian activity in Germany and other countries. Another possible cause for World War number three might rise out of our willingness to repeat mistakes made after World War number one. When a creditor nation raises its tariffs and asks foreign nations to pay up and at the same time refuses to let them pay in goods, the result is irritation of a sort which sooner or later leads first to trade war and then to bloodshed."

(Speech made in Delaware on 8th March 1943)

Jimmy Carter Provides Putin With Maps For ISIS Strikes

"I sent [Putin] a message Thursday and asked him if he wanted a copy of our map..."

By **Loren Gutentag**
News Max
October 21, 2015

Claiming that he knows Russian President Vladimir Putin "fairly well" because they once discussed their "common interest in fly fishing," former President Jimmy Carter took the initiative to provide maps of Islamic State positions in Syria to the Russian embassy in Washington — a move at odds with the Obama administration, The Washington Free Beacon reports.

"I sent [Putin] a message Thursday and asked him if he wanted a copy of our map so he could bomb accurately in Syria, and then on

Friday, the Russian embassy in Atlanta — I mean in Washington, called down and told me they would like very much to have the map," Carter said at his Sunday school class in Georgia, according to a video of his remarks first aired on NBC News.

"So in the future, if Russia doesn't bomb the right places, you'll know it's not Putin's fault but it's my fault," he added.

The Carter Center claims that they sent maps of the Islamic States location to Russia in an attempt to help improve their airstrike accuracy where U.S. officials have said that **Russia has bombed rebels and CIA-backed groups** rather than the Islamic State terrorist group.

"We are not prepared to cooperate on strategy which, as we explained, is flawed, tragically flawed, on the Russians' part," said U.S. Defense Secretary Ash Carter, earlier this month.

According to The Washington Free Beacon, neither the White House nor the Carter Center have commented on Carter's recent actions and Cmdr. Elissa Smith, the spokeswoman for the Department of Defense said in an email, "I can't speak to whether anyone in the Pentagon was aware the Carter Center provided maps to the Russia Embassy."

The Washington Free Beacon notes that this is not the first time Carter has shown his support for Russia.

Last year, he said that the United States should not impose more sanctions on Russia and that "Putin is not going to use military force" in eastern Ukraine.

He also said, "I don't think there is anything we can do that is going to deter Putin."

The Pentagon announced Tuesday that the U.S. signed an agreement with Russia to avoid incidents in Syrian airspace where American planes are also bombing Islamic State positions.

However, the memorandum with Russia "does not establish zones of cooperation, intelligence sharing, or any sharing of target information in Syria" and does "not constitute U.S. cooperation or support for Russia's policy or actions in Syria," Pentagon Press Secretary Peter Cook said, according to The Washington Free Beacon.

Russian President Vladimir Putin went underwater to view the Byzantine-era wreckage in the Black Sea off Crimea that included a trove of 10th century pottery.

Who keeps slandering Russia?

By **Cushman Cunningham**

Our TV and newspapers continue to lie to us about "Putin's invasion" of the Crimea "last year".

The fact is that Russia has "owned" the Crimea for hundreds of years. The naval base and adjoining port of Sevastopol in Crimea have been in Russian hands for centuries. Check the date of the Crimean War (1853-56) when Britain and France sent armies to invade Crimea. Less than a century ago all American high school students had to memorize "The Charge of the Light Brigade", which took place during the Crimean War. I could still quote much of it, if necessary.

I am not pro-Russian, but I am pro-truth in our press and media. Whoever it is that keeps on lying to us about Russia in our press and media, it is obvious that they always hate Russia.

The Charge of the Light Brigade

by **Alfred Lord Tennyson**

Half a league, half a league,
Half a league onward,
All in the valley of Death
Rode the six hundred.
"Forward, the Light Brigade!
"Charge for the guns!" he said:
Into the valley of Death
Rode the six hundred.a

"Forward, the Light Brigade!"
Was there a man dismay'd?
Not tho' the soldier knew
Someone had blunder'd:
Theirs not to make reply,
Theirs not to reason why,
Theirs but to do and die:
Into the valley of Death
Rode the six hundred.

Cannon to right of them,
Cannon to left of them,
Cannon in front of them
Volley'd and thunder'd;
Storm'd at with shot and shell,
Boldly they rode and well,
Into the jaws of Death,
Into the mouth of Hell
Rode the six hundred.

Flash'd all their sabres bare,
Flash'd as they turn'd in air,
Sabring the gunners there,
Charging an army, while
  All the world wonder'd:
Plunged in the battery-smoke
Right thro' the line they broke;
Cossack and Russian
Reel'd from the sabre stroke
  Shatter'd and sunder'd.
Then they rode back, but not
  Not the six hundred.

Cannon to right of them,
Cannon to left of them,
Cannon behind them
  Volley'd and thunder'd;
Storm'd at with shot and shell,
While horse and hero fell,
They that had fought so well
Came thro' the jaws of Death
Back from the mouth of Hell,
All that was left of them,
  Left of six hundred.

When can their glory fade?
O the wild charge they made!
  All the world wondered.
Honour the charge they made,
Honour the Light Brigade,
  Noble six hundred.

The Relief of the Light Brigade, 25 October 1854. *Oil on canvas by Richard Caton Woodville (1856-1927), 1897.*

Byzantine shipwreck found off Russia's Black Sea coast

[CREDIT: NATIONAL GEOGRAPHIC]

A treasure of ancient coins, adornments and over 100 amphorae were discovered by Russian divers on the site of a Byzantine shipwreck said to be at least 1,000 years old off the coast of Sevastopol on the Crimean (Taurica) Peninsula.

PHOTO: TV GRAB FROM ZVEZDA TV

The Khazarian Mafia has had long term plan to enslave and destroy Russia and Persia (now called Iran). They infiltrated Russia and hijacked it in 1917 with their Bolshevik Revolution funded by the RKM Banksters of the City of London and Wall Street.

Rothschild Khazarian Mafia Banksters

In 1917 Russia they were commonly known to the world as "the Jewish Bolsheviks"

Real Reason for ISIS and the war against Assad

By **Preston James, Ph.D**
October 26, 2015

The real reason behind ISIS and their war against Assad and Syria is a secret 995 year old Blood Feud of the Khazarian Mafia against the Persians and the Russians.

The Khazarian Mafia Bolsheviks stripped mother Russia of billions in Gold, Silver, jewels and artwork, while beginning a bloodbath of rape, torture and mass murder of about 100-200 million non-Khazarian Russians.

This Blood Feud against Russia is based on the Khazarians unmitigated inter-generational rage against the Russians for helping the Persians (now Iran) destroy Khazaria in about 1020 AD because it had become a criminal nation of robbers, murderers and identity impersonators and had not heeded its warnings to clean house from top to bottom.

This Khazarian Mafia Blood Feud against Russia was also accompanied by a blood feud against Persia for helping Russia destroy Khazaria in about 1020 AD.

This plan involves destroying Syria then using it as a staging area for the destruction of Iran. Iran is an essential step in the construction of Greater Israel (Eretz Yisreal) which will engulf the whole Mideast for the Khazarian mafia and Israel its main action-agent.

The Greater Israel (Eretz Yisreal) Land Plan

This plan also involves using NATO and the US Military to surround the Russian Federation with offensive missiles and missile defenses while making international manipulations to destroy Russia economically.

The plan always is to use false-flag terror to serve as a trigger to justify the deployment of the American military as the Khazarian Mafia's enforcer. Once the targeted nation's governments are destroyed and the citizens uprooted and driven from their lands, the Khazarian Mafia associated large corporations come in and cheaply acquire any and all natural resources in order to make massive profits.

This is little more than high tech Khazarian Mafia PIRACY, but instead of piracy on the high seas, it is piracy against sovereign nations and all done to mass-murder in order to access their natural resources as cheaply as possible. This type of international piracy on land is merely an extension of the road warrior behavior that the nation of Khazaria and its leaders were known for that finally ended up with Russia and Persia attacking and destroying Khazaria.

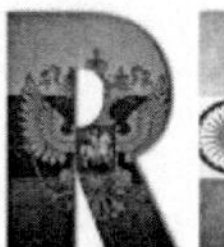

The Russian Federation has seen all this coming and has now taken major steps working with most of the World to set up major financial and economic firewalls against the US Petro Dollar which is actually owned and controlled by the Khazarian Mafia Banksters working out of the City of London.

All the recent Mideast war beginning with Iraq1 by Bush1 are actually part of an elaborate Khazarian Mafia plan to use the infiltrated and hijacked American Military to fight proxy wars for the Khazarian Mafia and its Cutout Israel in order to institute its "Greater Israel" (Eretz Yisreal) expansion plan designed to eventually destroy Syria, Iran and then surround and destroy the new Russian federation.

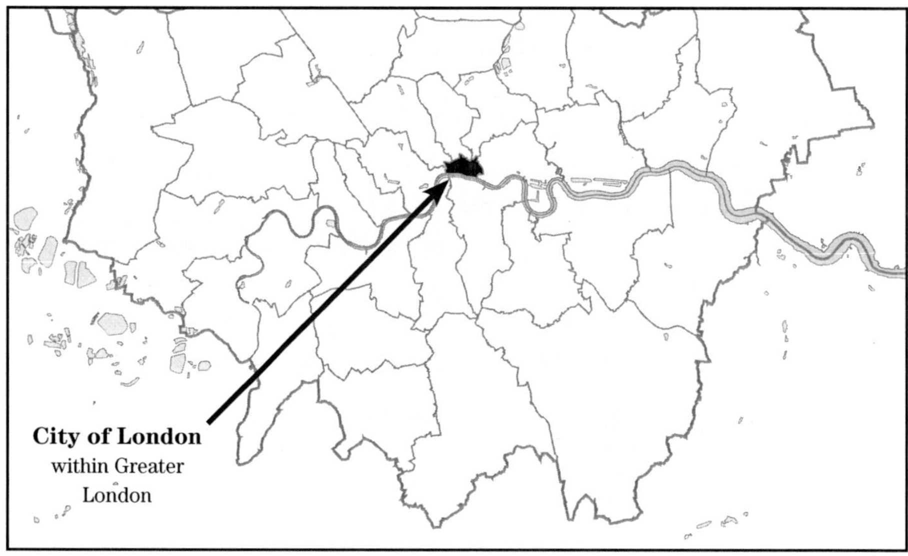

The City of London

But the actual underlying motivation for the Khazarian Mafia top leaders for creating all the Mideast Wars beginning with Bush1 is their inter-generational Blood Feud with Russia and Persia.

This Khazarian Mafia Blood Feud is also based on the Khazarian Mafia's extreme and unmitigated hatred of Russia for twice aiding America in its resistance to their private City of London Fiat based central Banking System, the first time blockading England from America in the Revolutionary War and the second time blockading England in the Civil War.

They used the Cold War to try and set off a nuclear WW3 that would have totally destroyed Russia, but this was stopped by President Reagan using his personal Secret Agent Lee Wanta, who negotiated a win/win settlement which has resulted in a new Russian Federation. A new Russia which is a non-communist, non-fascist nation and has been restored economically.

Ambassador Lee Wanta, *President Reagan's Secret Agent under the Totten Doctrine–negotiated a non-violent win/win solution and a quick end to the Cold War that prevented WW3.*

Ronald Reagan, *40th President of the United States*

The leaders of the Khazarian Mafia are part of a "bloodline family" system that never forgets when any group or nation thwarts its evil empire agendas. When the Khazarian Mafia is blocked in the attainment of any of their goals or blocked by any nation of group, they harbor continuing revenge and plots against its enemies (secretly referred to as "Goyim") forever until they are completely infiltrated, hijacked and preferably destroyed after being completely asset stripped.

The RKM has not been able to destroy Russia and mass-murder the non-Khazarian Russians so far as was its goal as a part of a 995 year old blood feud against Mother Russia.

Part of its Greater Isrel (Eretz Yisreal) expansion plan to destroy seven Middle East nations in five years has involved Iran. Persia was one of its targeted because the RKM's 995 year old blood feud against Russia also targeted Persia.

A very strange 995 year old Khazarian Mafia Blood Feud against Persians and non-Khazarian Russians.

This 995 year old Khazarian Blood Feud goes all the way back to approximately 1020 AD, when after hundreds of years of warnings, the Persians and Russia attacked Khazaria and destroyed it for refusing to stop their frequent road warrior crimes against travelers and neighbors in Persia and Russia.

In about 780 AD the Russians and Persians warned the Khazarian King that this road warrior behavior of murdering and robbing travelers and stealing their

The Khazarian Mafia's Greater Israel (Eretz Yisreal) Plan, a stepping stone to use as a staging area to eliminate Iran and then Islam, while serving as an essential step in encircling and destroying the Russian Federation. Saudi Arabia and Turkey will be then destabilized by RKM engineered "Color Revolutions", thus tightening the circle around the Russian federation.

identities must stop. They were given an ultimatum, make one of the three Abrahamic religions their official national religion or else they would be dealt with and destroyed.

The Khazarian King declared that he selected Judaism as the Khazarian national religion, but in the upper ruling circles secret Baal Worship was continued. Baal worship is also known as High Babylonian Talmudism (secet Luciferian Black Magick) and involves the sacrifice of Children to Lucifer as well as the use of Babylonian Money-Magick which is "making money from nothing". This is done by charging pernicious usury lending folks private money which should have been their own in the first place. This inner Khazarian circle of rulers began to function as a large national organized crime group, a type of organized crime which has gained control of a nations ruler-ship.

Baal, right arm raised. Bronze figurine, 14th-12th centuries, found in Ras Shamra (ancient Ugarit). Baal, properly Ba'al, was a title and honorific meaning "lord" in the Northwest Semitic languages spoken in the Levant during antiquity. From its use among people, it came to be applied to gods.

Baal aka Moloch, Lucifer, Satan. Take your pick it's the same evil spirit that wants to mass-murder all humans. In exchange for doing his "dirty work" he rewards those who allow him to snatch their souls by giving them incredible riches, fame and power. This is the secret blood contract called "selling one's soul."

"Christ Cleansing the Temple"
Carl Heinrich Bloch, 1875

In about 1020 AD when the Russian and Persian leaders agreed that the Khazarians had not changed their ways and their national Judaism had made absolutely no difference, they invaded Khazaria and destroyed it as a nation. However, before they were able to invade the Khazarian King and his top circle of Money-changers were able to take their vast wealth earned by criminal activities and leave Khazaria fleeing mostly to Europe.

They were eventually able to create a significant money-changing empire in Germany and then used trickery to manipulate the English stock market and take it over. This allowed the Rothschild banking Family to take over the City of London and assume leadership over the British Empire which was beginning to decline.

Geographically, this war was with the Caliphate on one side and the Byzantine Empire on the other side; the Khazars were caught in the middle. This occurred after the Khazars conversion to Judaism between 600-800 A.D. The reason was despite their conversion they continued their warrior attitude toward travelers. The Khazars fled to Eastern Europe, Prussia, the Baltic states, and Poland. That's why they speak Yiddish, a German dialect. The reason that the Khazar Jews hate the Russians and the Persians (Iranians) is because they exposed the Ashkenazim as not having any religious rights in the Levant due to the fact that there is no blood relation to the Hebrews. Over 97% of the Jews in the world today are Ashkenazim not Hebrew (according to the Jerusalem Post) which would be Bibically relevant to the Levant.

DEFINITION of 'Fiat Money'

Currency that a government has declared to be legal tender, but is not backed by a physical commodity. The value of fiat money is derived from the relationship between supply and demand rather than the value of the material that the money is made of. Historically, most currencies were based on physical commodities such as gold or silver, but fiat money is based solely on faith. Fiat is the Latin word for **"it shall be"**.

Once the Khazarian Mafia infiltrated and hijacked British City of London Banking and could manufacture all the money it wanted and distribute it to whomever they wanted, they became the largest and wealthiest Organized crime syndicate in the World.

The Rothschild Khazarians came up with a very crafty plan to transform the waning British Empire into a secret worldwide Khazarian Mafia Banking Empire based on central Fiat Banking franchised out of the City of London. Once this Khazarian Mafia private FIAT based central Banking system was franchised to America in 1913 by the illegal, unConstitutuional passage of the Federal Reserve Act, the die was set. The Khazarian Mafia was then able to buy, bribe and human compromise almost every single elected Official and USG official and federal Judge in America.

***Israel attacked America** on 9-11-01 with the help of stateside American Traitors.*

Russian fighter.

Right now every member of Congress except one, Rep. Walter Jones, R-NC, has apparently signed an AIPAC Loyalty Oath to place Israel first even before America. Apparently AIPAC (American Israel Political Action Committee) has rewarded each signer with massive campaign funding and very large perks. Signing such an AIPAC agreement is Treason and Sedition because AIPAC is an espionage front for the Khazarian Mafia which has proven itself to be an active enemy of America. They attacked America on 9-11-01 with the help of Israeli-American "Israeli-first" Dual Citizen Traitors in PNAC, top NeoCons, and Traitors in the Administration, JCS, USAF, NORAD and the FAA. Last time I checked Treason was defined as aiding and abetting an enemy of the United States of America. Certainly taking an AIPAC Loyalty Oath to place Israel first is a direct and clear violation of one's Oath of Office for any member of Congress.

Once the Khazarian Banksters used their endless supply of money (they can print or issue all they want and have no oversight at all) to gain control over Congress, the Administration, and the Pentagon, it was then easy to deploy the the CIA, Israel and Saudi Arabia trained, supplied and paid mercenaries to create Mideast terror to start wars. Once this Terror Machine was deployed and used to create chaos, death and destruction of innocent civilians

Map of the federal subjects of the Russian Federation

Oblasts
1 - Astrakhan
2 - Chelyabinsk
3 - Ivanovo
4 - Kaluga
5 - Kemerovo
6 - Kostroma
7 - Leningrad
8 - Lipetsk
9 - Moscow
10 - Nizhny Novgorod
11 - Novgorod
12 - Oryol
13 - Penza
14 - Ryazan
15 - Samara
16 - Sverdlovsk
17 - Tambov
18 - Tula
19 - Ulianovsk
20 - Vladmi
21- Volgograd
22- Voronezh
23 - Yaroslavl

Republics
24 - Adygeya
25 - Bashkortostan
26 - Chechnya
27 - Chuvashia
28 - Ingushetia
29 - Kabardino-Balkaria
30 - Khakassia
31 - Kalmykia
32 - Karachay-Cherkessia
35 - North Ossetia-Alania
36 - Tatarstan
37 - Udmurtia

Krais
38 - Stavropol

Federal Cities
39 - Moscow

in the Mideast and in America on 9-11-01, it was easy to motivate the American masses to support the deployment of the American Military to fight these wars for Israel and the Khazarian Mafia.

It is very hard to come up with the exact dates in the history and dissolution of Khazaria as a nation or other details because most of this history has been scrubbed from the libraries by the Khazarian Mafia, the World's largest, most powerful organized crime syndicate. So we have used approximate dates. As more an more history is uncovered, we will attempt to establish the actual dates.

Vladimir Putin

Right now Putin and the Russian Federation have created a complete checkmate against the Khazarian Mafia's ISIS and the Israeli-American

Terror Machine and has fully exposed America, Israel, Saudi Arabia and Turkey as those who created, supplied and paid the mercenaries making up ISIS (aka the Islamic State which is anything but that).

The Russian federation was invited to help defend Syria from ISIS and has every right under international law to be there. Right now the Russian federation is decimating ISIS by its sophisticated air power and very good Intel.

A good bet is that Putin and the top leaders of Russia think that it is a good time to checkmate and unravel the Khazarian Mafia and the Israeli-American Terror Machine before it completely surrounds Russia and can become powerful enough to threaten Russia's future. Beside, Russia has a lot of money invested in its loyal ally Syria and is certainly motivated to help protect its investment especially when formally invited by Syria to do so.

Summary:

Bottom line is that the 995 year old Khazarian Mafia Blood Feud against Russia and Persia is the real reason for the deployment of the Israeli-American Terror Machine which has deployed mercenaries hired, trained, supplied and paid by the CIA, Israel, Saudi Arabia and Turkey to attack the nation of Syria. These mercenaries are labelled as ISIS, ISIL, Daesh, Al Nusra, Al Qaeda (aka Al CIA Duh) and the like but they are all part of the Khazarian Mafia's Israel-American Terror Machine.

And now Putin has shown himself to be a very resourceful statesman and diplomat in his ability to checkmate the Israeli-American terror machine in Syria after being officially invited by President Assad to assist Syria. This of course is all legal under international law and is actually on the up and up, whereas the CIA and the Israeli-American Terror machine is a criminal action of the Khazarian mafia

and has now been fully exposed to the World. The US Administration and several retired US Generals have even admitted all this publicly that the USG started and is running ISIS.

*** The Khazarian Mafia is an abbreviation to represent the organized crime group that later morphed into the Rothschild Khazarian Mafia, a term coined by VT Financial Editor Mike Harris whose VT radio show is on Tuesdays and Thursdays 7-9 PM CST. Mike Harris started using this descriptive term Khazarian Mafia after extensively researching the true but hidden history of the nation of Khazaria and its connection to Rothschild World Zionism now centered in the City of London. He also discovered the long held hatred that the RKM has harbored since about 1020 AD for the non-Khazarian Russians that is still a major motive for the Khazarian Mafia today in its quest to destroy Persia (Iran) and then encircle and once again destroy Russia. Their demonic goal is to steal all of Russia's assets like in 1917, and to mass-murder any non-Khazarian Russians remaining alive, as a replay of their Bolshevik (JEWISH) Revolution of 1917.**

The Khazarian Mafia operates out of the City of London, a separate nation inside the UK which has its own police force and diplomats and pays no taxes to the UK government, like the Vatican, but has worldwide power through its private central banking system which uses FIAT money issued and placed in circulation (lent out for use at interest/pernicious usury).

The Khazarian Mafia has deeply infiltrated America and hijacked its manufacturing and distribution of money and most of its institutions of government, then uses the US military to fight its proxy wars for Israel

and to earn massive profits. The Khazarian Mafia uses UK, Israeli and American Intel factions and especially the Pentagon to traffick in massive quantities of illegal narcotics to generate massive "off the books" money for black ops and payoffs to politicians and government officials they "own".

The big question remains: Was the true cause of leaders of the Khazarian Mafia's incredible evil and savagery toward the human race a byproduct of nature or nurture?

veteranstoday.com

Preston James, Ph.D.

Social Psychologist with Doctorate from Major Midwest Big Ten University. Retired after serving the community for over 36 years during which time there were numerous contacts with those associated with Intel and Law Enforcement.

British Foreign Secretary Says "Bomb," which means "Missile"

Gordon Duff, Senior Editor - Veterans Today
November 10, 2015

"That means that the missile was fired from the Israeli side of the border"

The really good photos showing the key damage were hidden in the first few days

By **Gordon Duff, with Jeff Smith**

The imperative to push the bomb theory and put the blame on "ISIS" is now seen everywhere. There is one thing to be assumed safely from this, not a word of it is true. The scam job done over MH17, particularly the Dutch role in the cover up, was predicted to make civilian air transport an open target. We are seeing it pay off today.

With quality crash photos in the hands of VT experts, we now know that it only took those on the scene less than 5 minutes to have the answer, it was a missile. Anyone who thinks a missile can be mistaken for a bomb or can't be noticed in seconds, not "minutes" or "months" as with MH17, is a joker.

The forensics here are childishly simple, holes punched through by steel objects that planes don't carry, childishly simple "directionality" and enough external residue, much of it "taggant" that the culprit, like as not in the end companies like Raytheon or Rafael left more than a "calling card."

From Jeff Smith:

Photos clearly show a shrapnel hit from a missile. The steel ball bearings or cubes will go completely through the fuselage and exit on the other side of the plane. This imply's a hit on the lower right rear section with an exit on the upper left side of the plane. That means that the missile was fired from the Israeli side of the border.

When they use the term "External mechanical damage" it means a missile strike. Bombs are planted either in the well area or the aft cargo bay. They usually are made of high explosives only. They do not use ball bearings or metal cubes as a shrapnel device because it is unnecessary.

So we can rule out for sure tail damage decompression and or an onboard bomb. Also to high for a manpad. It would be impossible to get a vehicular mounted radar guided missile system in or out of this area without being seen by the many military patrols both by the UN and the MNF or the Egyptians or the Israelis. There are probably more fake plastic rocks loaded with motion sensors and antennas sticking out of them per mile than any other place on earth, not to count the multiple Israeli radar defenses units located just on the other side of the border.

As VT went over this evidence, there was considerable curiosity in both Syria and Russia. No one will know anything of the real Russian inquiries unless Russia wants them to. This was a huge mistake.

From Al Alam:

Lone-Wolf ISIS Maniac Planted Bomb in Russian Jet: Hammond

Britain's Foreign Secretary Philip Hammond believes there is a "high probability" a bomb planted by an ISIS supporter caused the Russian plane crash over Sinai, Egypt, October 31, 2015. Philip Hammond said it is likely the airliner, which was carrying 224 people, was brought down by a follower of the terrorist group.

He said: "It may have been an individual who was inspired by ISIS who was self-radicalised by looking at ISIS propaganda and was acting in the name of ISIS without necessarily being directed."

Mr Hammond's comments came as Russia also believes the plane was blown up by a bomb, according to US sources who reportedly intercepted Russian communications.

The Pentagon's intercepts are among other pieces of evidence leading US officials to believe the bomb was planted on Metrojet Flight 9268 – which exploded shortly after taking off from Sharm el-Sheikh.

All 224 people on board the plane – bound for St Petersburg, Russia – were killed.

From the Left VT Financial Editor Mike Harris, VT Managing Editor Jim Dean, VT Senior Editor Gordon Duff and VT Director Colonel James Hanke

Gordon Duff is a Marine combat veteran of the Vietnam War. He is a disabled veteran and has worked on veterans and POW issues for decades.

Gordon Duff is an accredited diplomat and is generally accepted as one of the top global intelligence specialists. He manages the world's largest private intelligence organization and regularly consults with governments challenged by security issues.

Gordon Duff has traveled extensively, is published around the world and is a regular guest on TV and radio in more than "several" countries. He is also a trained chef, wine enthusiast, avid motorcyclist and gunsmith specializing in historical weapons and restoration. Business experience and interests are in energy and defense technology.

Wreckage from the nose section of the MH17 plane is seen near the village of Rozsypne, in the Donetsk region July 18, 2014. | REUTERS

Did Ukraine Fabricate Evidence to Frame Russia for MH-17?

By **Paul Joseph Watson**
Report for infowars.com
July 18, 2014

Well, the Ukraine government has released the evidence which it claims implicates pro-Russian rebels and indeed Russia itself in the downing of the Malaysia airlines flight.

The evidence is not in the form of radar recordings or images of fire from said rebels but in the form of a U-Tube video which is attracting many, many questions.

This is basically a conversation between separatist rebels and a Russian armed forces Commander, the Ukrainian government claims. According to Kiev, this rebel separatist admits, "We have just shot down a plane and that it was indeed the Malaysian airlines flight.

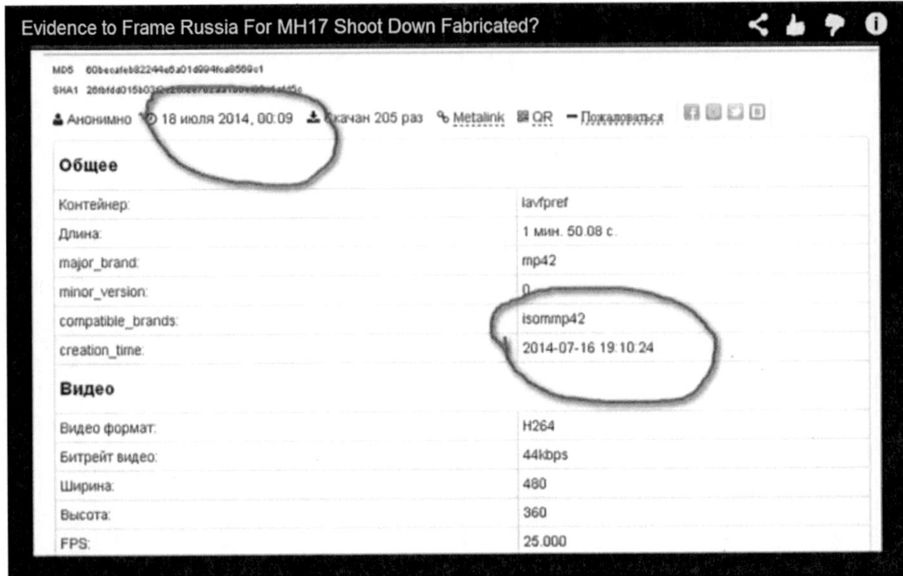

This is the time-stamp encoding information on the video file itself.

The video appears to have been created the day before the Malaysian flight went down according to the time-stamp linked to the livejournal.com website ... unconfirmed but being widely supported by outlets such as Zero Hedge ... and here we see the video was uploaded originally by the Ukraine government in the early hours actually minutes of July 18th. But if you go into the encoding information of a video or file itself on a computer (you can go on any computer and see when it was created) it gives us July 16th the day before flight MH-17 was shot down.

If this is accurate ... of course ... not confirmed, it appears as though they created the tape of the rebel commander talking to the Russian forces commander the day before the actual plane was down; this way they had evidence lined up to implicate Russia in the downing of the aircraft. This is different from what is seen in the past for example if a happening is on Facebook. It is explainable for Facebook because you can create and change to something else on Facebook after the fact. This is different as you cannot do that with the encoding time-stamp of a video as the time and date on which it was created is locked in. How do we know that these two individuals aren't just actors reading off a

This is the flight path map from days before where aircraft flew over non-restrictive and non-conflict zone air space.

script? Because the Ukraine separatists would have known that these conversations were potentially being recorded by the Kiev authorities. Back on June 5th a separate recording implicating another separatist in an incident was released by the Ukraine government. If this original recording were genuine they took no steps whatsoever to encrypt their communication in the month and one-half that followed allowing the Ukraine to then frame them for this downed airliner.

Another question is why was MH-17 diverted so it flew directly over restricted air space over a conflict zone? See the flight path map on the next page. Ten flights beforehand flew over non-restrictive and no conflict zone air space. Only on July 17th the first time it appears this flight flew over the region where there was a threat of flying over a conflict zone. Flights from two days before and one day before avoided the conflict area in Eastern Ukraine but flight 17 flew directly over it. Was the plane diverted? It looks as though it was. If so then who gave order to divert the airliner?

The only missile system according to Ukraine authorities that could have downed the plane was the Russian made BUK Missile

System which they claim Ukraine rebels had seized control of shortly before this incident. The BBC reports Ukraine Prosecutor General Vitaliy Yarema has cast doubt on this telling local media on Friday, "The military told the president after the passenger plane had been shot down that the terrorists did not possess our BUK Missile Systems." That's not coming from the separatists or pro-Russian propaganda; that is the Ukraine prosecutor general admitting that the military told the president immediately after the incident that these terrorists did not possess the capability or even the possession of the missile system itself to shoot down the airliner.

We look at the Twitter account of a Spanish air controller working at Kiev's Borispol Airport at the time of the incident. His

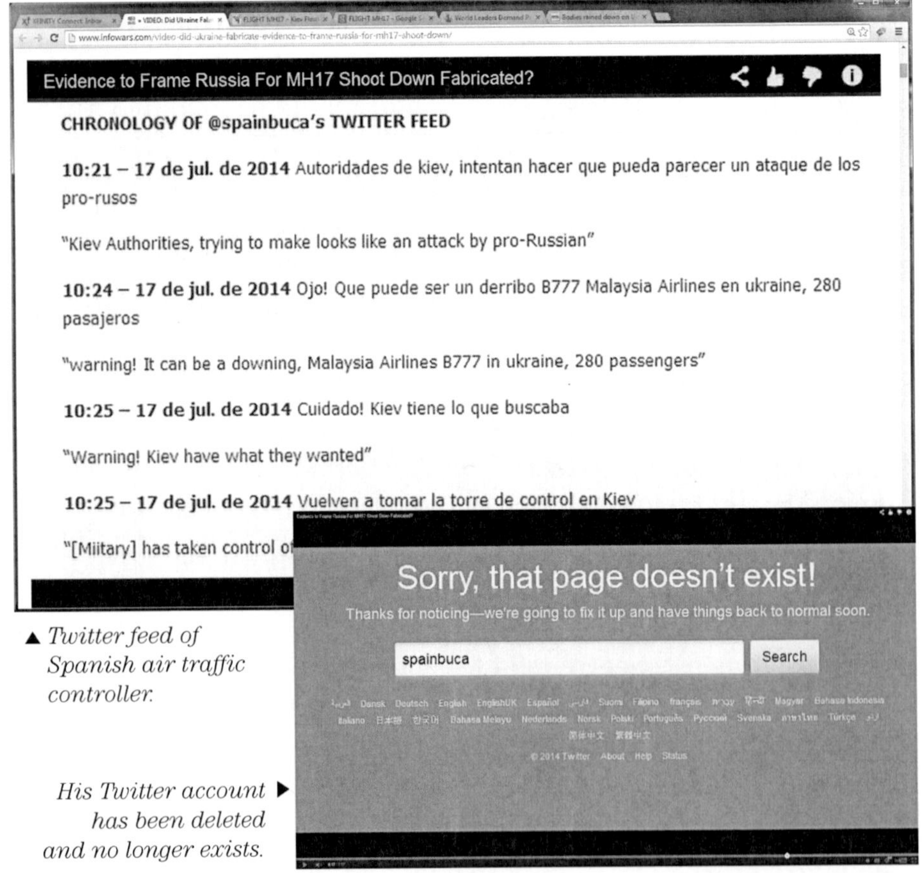

▲ *Twitter feed of Spanish air traffic controller.*

His Twitter account has been deleted and no longer exists. ▶

Twitter feed says, "The Ukraine authorities knew immediately that the plane had been shot down. He claims Ukraine fighter jets were in the vicinity of the Malaysian jet three minutes before it was shot down. Then when it was shot down he claims that Kiev authorities entered the tower and started making threats to the air traffic controllers in that control tower to basically follow orders and shut-up. He was frantically tweeting saying, "They will take from us our phones and other stuff at any moment. Before they take my phone or break my head. Shot down by Kiev." This is the apparent testimony of an air traffic controller working at Borispol Airport at the time of the downing. As you would expect, his Twitter account has been deleted and no longer exists.

Question: Was this a 'false flag'? Was the shoot down a 'false flag'? The sniper attack which started the regime change in the Ukraine was admittedly a 'false flag' attack; we don't know if it was by the Ukraine or Russia. Both the Ukraine and Russia have been caught carrying out 'false flag' attacks in the past.

Cui bono? Who benefits? Certainly not Russia … in days before the downing of the airliner we had the big BRICS announcement the alternative to the IMF (International Monetary Fund) the anti-dollar systems representing a major threat against the New World Order pushed by the U.S. and NATO. We've got the sanctions against Russia proving to be completely inept and in 48 hours before the incident we saw Ukrainian soldiers being killed, basically separatist rebels gaining an upper hand in the region where the plane was shot down.

So when you look at the context of this bombshell evidence that the Ukraine has presented to blame Russia it really doesn't seem to stack up at this point, of course, everything keeps evolving.

BUK Manufacturer Test Exposes Dutch MH17 Terror Cover Up by GPD | October 14, 2015

BUK manufacturer says Russian-made air defenses 'absolutely' not involved in MH17 crash

Journalists attend a news conference, organized by officials of Russian missile manufacturer Almaz-Antey and dedicated to the results of its investigation into Malaysia Airlines flight MH17 crash in eastern Ukraine, in Moscow, Russia, October 13, 2015.

The damage caused by shrapnel to the aircraft involved in flight MH17 could not have been caused by a modern Russian BUK missile, the manufacturers of the weapon Almaz-Antey have stated.

The manufacturer staged two real-life tests involving decommissioned aircrafts and BUK anti-aircraft missiles to see whether missile complexes currently deployed by Russian troops could have been involved in the downing of the Malaysian Airlines aircraft on July 17, 2014.

The experiments were carried out on July 31 and October 7 with the help of 9N314M BUK missile warheads, which are currently deployed by the Russian military. The results of the tests *"decisively indicate"* that an explosion from such a missile leaves a distinctive *"butterfly-shaped"* puncture holes due to the shape of the shrapnel, Almaz-Antey, the manufacturer of Buk air defense missile complexes, said.

"The Boeing 777, which carried out the flight, did not have a single hole like this and as a consequence, this absolutely excludes the possibility of a missile with double T-shaped shrapnel being used to strike this aircraft," Almaz-Antey stressed in a statement on Wednesday, following the final report of the Dutch Safety Board that looked into the causes of the crash.

The Dutch Safety Board concluded the plane, which was carrying almost 300 people, was hit with a 9N314M-model warhead mounted on the 9M38-series missile. The weapon was fired from a BUK surface-to-air missile system from an area in eastern Ukraine.

Almaz-Antey maintains that in fact a 9N314 warhead was responsible. On Wednesday, they commented on the differences between the two warheads and whose defense forces may have been using the missiles mentioned by the Dutch investigators.

The manufacturer said the Russian army has not been using BUK missiles with 9N314 warheads filled with shrapnel different from a double T-shape, as these are *"outdated,"* while the production of such warheads was halted in 1982, Almaz-Antey stressed.

Almaz-Antey also noted that as of 2005, there were 991 missiles armed with 9M38M1 warheads in arms depots in Ukraine.

"We obtained this information through official channels. Back in 2005, the company conducted a pre-contractual engineering study of how long these types of missiles could be used for in Ukraine," Almaz-Antey said, adding that they had a shelf-life of around 25 years.

"We also have data that 502 missiles of the outdated 9M38 modification were used by Ukraine's armed forces during the same year," the company added.

On October 13 the Almaz-Antey defense company presented the results of two full-scale experiments aimed at recreating the MH17 crash. The company concluded the missile that downed the flight was an old BUK model fired from a Ukrainian government controlled area, contesting the preliminary theory by Dutch investigators.

"Our Constitution assumed our self-government would function with the cooperation of transparency about federal activities."

Cushman Cunningham

9/11: Russia Presents Evidence Against USA, UK And Israel Co-Conspirators?

By **Michael Thomas**

"9/11 was an Anglo-American black operation executed in collusion with Israeli Secret Services."

9/11 Investigator

Undoubtedly the 9/11 attacks on New York City and Washington DC are the most misrepresented by officialdom in US history.

Whereas the assassination of John F. Kennedy is now understood to have been a classic CIA Public Execution Plan, it does not come close to 9/11 in terms of the number and magnitude of outright falsehoods, misleading statements, fake science and fraudulent facts submitted by officials and agents of the US Government. **The 'official' 9/11 Commission Report stands as the most fabricated document ever produced by US tax dollars.** Not only did the investigation avoid every serious inquiry about how two steel frame buildings came down after being dustified in NYC, it also subverted every initiative to ferret out the truth.

That's all about to change in 2014.

It appears that Russia has been conducting systematic data dumps on 9/11, the release of which represents more factual information on the attacks than any US Government source. In the wake of the Anglo-American coup d'état conducted by the CIA and MI6 in Kiev, it appears that Russia has no more patience for Western interference. Especially when nations are destabilized on Russia's borders do the stakes in this highly consequential geopolitical chess match go up.

Since Vladimir Putin has no intention of starting World War 3, he can only respond to US-EU meddling by using asymmetric warfare on the internet. **Were the American people to understand that elements within the US Federal Government were behind the 9/11 attacks, EVERYTHING would change in a heartbeat.** Because the Obama Administration has shown no sign of aborting its planned takeover of the Ukraine, Russia is now left with fewer, but still quite potent options.

The following excerpt recently appeared on an alternative news website – Veterans Today – under the subtitle **"Too Classified to Publish."** Essentially this unprecedented release of ultra-secret and highly classified information illustrates Putin's new tack toward Western intractability. Simply put, Russia will no longer stand by idly while the Anglo-American Juggernaut projects it power wherever it so chooses.

Too Classified to Publish

According to a retired FXX agent specializing in Israeli counter intel: The type of nuclear devices used on 9/11 were a modified version of the W-54 nuclear artillery shells that were covertly provided to the Israelis between 1988 and 1998 from US surplus stockpiles illegally exported during the Bush/Clinton era.

Chemical analysis done by DOE Sandia was able to identify the chemical/radiation footprint or fingerprint of the warheads based on samples taken after 9/11 of the fallout at ground zero. (Editor's note: Nuclear weapon use at ground zero is confirmed from multiple sources.)

All plutonium based warheads have a chemical fingerprint that can identify the type of design and where the PU was made and how old it is. ***This was the 9/11 blackmail on Bush 1 and 2, the illegal transfer of surplus US nuclear weapons to the Israelis and why the continued cover up, along with the stolen gold and stock fraud that was going on at Wall Street, etc. according to file ENW57.pdf on page 66. (Editor's note: Document received and confirmed.)***

Only a 2 kiloton device was needed to drop the buildings. A 2 kiloton device will produce a fireball of apx 150 to 200 feet in diameter at over 4000 degrees Centigrade. Just large enough to melt the I beams of the central core of the building and drop them in place. The light flash would last less than 1 second and primarily be in the UV light range. Overpressure would only be at 60PSI max and directed upwards with the blast. See underground effect.

Fallout would be minimal and located to within ground zero range only. Radiation would drop to acceptable levels within 72 hrs. after the blast. Most fall out was trapped in the cement dust thus causing all of the recent cancer deaths that we are now seeing in NYC amongst first responders. (Editor's note: Consistent with site data.)

Melted steel and iron oxide or "nano thermite" is a byproduct of the very high gamma ray / Neutron flux induced into the central steel core. The radiation dissolves the steel into iron oxide consuming the carbon and silicone in the steel.

This explains the missing steel columns and the very important clue of the "vaporized" 20 ton antenna tower atop the south tower. The upward blast of radiation literally vaporized it. Video evidence proves this to be true. (Editor's note: Tower issue a vital one.)

The total XXOO data file from DOE Sandia on the 9/11 event is well over 72 MB. P.S. Snowden didn't have a Q clearance so he missed this one. Carnaberry had a pretty good stash of documents on the subject. (All under the transit stuff.) The

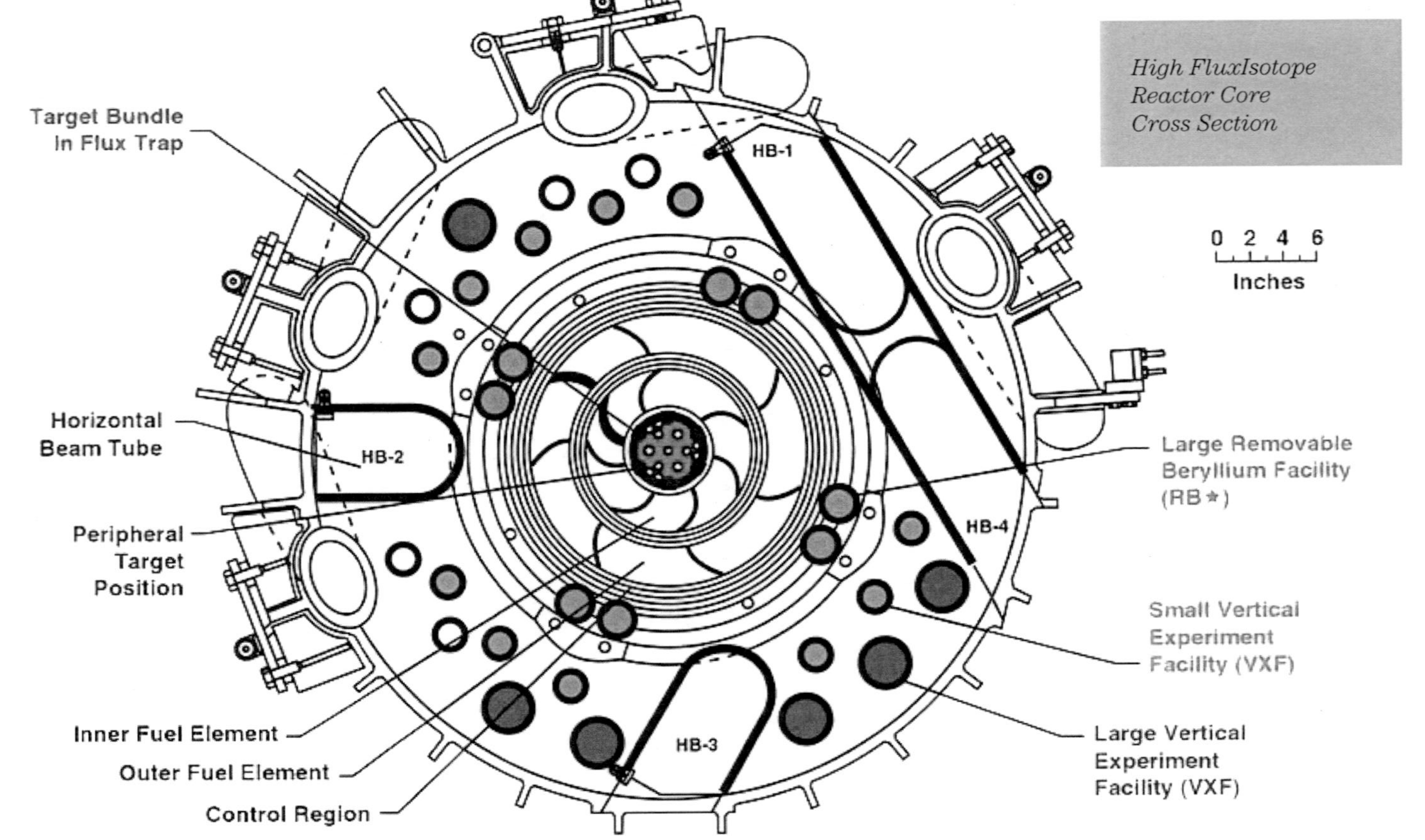

The type of nuclear device used on 9/11 was a modified version of the W-54 nuclear artillery shells that were covertly provided to the Israelis between 1988 and 1998 from US surplus stockpiles illegally exported during the Bush/Clinton era.

entire nuclear nonproliferation story of stolen nuclear material coming from Russia was an Israeli cover story to hide the original source of weapons material coming from the US stock piles. (Editor's note: Fully confirmed.)

Illegal distribution of US nuclear material to foreign allies was not limited to Israel. Virtually all NATO allies were in on this scam too. ***Dick Cheney was the bad guy on this one. Bush2/Cheney traded nuclear pits to foreign countries as IOU's in order to get what they wanted. Tom Countryman a well-known Israeli operative is curiously now in charge of N.N.P. at the State Department under Obama.(?) He was put there by Rahm Emanuel.***

It appears that the weapons of choice for the Israelis were the W-54 and follow on series of nuclear pits taken from the Amarillo, TX storage dump. This was what Carnaberry was working on for Bush senior in Houston.

A total of over 350 pits were transferred to the Israelis over a 10 to 20 year period of time. The W-54 type of pit design was the most desirable due to the 2 point implosion pit design. This is the easiest to remanufacture and modify as compared to other circular pit designs.

Early Israeli core model – Vannunu photo

The pill shaped design of the W-54 type weapon contains over 1.5 times more plutonium than a standard pit. This would allow enough plutonium 54 to be recovered that was still of weapons grade use even after 32 plus years of age. Americium (Am) build up in the pit over time eventually makes the Pit unusable as a weapon so they have a limited shelf life based on how fast or slow the plutonium was produced in the reactor at Stanford.

Khazelov confirmed this a micro nuke bombing.

Usually it was about 150 days max. Irradiation time in the reactor during production determines the shelf life of the pit as weapons grade material. ***All of the micro nukes used by the Israelis are re-manufactured W-54 type series devices.***

These devices were used in the Bali bombing and the London bombing and in Japan on their reactors. (Editor's note: Nuclear weapon use in Bali confirmed) Also used in Damascus, Iraq and Afghanistan by the US. (Editor's note: Multiple confirmations including site samples.)

These are stored in most Israeli embassies for ease of deployment. The ones used on 9/11 were kept at the Israeli consulate in NYC until put in place. After 9/11 the FBI now checks all diplomatic pouches with a Geiger counter before entering or leaving the US. *The South African weapons were also surplus W-54 artillery shells acquired from Israeli and final assembly and testing was done in South Africa with Israel assistance. (Editor's note: This explains Pelendaba production issues.)*

This was done because the Israelis needed a testing ground in order to make sure that their rebuilt weapons would work

Dimona Nuclear Facility in Israel: Dimona is a standard 75 megawatt thermal open top reactor as used in France for their plutonium weapons production program.

as designed. (Editor's note: Testing on Sept. 22, 1979 multiple confirmations.) The North Korean weapons are also of the 155 mm artillery design as provided by Israel.

The true North Korean nuclear weapons program is based on nuclear artillery use and not missiles. The plan is to use a massive artillery barrage on South Korea if war breaks out, this would include the use of small nuclear artillery shells to counter US tanks, rockets and artillery.

The Saudi's also have a stash of W-54's acquired from the US under Bush2. (Editor's note: Confirmed) The Israelis have also provided them to India, Brazil, China, Taiwan, Japan, North and South Korea, etc. (Editor's note: All but South Korea confirmed. Canada had been believed to be the source of Brazilian nuclear weapons.) Dimona is a standard 75 megawatt thermal open top reactor as used in France for their plutonium weapons production program).

Due to over use as a fast breeder reactor by the Israelis, Dimona suffered a "steam explosion" i.e. a flash over incident due to neutron criticality back in the late 1980's under Bush 1. This shut down its operation for many years until repairs could be made.

It now only operates at very low power levels due to neutron absorption damage to the containment vessel and is mainly used for isotope production. This forced the Israelis to turn to stolen nuclear stock piles from the US for the continuation of their nuclear program.

The Israelis, knowing that the nuclear material that they had acquired only had a limited shelf life left before it was no longer usable as weapons grade, then tried to dump it on the surplus market as fast as possible before it was of no use to them. So they dumped it on unsuspecting nations who would only sit on it and not be able to test it. These were the fissile tests in North Korea. (Editor's note: Confirmed, multiple sources.)

When everybody caught on to the scam such as Japan and Korea (i.e. the Korean sub sinkings, etc.) they were angry because they paid big bucks for junk. This started a mini cold war with Israel and her old clients. However the micro nukes, even as the plutonium ages, will still fissile, producing a smaller size detonation well under 2 kilotons in size.

So they can still be used as small dirty bombs or as very small tactical nukes such as the nuclear artillery strikes on Damascus with rocket assisted W-54's. (Editor's note: Confirmed strike, May 4, 2013.) On the W-54 pit design it is pill shaped and it is only about 4 inches in diameter and weighs about 24 pounds.

Most of the fuel is consumed in the plasma fire ball when detonated so there is very little plutonium fallout left to escape. If it is salted with other materials the fallout can be even reduced to lower levels such as in an enhanced radiation device or the so called neutron bomb. This is what was used on 9/11.

Falling man – 911

The primary purpose of the nuclear weapon used on 9/11 was to produce a massive Gama ray / neutron flux that would vaporize about 150 to 300 feet of 6 inch thick steel I-beams that constituted the central core of the WTC buildings. This created a free fall event as seen on TV that day. (Editor's note: Critical information here.)

The flash would be hidden from sight due to the underground detonation. Most of the light was in the

non-visible light spectrum any way. Over pressure would be reduced to 6 psi due to the blast traveling up the central core and neutron radiation vaporizing the TV antenna at the top of the building as seen on TV.

The fallout would be mainly vaporized concrete cement and iron oxide. This is why after 9/11 they told everyone on TV that the beta radiation burns that people were getting were due to the caustic cement dust and not due to the radiation effects from the radioactive cement fallout. (Editor's note: Fully confirmed.)

The iron oxide found all over the place was what was left of the steel I-beams. This was the so called Nano Thermite that was found everywhere. Fallout was limited to a 1 mile area around down town NYC. See charts. (Editor's note: Received)

Radiation decay was reduced to safe low levels after 72 hrs. (Editor's note: Fully confirmed) outside of ground zero itself. This is why the area was blocked off from the public for 3 days after the event, in order to let the radiation drop to safe levels.[1]

If you read this excerpt closely, you can clearly see that Russia means business. It is what they did not say – directly – that makes this data-dump so poignant ... and dangerous to the Anglo-American power structure.

Michael Thomas
May 29, 2014
StateoftheNation2012.com

Footnotes:

[1] Too Classified to Publish: Bush Nuclear Piracy Exposed | Veterans Today by Gordon Duff, Senior Editor

References:

9/11: The Ultimate Inside Job And False Flag Operation

9/11 Commission Report: The Most Ridiculous Conspiracy Theory Of All Time

BANKSTERS:

WAR AGAINST THE PEOPLE

A chilly Paris, as seen from our balcony

Bill Bonner

End the Fed

By **Bill Bonner, Chairman**
Bonner & Partners
October 15, 2015

PARIS – Suddenly, it has turned very cold in Paris.

The sky is gray. People wear coats and scarves. It almost feels as though it could snow.

Seeing the weather turn against us, we wonder what else might be coming.

As we predicted, the Dow fell back below 17,000 yesterday, after Walmart warned that it was having trouble selling things to people with no money – at least online.

Its e-commerce efforts don't seem to be paying off as quickly as it hoped.

Why?

There are about 100 million people in the U.S. who earn about the same average wage as the people of Argentina, Estonia, or Bosnia-Herzegovina.

Here's President Reagan's former budget advisor David Stockman in the *Daily Reckoning*:

> **"[A]ccording to the Social Security Administration's wage records, there were 100 million workers who held any kind of paying job during 2013, who earned a collective total of just $1.65 trillion that year.That amounts to the incredibly small sum of just $16,500 per average worker. And not for a small slice of the labor force but fully two-thirds of all Americans with a job."**

A Dismal Share

And according to our old friend Jim Davidson, the U.S. now has wealth inequality rivaled only by Russia.

There are a few people at the top earning a lot of money. And there are a lot at the bottom earning little money.

Jim elaborates in his soon-to-be-released book, tentatively titled *The Breaking Point*:

> **"Evidence of how far the bottom 50% of America's wealth distribution has fallen comes from Credit Suisse in its 2014 Global Wealth Report.**
>
> **As interpreted by Mike Krieger, the data show that the bottom half of America's wealth distribution ranks dead last among 40 major economies, with "just 1.3% of national wealth. Only Russia comes close to that dismal share, at 1.9%."**

At the *Diary*, how much other people earn is none of our business. And we have no truck with those who urge the feds to "do something" – by which they mean take away money from rich Peter and give it to poor Paul.

The feds are not very good at it. Much of the money sticks to their hands. Also, Peter has friends in high places. Speaking fees, lobbying jobs, campaign contributions – when Peter talks, the feds listen.

Besides, we're suspicious of the feds' motives. The common critique of Fed policy is that it was a "mistake" to push down rates so low for so long. And now, the poor federales are having trouble getting rates up off the floor.

Last month, Janet Yellen – supposedly in good faith – believed the world was not ready for it.

Larceny and Fraud

At the *Diary*, we don't believe the feds have committed an error; we believe they've committed a crime.

Larceny and fraud are the ones that spring to mind. Though we suspect a good prosecutor could tag them with counterfeiting and embezzlement, too. Throw in money laundering, conspiracy, and jaywalking – now you're looking at 10 to 20 in the big house.

The essence of larceny is taking something that doesn't belong to you without permission.

Imagine the poor retiree. He has saved his money all his life. Now, in his twilight years, is he not entitled to his recompense?

But instead of earning a decent rate on his savings, he gets the ultra-low rate that is fiddled by the feds. He gets almost nothing.

This is not just an abstract point to be argued by economists. It is theft.

Think of the aging person who had $100,000 saved in 2007. If he had earned 4% a year on his money, he would

have earned $28,000 in interest since then. But if he got only 1% (or less), he would be short $21,000.

What happened to it? Who took it?

End the Fed

There are two parties to robbery – the taker and the takee.

We have seen what happened to the victims. They are too busy picking through trash bins to go to the Walmart website.

But what about the takers?

They are busy too – lobbying … eating foie gras and caviar… and offering to save the world with increasingly radical monetary policies. They are, of course, those who pay net interest, not those who earn it.

Who exactly?

The U.S. federal government is the biggest debtor in the world (in terms of the total dollar amount owed).

Who gained the most from the federales' policy?

The federales themselves.

And who else?

The cronies, of course – Wall Street and corporate America. They were rich before the massive intervention began in 2008. Now, they are much richer.

"You complain about all this stuff," said one of the attendees on our *MoneyWeek* investment cruise last week, probably speaking for thousands of readers.

"But you never offer any solutions. What would you do about it?"

"We would do nothing. We would undo a lot," we replied.

The first thing we would undo is the Fed's control of the financial system. Let the takee's get the interest they are entitled to. And let the takers get what they've got coming to them.

Regards,

Bill

US Military Uses IMF and World Bank to Launder 85% of Its Black Budget

By **Jake Anderson**

The Anti-Media | August 13, 2015

Though transparency was a cause he championed when campaigning for the presidency, President Obama has largely avoided making certain defense costs known to the public. However, when it comes to military appropriations for government spy agencies, we know from Freedom of Information Act requests that the so-called "black budget" is an increasingly massive expenditure subsidized by American taxpayers. **The CIA and and NSA alone garnered $52.6 billion in funding in 2013 while the Department of Defense black ops budget for secret military projects exceeds this number. It is estimated to be $58.7 billion for the fiscal year 2015.**

What is the black budget? Officially, it is the military's appropriations for *"spy satellites, stealth bombers, next-missile-spotting radars, next-gen drones, and ultra-powerful eavesdropping gear."*

However, of greater interest to some may be the clandestine nature and full scope of the black budget, which, according to analyst Catherine Austin Fitts, goes far beyond classified appropriations. Based on her research, some of which can be found in her piece "What's Up With the Black Budget?," **Fitts concludes that the during the last decade, global financial elites have configured an elaborate system that makes most of the military budget unauditable. This is because the real black budget includes money acquired by intelligence groups via narcotics trafficking, predatory lending, and various kinds of other financial fraud.**

What's Up With...

The Black Budget?

- The $64 Question -

Catherine Austin Fitts former Assistant Secretary of Housing – Federal Housing Commissioner in the first Bush Administration

The result of this vast, geopolitically-sanctioned money laundering scheme is that Housing and Urban Devopment and other agencies are used for drug trafficking and securities fraud. According to Fitts, the scheme allows for at least 85 percent of the U.S. federal budget to remain unaudited.

Fitts has been researching this issue since 2001, when she began to believe that a financial coup d'etat was underway. **Specifically, she suspected that the banks, corporations, and investors acting in each global region were part of a "global heist," whereby capital was being sucked out of each country. She was right.**

As Fitts asserts,

"[She] served as Assistant Secretary of Housing at the US Department of Housing and Urban Development (HUD) in the United States where I oversaw billions of government investment in US communities ... I later found out that the

government contractor leading the War on Drugs strategy for U.S. aid to Peru, Colombia and Bolivia was the same contractor in charge of knowledge management for HUD enforcement. This Washington-Wall Street game was a global game. The peasant women of Latin America were up against the same financial pirates and business model as the people in South Central Los Angeles, West Philadelphia, Baltimore and the South Bronx."

This is part of an even larger financial scheme. It is fairly well-established by now that international financial institutions like the World Trade Organization, the World Bank, and the International Monetary Fund operate primarily as instruments of corporate power and nation-controlling infrastructure investment mechanisms. **For example, the primary purpose of the World Bank is to bully developing countries into borrowing money for infrastructure investments that will fleece trillions of dollars while permanently indebting these "debtor" nations to the West. But how exactly does the World Bank go about doing this?**

John Perkins wrote about this paradigm in his book, "Confessions of an Economic Hitman." During the 1970s, Perkins worked for the international engineering consulting firm, Chas T. Main, as an "economic hitman." He says the operations of the World Bank are nothing less than ...

John Perkins is an American author, best known book is *Confessions of an Economic Hit Man* (2004).

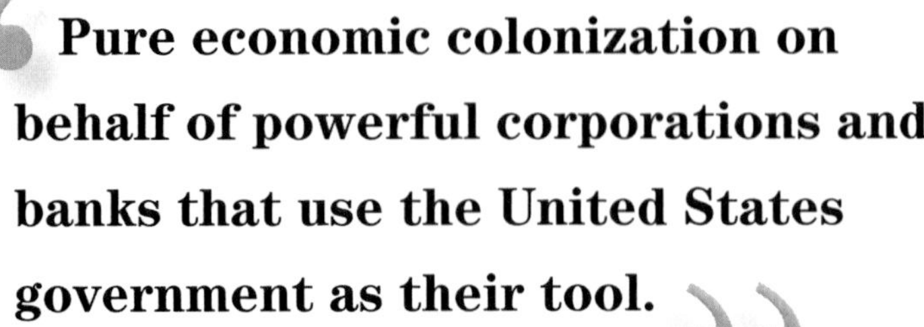

> **Pure economic colonization on behalf of powerful corporations and banks that use the United States government as their tool.**

In his book, Perkins discusses Joseph Stiglitz, the Chief Economist for the World Bank from 1997-2000, at length. Stiglitz described the four-step plan for bamboozling developing countries into becoming debtor nations:

Joseph Stiglitz

Step One...

according to Stiglitz, is to convince a nation to privatize its state industries.

Step Two...

utilizes "capital market liberalization," which refers to the sudden influx of speculative investment money that depletes national reserves and property values while triggering a large interest bump by the IMF.

Step Three...

Stiglitz says, is "Market-Based Pricing," which means raising the prices on food, water and cooking gas. This leads to **"Step Three and a Half: The IMF Riot."** Examples of this can be seen in Indonesia, Bolivia, Ecuador and many other countries where the IMF's actions have caused financial turmoil and social strife.

Step Four...

of course, is "free trade," where all barriers to the exploitation of local produce are eliminated.

There is a connection between the U.S. black budget and the trillion dollar international investment fraud scheme. Our government and the banking cartels and corporatocracy running it have configured a complex screen to block our ability to audit their budget and the funds they use for various black op projects. However, they cannot block our ability to uncover their actions and raise awareness.

Cursed Are the War Makers

Cursed are the war makers
They shall be called children of hell
Cursed are the war makers
For every life they take and every lie they tell.

Their false flags have set the world on fire
Turning it into a funeral pyre
Pushing the stakes higher and higher
Universal dominion is their demonic desire.

They leave nations in rubble and ruin
Brainwashing the masses with their martial tune
Promoting war so a new world can bloom
But only nightshades thrive in a realm of gloom.

Puppet politicians are ringing the bell
Clamoring for the death of the infidel
Cursed are the war makers
for every life they take and every lie they tell
Cursed are the war makers …
they shall be called children of hell.

Edward Moran

They are all wrong

By **Adrian Krieg**

April 07, 2015

Yes, it's a fact, the economists, banksters and politicians have been wrong in their economic predictions and their proposed solutions for the last 50 years, certainly since the Bretton Woods Conference.

The basic economic theory being; that based on economic trends they are able to stimulate economic growth by manipulating the value of fiat, and interest rates. These short-term efforts used by banking and government has never in history succeeded and never will. The most pronounced failure has been Japan which has attempted to QE itself out of a failing economy for 20 years. Standing in a bucket and pulling on the handle does not raise the bucket or its occupant.

Politicians in an inane desire for re-election press QE monitory expansions in desperate attempt to stave off the inevitable economic downturn. All economic activity in free markets is cyclical, but bankers in 1913 claimed that they could control free markets by manipulating interest rates, government borrowing, and capital availability, preventing economic up and down turns, they failed every single time. The American economy is about $14.7 trillion dollars; for bankers to imagine that they are able to control cyclical economic action through financial stimulus is akin to a flea threatening an elephant with rape. QE simply explained; is purchasing your own debt by writing cheques on bank accounts that have no asset. But they don't even bother with that; all they do is to instruct their 12 FRS branch banks to increase their credit side balance sheet, the total amount to date is about $ 4.4 trillion, not one cent of which is listed in the national debt accounts. This in fact makes the national debt $22.37 trillion, not the reported $18.17 trillion; just as I predicted five years ago, more smoke and mirrors.

It is really difficult to understand that in view of the fact that since the Weimar Republic of the early 30's, every effort to control markets by democrats, socialists, republicans, and communists has totally failed, regardless they keep trying. The only exception was Hjalmar Schacht, who under the Nazis opted out of the Rothschild dominated banking industry; the Jews then declared war on Germany for that act in 1933. Interference with the markets has the same inevitable result; it makes things worse. It's not that difficult to understand, the sheer number of issues impacting the rise and fall of economies encompasses so many issues that not even a super computer can make predictions. Many of the affecting emanates are impossible to predict, for example, population age, weather, crop growth, consumer demand, new products replacing old ones and new inventions. Additionally these people ignore population demographics.

For the past six months government economists have been pontificating that the economy is recovering and we are on the way to a bright and glorious future. There are unfortunately several real facts contradicting this prediction. The Atlanta Fed has just downgraded their economic prediction for the first quarter of 2015 to a growth rate of 0.0%, down from their bogus 2.3% prediction. The new adjusted prediction indicates no economic growth for 2015. Meanwhile the Kansas City Fed stated "we do not see the economy as being as strong as portrayed in national media reports" by the way, all those reports come from 1600 PA Ave. Employment stats were also changed to 126K from a prediction of 225K the lowest new jobs statistic since Jan. 2014. By the way if the new jobs are not over 220K there is an actual loss because 220K new workers come into the economy every month. This is the worst report in four years. The statistics were intensely massaged by various government agencies. The Department of labor postulated that dismal U.S. Jobs sector statistics were due to bad weather and would rebound shortly--- not so, they did not rebound, and blaming the weather for the loss of new jobs is just plain silly. The really telling issue is US S&P

profits and Sales, which are both, stalled at 0% growth.

Why are they continuously and relentlessly wrong? Demographics of population. The most pronounced occurrence is Japan. Beginning in 1989 the Japanese economy began to collapse. Japan realized a 0% inflation rate and a 0% growth rate, which has continued well into the 21st century. The problem in Japan, which is the same problem we now have here and the one that is appearing in Europe, is reduced population growth, an increase of age, coupling to produce lower consumer demand. Westernized economies are over 60% based on consumption by consumers. As the population increases in age it consumes at lower rates. In Europe and America politicians have tried to reverse that problem through increased legal and illegal immigration. In Europe with people from North Africa, mostly Muslims, in America with people from Central America, mostly Mestizos. In both cases the increase of population by lower intelligence, less educated has had deleterious effect on not only the economies but also increasing crime, and terrorism.

Coping with these issue by governments have been stupid and totally ineffective. Due to political correctness (Cultural Marxism) they absolutely refuse to identify people by race or national origin. They bulk the entire population into a single classification of humans, completely discounting the reality of age demographics, buying power and crime statistics by race and national origin. Minorities, are statistically suppressed even by the FBI crime statistics reportage, minorities commit 86% of all crime. Exactly the same error is made by economists in attempted future predictions. Based in CM it is incorrect to tell the truth and society must suffer the consequences of the misinformation released by the bureaucracies.

In economics this is more harmful than in social issues because it affects the entire society, rich as well as poor. The idea that immigration of low educated, poor, will reverse the demographic downturn is wrong. Demographic bell curves do not change with a stimulus that differs from the existing norm. Bell curves are only usable if the existing human product is constant; if it is not then the predictions are not workable. And no Milton Freedman economic cycles are not driven by inflation or monitory policy, they are motivated by population age, and population volume. One of the most ill conceived demographic assumptions is related to total population, the 2010 census was bogus and thus economic and demographic assumptions based on the 2010 census are wrong.

The US Census bureau counted every resident in the country; this caused a population assumption of about 318.7 million, they counted, every living resident including; illegals, green card holders, foreign diplomats, all children over 10 months old, and they counted most hospital interred, living in barracks, and military twice. By this they distorted the American population by at least 24 million. Demographics and economic behavior between citizens and non-citizens especially illegals vary vastly. This produces false statistics and bad economic perditions.

In order for the American economy to retain health it must produce about 220,000 new jobs every month, which would be enough to accommodate new entrees, children coming of age, college and HS graduates, and immigrants, both legal and illegal. For the last decade we have almost constantly been below that number, or the number was misrepresented by the Department of Labor. Additionally, under the table paid workers, are not counted at all. In the mean time they have also misrepresented unemployment now reported at 5.5% at 8.5 million, completely false, real unemployment remains at 24.3% or about 57 million based on their 318 million total population number of the 2010 census. If in fact our unemployment level was actually 8.5 million how could we have 47 million on food stamps?

All reported numbers are based on political expediency to get a Democrat elected in 2016, and the Republicans are too stupid to bring this issue to public information. Republicans will again run a RINO in 2016, snatching defeat from the jaws of victory yet once again. The time is at hand for a new political party that represents the people not the politician republocrats and their bureaucrat toadies.

Black-Listed by Banksters

By **Cushman Cunningham**

I have had repeated evidence over the decades that I am being black-listed by some powerful international force which has destroyed various businesses I have tried to start up. That happened to University European Villages {UEV) which I tried to organize in Europe and to several other projects which were blasted out of the water even before they got underway. You had asked me to repeat the sad story of South Seas Catamaran, Inc. (SSC, Inc.) which I started in Cape Coral, Florida. We (SSC) manufactured large high-speed commercial passenger catamarans for use in semi-protected waters such as the Mediterranean, the Baltic, the Caribbean and the Islands between Southeast Asia and Australia.

Many boat operators came to visit our factory and told us that they wanted to buy our catamarans. But as most of them later explained to me why they could not: **they told us that when they asked for financing from their bank (which had**

previously financed boats for them) their bank told them: "We will finance a boat for you built by any boat builder, except South Seas Catamaran."

I had earlier always had a spotless credit record confirmed by one of the most-reputable large banks in New York (Bank of New York Mellon) when necessary.

Now, back to South Seas Catamaran: Two partners, owners of several resort hotels and condo buildings on Venice Beach in Florida wanted to buy a large catamaran from us. **They had a signed letter of credit from the SunTrust Bank in Florida for that purpose.** They came to us one day very distressed, saying that Sun Trust refused to honor that letter-of-credit. That was unimaginable. A letter-of-credit from a bank is rock-solid legal guarantee for a loan. I went with them to talk to the SunTrust Bank office manager with whom they had been dealing. The poor fellow was so embarrassed he could hardly reply intelligibly, so he called the regional SunTrust Bank office. He then told us the SunTrust bank executive Vice-President would be there in just a minute. **It turned out to be about an hour before a very large man with a Jewish name in an elegant business suit stormed**

in. He yelled at me in a threatening voice that Sun Trust Bank would not honor that letter-of-credit ... we could sue them if we wished ... but Sun Trust Bank would NOT honor that letter-of-credit. Then he stormed out slamming the door.

I called our attorney when I got back to the South Seas Catamaran office. **He was incredulous! A reputable bank <u>not honoring</u> a letter-of-credit! He had never heard of such a thing.** He said he would investigate and call me back. A couple of hours later he called. His voice was low and different. **He seemed frightened. He advised me not to talk to anyone else about it.** He said he would continue to investigate it and report back to me. But again he advised me not to talk to anyone about it ... not even family members! There was a convincingly urgent tone to his voice. Sun Trust Bank never did honor that letter-of-credit and I never saw the partners from Venice Beach again. They had disappeared.

South Seas Catamaran had all kinds of other unusual problems ... with disappearing employees, heavy pressures on our factory-building owner to kick us out (he did not) ... and we constantly had problems getting our cats to water to launch them. The sights where we launched them were constantly being closed to us, so we had to find new launch sites with access to the open sea. Our launch sites were closed something like a dozen times. Towards the end we had to have our cats hauled many miles to launch them at 3 to 4 o'clock in the dark of early morning when traffic was minimal.

Our problems with the banks were continuous, though always petty and minor. Often a cashier or low-level bank employee made a "mistaken with our account. We had to personally escort our employees with their SSC paychecks to the bank; otherwise they had problems and were forced to wait. Of course this led our employees to wonder how long we would stay in business.

The advantages of the catamaran hull design have been shown

across the world in the last couple of decades by the fact that most passenger boat operators across the world are now using catamarans … in the Mediterranean, in Mexico's Baja, California and elsewhere.

The narrow twin hulls of the catamaran have a much higher "hull-speed" than the earlier mono-hull boats. **They use much less fuel and travel much faster.**

The use of fiberglass in hull manufacturing is much faster, cheaper and more durable than riveted aluminum. The bow of the fiberglass hull can be laid up so as to resist the pounding of waves (especially important for high-speed boats) whereas all aluminum hulls have a memory that leaves minute footprints as the hull speeds across the waves and eventually the aluminum cracks up in the bow in high-speed boat operations.

South Seas Catamaran, Inc. with its advanced research and development was way ahead of other manufacturers in the field and a threat to monopolistic tendencies of the Federal Reserve banking system (world-wide). So much for free enterprise.

Usury, The Bible & Financial Conduct

By **Peter Jon Simpson**

Peter Jon Simpson, August 1995

Hidden from history is the truth about Europe coming out of the Dark Ages and The Bubonic Plague, or "Black Death".

As one-third of Europe succumbed to the disease, the Church sought answers to stop the plague. The line between civil and ecclesiastical governance at the time was blurred, and the Church controlled many civil government functions in European Societies.

It is recorded but seldom repeated that a group of monks, searching for a solution, stumbled upon an obscure military sanitation statute in the Book of Deuteronomy. This statute controlled sanitation and human waste:

KJV Deuteronomy 23:13

And thou shalt have a paddle upon thy weapon; and it shall be, when thou wilt ease thyself abroad, thou shalt dig therewith, and shalt turn back and cover that which cometh from thee:

The short version is the monks brought forward this law, and the Church, for whatever reason, imposed it upon Christian Europe. In hamlet and village, town and city, the morning chamber pots were no longer emptied onto the streets to be tracked all over everywhere. As soon as this enactment was accomplished, the

Black Death began receding and disappeared. Encouraged and intrigued by this turn of events, the monks returned to the Law of Moses, searching for other ideas to improve society. They came upon the financial conduct laws, especially those focusing on usury. And they made them law as well.

Today the definition of usury has been changed from it's Bible definition. From any rate of interest on a loan of money, the Bible definition, usury has today become an illegal or exorbitant rate of interest. Today's bankers escape penalty, and the people are enslaved financially. This is true "verbicide"; we are being killed with words.

The Church of this day, circa 1300 to 1350, outlawed usury. The idea swept across Europe.

If you were caught in a contract of loaned money with a rate of interest, the following ensued:

- **Borrower and lender were ordered to cease and desist and were given 30 days to do so.**
- **Borrower return all loaned monies, Lender returned all "interest" paid.**
- **If borrower or lender did not cease and desist, they were given the opportunity to leave the jurisdiction within a narrow time window, usually 30 days.**
- **If they remained in the usury contract, they were apprehended and tried as Capital Felons. The Penalty was death at the gallows.**

The result of the implementation of these statutes led to what you know as "The Renaissance". Guilds began, trade unions began, both flourished. The Economy exploded and business expanded. Money was what the Bible proscribed, "silver".

The great Gothic Cathedrals in Europe were started and completed in this period, and there was so much wealth those great edifices were built with donated materials and volunteer labor. Men with one-skill set volunteered to

work on the Cathedral to learn a new, different skill-set. Europeans wore leather boots and had plenteous meat and bread and beer. The Dark Ages faded into history.

The average working man in those days worked 14 weeks to supply his family with one full year's worth of food, shelter, clothing, medication [such as it was] and recreation. England had 200 National Holidays; Germany had 180, France had 160 or more. The only difference between then and now was they had no electricity and usury was a death penalty felony. Compare that life for the average working man to today ...

The Hebrew word rendered **"usury"** in English Bibles today is a word worth examining. It has nothing to do with financial conduct. It translates **"the serpent's bite"** or **"the scorpion's sting"**. Few readers will need to learn who **"the serpent"** is ... In Strong's Exhaustive Concordance of the Bible, check Hebrew words #5391 and #5392 in Deuteronomy 23:19, translated in English as **"usury"**.

If you think about it a moment, it is common sense, or it was in the Bible. Bankers will always lend you the principal but never **"the serpent's bite"**, or interest.

Put another way, if there are 100 units of money worldwide, and you lend them to me on a contract promising that I repay you 110 units in one year, I've agreed to do the impossible. If there are only 100 units of money worldwide, where will I get the extra 10 units? Do you see?

Sharia Law on Financial Conduct

The abolition of usury in America today is a topic that takes us, with great peril, to the topic most call "Sharia Law". Sharia Law means different things to different people, and in our lame-stream media today, it is widely condemned, in so far as particular segments of that law are discussed. One segment of Sharia Law is banned from discussion in American Mass Media: **usury and financial conduct**.

Muslims hold, in the main, that the 5 Books of Moses in the Christian Bible are an adequate and satisfactory presentation of God's Laws for men on earth. Muslims certainly have added to and twisted God's Laws, as have most Christians, but it bears emphasizing that Sharia Law's treatment of usury matches up with the Christian Bible's treatment. Ezekiel 18:5-20 is the quick and easy reference.

The connection between Sharia Law and the GOD'S LAW through Moses cannot, and is not, ever presented, or parsed. It might prove fatal to the usurious dream-world in which America finds itself as it spirals into bankruptcy. Want to own a home in Detroit?

In 1990, the Sharia Banks in Egypt wrote more new commercial loan business than did the usury-Banks. Here's the real world, "in your face":

In usury-Banking, the usury-banker "creates money" out of thin air; out of his ability to "create money" out of nothing. **Creating "something out of nothing" is, of course, the Province of GOD alone.** See Genesis, Chapter One. It is, of course, not money but credit [from the usurer] or debt [to you]. The usury-Banker uses these terms interchangeably. Do you use them interchangably?

The Bankers' use of words is artful and ingenious. For you, it is fatal. "I'm eligible for credit down at the Bank, think I'll go into debt." I've got good debt-eligibility down at the Bank, think I'll go borrow some credit."

Debt ... **D E A T H**. Mortgage, mortician, mortuary. An etymological dictionary is very revelatory when reviewing the verbicide you are reading here and living daily in America.

The usury-Banker creates a checking account with what you think is, or call "money" in it. You get a nice book of checks with a hefty balance in the account. The usury-Banker has no cost or risk in the loan. You pledge collateral assets against the loan. If you don't pay, the usury-Banker forecloses, gets your property; if you are a success, you pay the usury. The usury-Banker can't lose,

only you can. Do you see that?

So you borrow $100,000 and open a car repair shop. At the exact mid-point of the life of the loan contract, an accident leaves you unable to work. Your venture fails, your friendly usury-Banker forecloses on your failure to perform the specifics of the loan contract, takes your property pledged and leaves you with nothing. On a loan of "money" in which the usury-Banker had no cost or risk. This is what your Federal Reserve calls "Modern Money Mechanics". Are we having fun yet?

In Sharia Banking, things are a bit more "Biblical".

Sharia Banks do not lend credit created from out of thin air. They loan money, the savings and deposits of their depositors and savers. The Sharia Bank reviews your proposal for your car repair shop, and agrees to lend you $100,000. But the terms are different.

Since they are lending you depositors savings, they carefully review your business venture. **They lend you the $100,000 at 0% interest, and instead negotiate with you a profit-sharing arrangement. If you're a success, the Sharia Bank succeeds; if you fall down, the Sharia Bank loses. The 0% interest loan runs for 7 years or less, per your Bible.** In the end, you own your business outright, the Sharia Bank shares profits for 7 years on mutually acepted terms for the use of their depositors' money. And if you have the same accident, above, resulting in foreclosure above, there's a slightly different outcome:

In the Sharia Loan, if you are disabled half-way thru the term of the contract, your payments to the Bank cease. Instead of taking all your stuff in foreclosure, the Sharia Bank finds another auto-repair guy and pitches him the same deal you signed. When he accepts, signs and makes his 1st profit-sharing payment to the Sharia Bank, the Sharia Banker pays you half of the profit-sharing payment he makes, because you were in for half the deal before your accident prevented you from continuing.

Oh, those wicked and evil, perverted Muslims. For shame!!

Try pitching that paradigm to your friendly, local

"neighborhood usury-Banker". When he or she looks at you like you're a Spider From Jupiter, you'll understand why the true history of the Black Plague, the Abolition of Usury in Christian Europe and the resulting Renaissance are never discussed in "polite company." Guess who holds the bonds on your school systems; guess who owns and controls your media outlets? The usury-Banks have a vested interest, pun intended, in your continued ignorance.

The Coming Police-State/ Slave State will be predicated on everyone being in debt to the Bankers. Your Voter ID, your bank and financial records, your driving records, your health and legal records will all be on an electronic personal data device. Don't get caught out of the house without that PDA; otherwise how can the COPS know you're mortgage, school, personal and business loans are current? **Your slavery will be assured, your chains will be electronic, your debt will be perpetual and never-ending.**

Meanwhile, back in your Bible, you can see what GOD thinks of all this. The word "usury" appears 24 times in the King James Bible; "usurer" appears once. If you dare, research all 25 texts thru a Bible Lexicon. Then take note of and pay special attention to Luke 19: 12- 27; Jesus' "Parable of the 10 Talents". That Luke 19 parable is the most scathing indictment of usury in the English Bible, till you let modern preachers explain it.

"Viv le differance'."

If you want more of this, in detail, up-front with no holds barred, get "Life Without Usury" in book form for one silver-weight dollar coin or for 25 Fraudulent Reserve Unit Accounting Devices, affectionately known as "FRAUD NOTES", from:

Peter Jon Simpson
c/o P.O. Box 211
Atwater Minnesota 56209-0211

This writer is so weird, he'll let you buy his work from him for money or he'll let you steal his book for bank credit.

Are we having fun yet?

Luke 19:12-27 New International Version (NIV)

12 He said: "A man of noble birth went to a distant country to
have himself appointed king and then to return. 13 So he called
ten of his servants and gave them ten minas.[a] 'Put this money to
work,' he said, 'until I come back.'
14 "But his subjects hated him and sent a delegation after him to
say, 'We don't want this man to be our king.'
15 "He was made king, however, and returned home. Then he
sent for the servants to whom he had given the money, in order to
find out what they had gained with it.
16 "The first one came and said, 'Sir, your mina has earned ten
more.'
17 "'Well done, my good servant!' his master replied. 'Because
you have been trustworthy in a very small matter, take charge of
ten cities.'
18 "The second came and said, 'Sir, your mina has earned five more.'
19 "His master answered, 'You take charge of five cities.'
20 "Then another servant came and said, 'Sir, here is your mina;
I have kept it laid away in a piece of cloth. 21 I was afraid of you,
because you are a hard man. You take out what you did not put in
and reap what you did not sow.'
22 "His master replied, 'I will judge you by your own words, you
wicked servant! You knew, did you, that I am a hard man, taking
out what I did not put in, and reaping what I did not sow? 23 Why
then didn't you put my money on deposit, so that when I came
back, I could have collected it with interest?'
24 "Then he said to those standing by, 'Take his mina away from
him and give it to the one who has ten minas.'
25 "'Sir,' they said, 'he already has ten!'
26 "He replied, 'I tell you that to everyone who has, more will be
given, but as for the one who has nothing, even what they have
will be taken away. 27 But those enemies of mine who did not want
me to be king over them—bring them here and kill them in front
of me.'"

---

a. Luke 19:13 A mina was about three months' wages.

ISLAM by Andrew (henrymakow.com)

For the last few months, I've reviewed accurate narratives about the life of Mohammed. The last great prophet died at the age of 63. On his deathbed, he attributed his premature death to his poisoning at the hands of an Arabian Jewess who successfully poisoned not only him but also other lieutenants who actually died immediately.

Mohammed died years later in 632 AD. The Jews of Arabia during Mohammed's day were the primary merchants of spirits and wines which Mohammed forbade his followers, so they naturally worked indefatigably to nip their Islamic problem "in the bud" so to speak. This poisoning of the Islamic leadership was only one of numerous attempts to eliminate the Muslims from Arabia while the movement was still in its infancy.

"American Freedom Defense Initiative" President, Pamela Geller.

Today, the attack is fiercer than ever except now it takes the form of THE BIG LIE in a relentless campaign of defamation against Islam. As Abdullah Ganji, the managing-director of an influential Iranian newspaper recently explained, the Jewish media continuously presents an ugly, violent, homicidal and false face of Islam to the world in order to prepare everyone for the gruesome Islamic genocide of World War III in a few years.

In order to counter the phony ISIS message of DEATH TO ALL INFIDELS, I thought it was time to tell the truth. What follows is a synopsis written in the 1930s of Essad Bey's biography, Mohammed.

THE LAST GREAT PROPHET Reviewed by Thomas Sugrue

"Mohammed was a prophet, but he never performed a miracle. He was not a mystic; he had no formal schooling; he did not begin his mission until he was forty. When he announced that he was the Messenger of God, bringing word of the true religion, he was ridiculed and labeled a lunatic. Children tripped him and women threw filth upon him. He was banished from his native city, Mecca, and his followers were stripped of their worldly goods and sent into the desert after him. When he had been preaching ten years he had nothing to show for it but banishment, poverty and ridicule. Yet before another ten years had passed, he was dictator of all Arabia, ruler of Mecca, and the head of a New World religion which was to sweep to the Danube and the Pyrenees before exhausting the impetus he gave it. **That impetus was three-fold: the power of words, the efficacy of prayer and man's kinship with God.**

A painting of Mohammed.

"His career never made sense. Mohammed was born to impoverished members of a leading family of Mecca. Because Mecca, the crossroads of the world, home of the magic stone called the Caaba, great city of trade and the center of trade routes, was unsanitary, its children were sent to be raised in the desert by Bedouins. Mohammed was thus nurtured, drawing strength and health from the milk of nomad, vicarious mothers. He tended sheep and soon hired out to a rich widow as leader of her caravans. **He traveled to all parts of the Eastern World, talked with many men of diverse beliefs and observed the decline of Christianity into warring sects.** When he was twenty-eight, Khadija, the widow, looked upon him with favor, and married him. Her father would have objected to such a marriage, so she got him drunk and held him up while he gave the paternal blessing. For the next twelve years **Mohammed** lived as a rich, respected and very shrewd trader. Then he took to wandering in the desert, and one day he returned with the first

◄ *The appointment of Mohammed through the angel.* PAINTING BY GABRIEL OLEH THEODOR HOSEMANN, 1847

verse of the Koran and told Khadija that the archangel Gabriel had appeared to him and said that he was to be the Messenger of God.

"The Koran, the revealed word of God, was the closest thing to a miracle in Mohammed's life. He had not been a poet; he had no gift of words. Yet the verses of the Koran, as he received them and recited them to the faithful, were better than any verses which the professional poets of the tribes could produce. This, to the Arabs, was a miracle. **To them the gift of words was the greatest gift, the poet was all-powerful. In addition the Koran said that all men were equal before God, that the world should be a democratic state Islam. It was this political heresy, plus Mohammed's desire to destroy all the 360 idols in the courtyard of the Caaba, which brought about his banishment. The idols brought the desert tribes to Mecca, and that meant trade. So the business men of Mecca, the capitalists, of which he had been one, set upon Mohammed. Then he retreated to the desert and demanded sovereignty over the world.**

"The rise of Islam began. Out of the desert came a flame which would not be extinguished--a democratic army fighting as a unit and prepared to die without wincing. **Mohammed had invited the Jews and Christians to join him; for he was not building a new religion. He was calling all who believed in one God to join in a single faith. If the Jews and**

Christians had accepted his invitation Islam would have conquered the world. They didn't. They would not even accept Mohammed's innovation of humane warfare. When the armies of the prophet entered Jerusalem not a single person was killed because of his faith. When the crusaders entered the city, centuries later, not a Moslem man, woman, or child was spared. But the Christians did accept one Moslem idea—the place of learning, the university."

Islam is a way of life, encompassing a religion, government and social rules. It is not a system adaptable to European concepts of democracy. In some respects it is better than our system in others it is worse. Regardless, any attempt to impose Western political concepts in Islamic nations is doomed to failure.

— Dr. A. H. Krieg

One of the best means to the introduction of any history is the historical novel.

Highly recommended for this time period...

At the center of *The Walking Drum* is Kerbouchard, one of Louis L'Amour's greatest heroes. Across Europe, the Russian steppes and through the Byzantine wonder of Constantinople, gateway to Asia, Kerbouchard is thrust into the heart of the treacheries, passions, violence and dazzling wonders of a magnificent time. ***The Walking Drum* is a powerful adventure of an ancient world.**

Author's Note – *The Walking Drum:*

The place names, titles of books, authors, and dates are factual, the descriptions of places and people are based upon the best contemporary and historical sources, as well as personal observation. On occasion I have referred to places by names now in use for purposes of clarity.

Unhappily, history as presented in our schools virtually ignores two-thirds of the world, confining itself to limited areas around the Mediterranean, to western Europe, and North America. Of China, India, and the Moslem world almost nothing is said, yet their contribution to our civilization was enormous, and they are now powers with which we must deal both today and tomorrow, and which it would be well for us to understand.

Photo of Louis L'Amour c. 1939

Louis L'Amour

February 1945, Germany

The film-clip insulting the Prophet Mohammed by Cushman Cunningham

With all the press attention now being focused on Hillary Clinton's role in the Benghazi tragedy, it is interesting that her first comment on it is now being assiduously ignored in the press.

She was first reported as saying that the CIA had just told her that the riot in Benghazi (in which Ambassador Stevens and three CIA agents had been killed) had been caused by a film-clip insulting the Prophet Mohammed, which the rioters accused "The Americans" of having made and circulated in major Muslim cities.

We have determined that such a film clip was indeed televised in cities all across the Muslim world, and did cause major anti-American riots in many such cities. The film-clip portrays the Prophet as a homosexual slobbering over two young boys.

In Hollywood, California, amongst the Jewish community, it was known exactly which Hollywood film studio had made it and which studio magnates had done it. It was gleefully applauded amongst the California Jewish community.

So why is that film-clip now never being mentioned in all the uproar over Hillary's role in the Benghazi tragedy? Obviously the Jewish owners of the press do not want us to think "the Jews" had intentionally caused those "anti-American" riots. Why? Did they want to foment war between the Muslim world and Christian West?

Kuala Lumpur, 21/09/2012. Malaysian Muslim demonstrators march towards the US embassy against an anti-Islam film, "Innocence of Muslims" and the publication of caricature of the Holy Prophet Muhammad
PHOTO: FIRDAUS LATIF

GLOBAL WARMING

Morning Roar: New Examples of Climate Data Fudged to Invent Global Warming

By **Brian McWilliams**
Lions of Liberty | February 10, 2015

Global Warming, or "Climate Change" as it was re-branded once the ample evidence started to emerge that this "settled" science was proving to be incorrect, still remains one of the topics that is viewed as unassailable by a wide swathe of the population.

"Climate change denier" is a term used by many to paint anyone who questions global warming as some sort of psychopath, intentionally bringing to mind the term "Holocaust denier," as if the two shared any semblance of overlap in any way, shape or form. This is a classic example of using slander when a rational argument can't be made. This dedication is in the face of publicly available climate models on which government policy and **papers were conceived, which have already been *proven* to be flawed at their core due to variables that couldn't be accounted for, and based on data sets that were exposed as having been doctored when the results didn't match what the scientists needed to keep their illusion – and funding – in place.**

Despite all of this, governments still funnel billions of dollars into green energy pet projects, technology for developing countries, and of course into the same scientists' pockets that have been riding the gravy train, even with their hypothesis being exposed as questionable at best. **In addition, policy changes alter the way we as private citizens live our lives, via coercive taxation and regulation, prohibition of products or technologies, and a hundred other ways which we don't even realize.**

When will this madness end? The Obama administration doesn't seem to understand or care that **climate science up to now has been unproven rubbish.** The President doubled down on this notion during his State of the Union Address just recently.

> **And no challenge, no challenge, poses a greater threat to future generations than climate change.**
>
> **2014 was the planet's warmest year on record.**

President Barack Obama delivers the State of the Union address in the House Chamber at the U.S. Capitol in Washington, D.C., Jan. 20, 2015. | OFFICIAL WHITE HOUSE PHOTO BY PETE SOUZA

Actually, according to the suspect data sets, it's tied with 2005 and 2010, and basically .02 degrees warmer or in the area of "uncertainty of measurement." **So it's really in line with the trend for the past 17 years of no statistically notable warming of the Earth.**

Now, speaking of those data sets – we come to the latest news. A noble soul has been going back through the climate data taken from weather stations across the globe and cross checking it with what has been published by our own government-funded climate organizations and scientists on the dole, and guess what? **They're at it again, increasing the temperatures in their**

published reports by a degree or more over what the actual data is. The Telegraph reports:

> **Two weeks ago, under the headline "How we are being tricked by flawed data on global warming", I wrote about Paul Homewood, who, on his Notalotofpeopleknowthat blog, had checked the published temperature graphs for three weather stations in Paraguay against the temperatures that had originally been recorded. In each instance, the actual trend of 60 years of data had been dramatically reversed, so that a cooling trend was changed to one that showed a marked warming.**
>
> **This was only the latest of many examples of a practice long recognised by expert observers around the world – one that raises an ever larger question mark over the entire official surface-temperature record.**
>
> **Following my last article, Homewood checked a swathe of other South American weather stations around the original three. In each case he found the same suspicious one-way "adjustments". First these were made by the US government's Global Historical Climate Network (GHCN). They were then amplified by two of the main official surface records, the Goddard Institute for Space Studies (Giss) and the National Climate Data Center (NCDC), which use the warming trends to estimate temperatures across the vast regions of the Earth where no measurements are taken. Yet these are the very records on which scientists and politicians rely for their belief in "global warming".**

Homewood has now turned his attention to the weather stations across much of the Arctic, between Canada (51 degrees W) and the heart of Siberia (87 degrees E). **Again, in nearly every case, the same one-way adjustments have been made, to show warming up to 1 degree C or more higher than was indicated by the data that was actually recorded.** This has surprised no one more than Traust Jonsson, who was long in charge of climate research for the Iceland met office (and with whom Homewood has been in touch). Jonsson was amazed to see how the new version completely "disappears" Iceland's "sea ice years" around 1970, when a period of extreme cooling almost devastated his country's economy.

Somehow this concept that the world is warming through manmade means has become a crusade, based upon a myth that refuses to die or rest, despite the evidence to the contrary.

I honestly feel that it's simply a matter of ego at this point, both for the scientists responsible for this movement and for those everyday people who for so long have stood behind it and now don't want to have to admit they were wrong. **It's mind boggling to say the very least, and the dangers to our liberties can't be understated as more legislation and taxation is piled up to "fight" climate change.**

There need to be more educated voices of reason in this debate, not blind believers in a dubious and very unproven "science" based upon money, deception, and politics.

* * *

Mind-Blowing Temperature Fraud At NOAA

By **Steven Goddard** | July 27, 2015

The measured US temperature data from USHCN shows that the US is on a long-term cooling trend. But the reported temperatures from NOAA show a strong warming trend (Fig. 1).

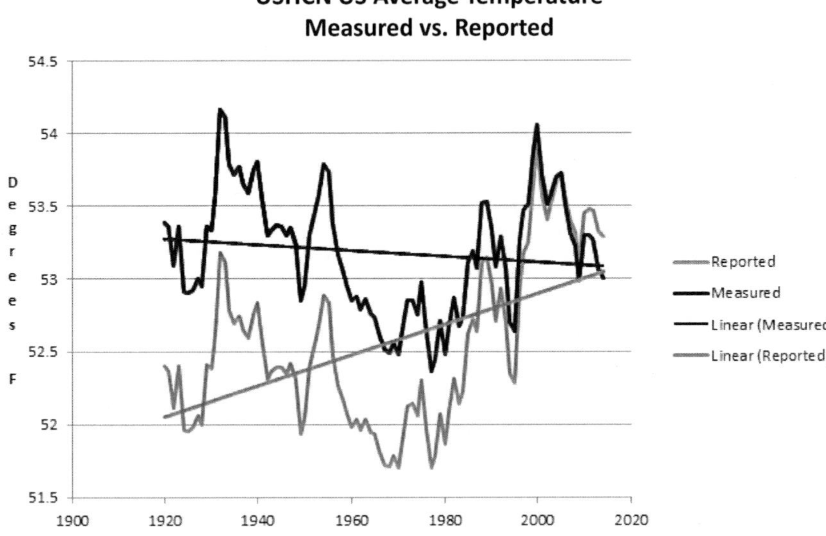

Fig. 1

They accomplish this through a spectacular hockey stick of data tampering, which corrupts the US temperature trend by almost two degrees **(Fig. 2)**.

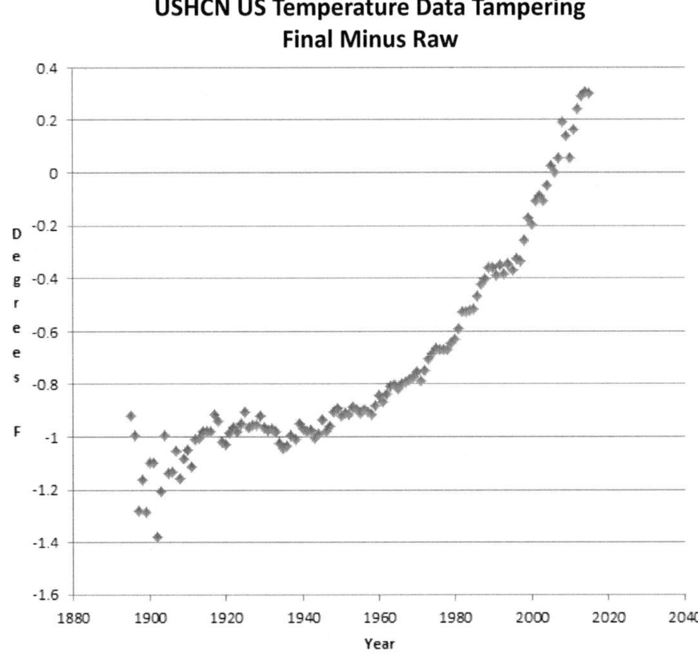

Fig. 2

The biggest component of this fraud is making up data. Almost half of all reported US temperature data is now fake. They fill in missing rural data with urban data to create the appearance of non-existent US warming **(Fig. 3)**.

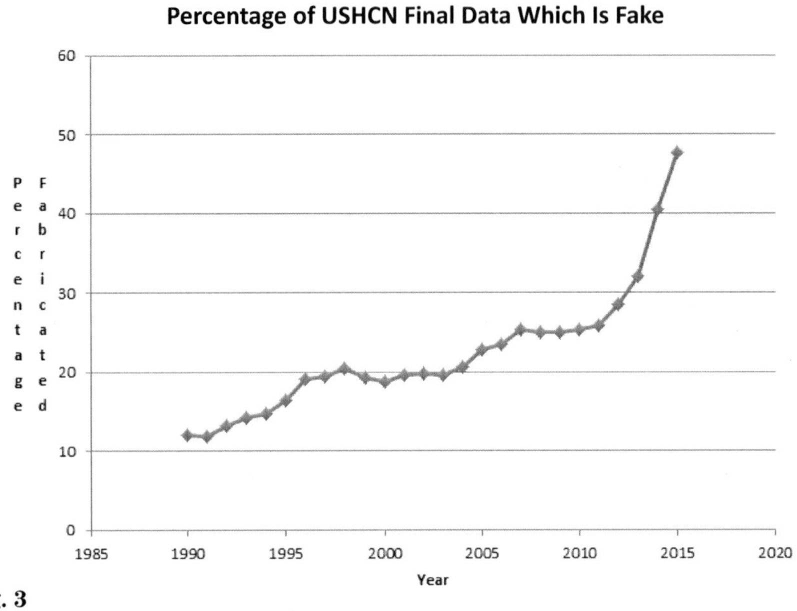

Percentage of USHCN Final Data Which Is Fake

Fig. 3

The depths of this fraud is breathtaking, but completely consistent with the fraudulent profession which has become known as "climate science."

"Science is the belief in the ignorance of the experts."

RICHARD FEYNMAN

Steven Goddard (pseudonym for Tony Heller) is a blogger and the publisher of "Real Science," a website he established to promulgate his assertions that concerns over anthropogenic global warming are unfounded. Before establishing his own blog, Goddard built his reputation as a challenger to anthropogenic climate change theories through frequent postings on the Watts Up with That? blog. Goddard wrote pseudonymously until 2014 when he revealed his true real identity on his blog. He has a BS in geology from Arizona State University and a Master's degree in electrical engineering from Rice University.

Climate of Fear

"Over the last 10,000 years it has been warmer than today 65 per cent of the time."

PROFESSOR GERNOT PATZELT, PHD
The international Climate and Energy Conference
Munich, 2011

"The whole hockey-stick episode reminds me of the motto of Orwell's Ministry of Information."

PROFESSOR WILLIAM HAPPER, PHD

On February 25, 2009 Professor Happer testified before the US Senate's Environment and Public Works Committee:

The existence of climate variability in the past has long been an embarrassment to those that all climate change is due to man and that man can control it. When I was a schoolboy, my text books on earth science showed a prominent "Medieval Warm Period" at the time the Vikings settled Greenland, followed by a vicious "Little Ice Age" that drove them out. So I was very surprised when I first saw the celebrated "hockey stick curve," in the Third Assessment Report of the IPCC. **I could hardly believe my eyes.** Both the Little Ice Age and the Medieval Warm Period were gone, and the newly revised temperature of the world since the year 1000 had suddenly become absolutely flat until the last hundred years when it shot up like the blade on a hockey stick...**the hockey stick was trumpeted around the world as evidence that the end was near. The hockey stick has nothing to do with reality** but was the result of incorrect handling of proxy temperature records and incorrect statistical analysis. There really was a Little Ice Age and there really was a Medieval Warm Period that was as warm or warmer than today.

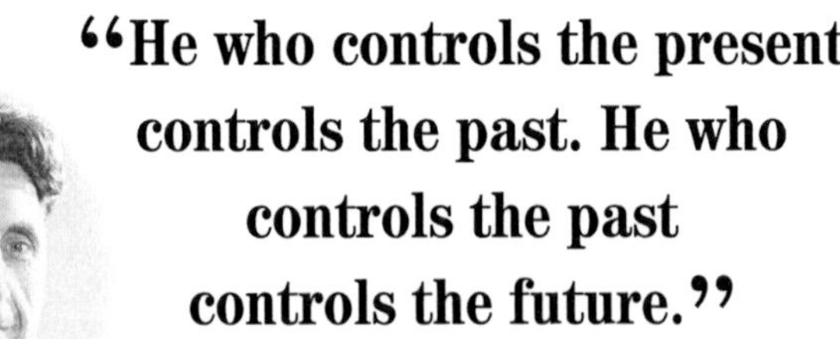

GEORGE ORWELL

And now it's global COOLING!
Record return of Arctic ice cap as it grows by 60% in a year

By **David Rose** | September 7, 2013

- Almost a million more square miles of ocean covered with ice than in 2012
- BBC reported in 2007 global warming would leave Arctic ice-free in summer by 2013
- Publication of UN climate change report suggesting global warming caused by humans pushed back to later this month

* * *

A chilly Arctic summer has left nearly a million more square miles of ocean covered with ice than at the same time last year – an increase of 60 per cent.

The rebound from 2012's record low comes six years after the BBC reported that global warming would leave the Arctic ice-free in summer by 2013.

Instead, days before the annual autumn re-freeze is due to begin, an unbroken ice sheet more than half the size of Europe already stretches from the Canadian islands to Russia's northern shores.

The Northwest Passage from the Atlantic to the Pacific has remained blocked by pack-ice all year. More than 20 yachts that had planned to sail it have been left ice-bound and a cruise ship attempting the route was forced to turn back.

Some eminent scientists now believe the world is heading for a period of cooling that will not end until the middle of this century – a process that would expose computer forecasts of imminent catastrophic warming as dangerously misleading.

The disclosure comes 11 months after The Mail on Sunday triggered intense political and scientific debate by revealing that global warming has 'paused' since the beginning of 1997 – an event that the computer models used by climate experts failed to predict.

In March, this newspaper further revealed that temperatures are about to drop below the level that the models forecast with '90 per cent certainty'.

The pause – which has now been accepted as real by every major climate research centre – is important, because the models' predictions of ever-increasing global temperatures have made many of the world's economies divert billions of pounds into 'green' measures to counter climate change.

Those predictions now appear gravely flawed.

The continuing furore caused by The Mail on Sunday's revelations – which will now be amplified by the return of the Arctic ice sheet – has forced the UN's climate change body to hold a crisis meeting.

The UN Intergovernmental Panel on Climate Change (IPCC) was due in October to start publishing its Fifth Assessment Report – a huge three-volume study issued every six or seven years. It will now hold a pre-summit in Stockholm later this month.

THERE WON'T BE ANY ICE AT ALL! HOW THE BBC PREDICTED CHAOS IN 2007

Only six years ago, the BBC reported that the Arctic would be ice-free in summer by 2013, citing a scientist in the US who claimed this was a 'conservative' forecast. Perhaps it was their confidence that led more than 20 yachts to try to sail the Northwest Passage from the Atlantic to the Pacific this summer. As of last week, all these vessels were stuck in the ice, some at the eastern end of the passage in Prince Regent Inlet, others further west at Cape Bathurst.

Shipping experts said the only way these vessels were likely to be freed was by the icebreakers of the Canadian coastguard. According to the official Canadian government website, the Northwest Passage has remained ice-bound and impassable all summer.

The BBC's 2007 report quoted scientist Professor Wieslaw Maslowski, who based his views on super-computer models and the fact that 'we use a high-resolution regional model for the Arctic Ocean and sea ice'.

He was confident his results were 'much more realistic' than other projections, which 'underestimate the amount of heat delivered to the sea ice'. Also quoted was Cambridge University expert

Professor Peter Wadhams. He backed Professor Maslowski, saying his model was 'more efficient' than others because it 'takes account of processes that happen internally in the ice'.

He added: 'This is not a cycle; not just a fluctuation. In the end, it will all just melt away quite suddenly.'

NEWS LIVE BBC NEWS AT ONE

Page last updated at 10:40 GMT, Wednesday, 12 December 2007

E-mail this to a friend Printable version

Arctic summers ice-free 'by 2013'

By Jonathan Amos
Science reporter, BBC News, San Francisco

Scientists in the US have presented one of the most dramatic forecasts yet for the disappearance of Arctic sea ice.

Their latest modelling studies indicate northern polar waters could be ice-free in summers within [illegible] years.

Leaked documents show that governments which support and finance the IPCC are demanding more than 1,500 changes to the report's 'summary for policymakers'. They say its current draft does not properly explain the pause.

At the heart of the row lie two questions: the extent to which temperatures will rise with carbon dioxide levels, as well as how much of the warming over the past 150 years – so far, just 0.8C – is down to human greenhouse gas emissions and how much is due to natural variability.

In its draft report, the IPCC says it is '95 per cent confident' that global warming has been caused by humans – up from 90 per cent in 2007.

This claim is already hotly disputed. US climate expert Professor Judith Curry said last night: 'In fact, the uncertainty is getting bigger. It's now clear the models are way too sensitive to carbon dioxide. I cannot see any basis for the IPCC increasing its confidence level.'

She pointed to long-term cycles in ocean temperature, which have a huge influence on climate and suggest the world may be approaching a period similar to that from 1965 to 1975, when there was a clear cooling trend. This led some scientists at the time to forecast an imminent ice age.

Professor Anastasios Tsonis, of the University of Wisconsin, was one of the first to investigate the ocean cycles. He said: 'We are already in a cooling trend, which I think will continue for the next 15 years at least. There is no doubt the warming of the 1980s and 1990s has stopped.

'The IPCC claims its models show a pause of 15 years can be expected. But that means that after only a very few years more, they will have to admit they are wrong.'

Others are more cautious. Dr Ed Hawkins, of Reading University, drew the graph published by The Mail on Sunday in March showing how far world temperatures have diverged from computer predictions. He admitted the cycles may have caused some of the recorded warming, but insisted that natural variability

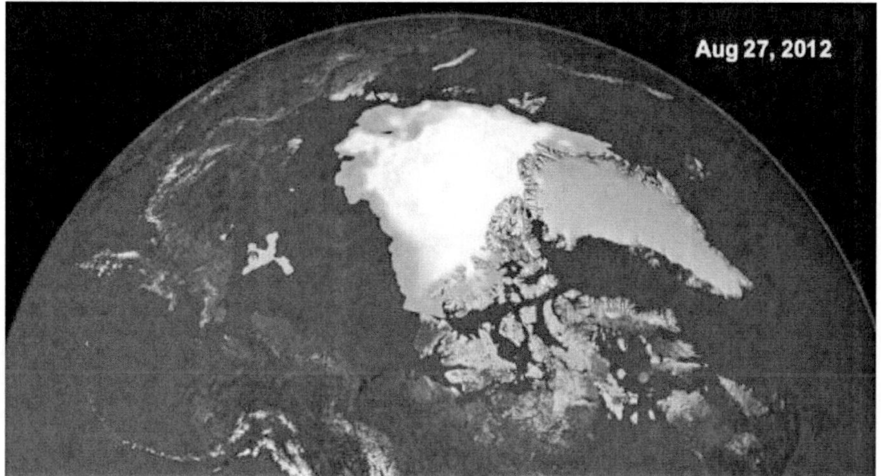

Then . . . NASA satelite images showing the spread of Artic sea ice 27th August 2012

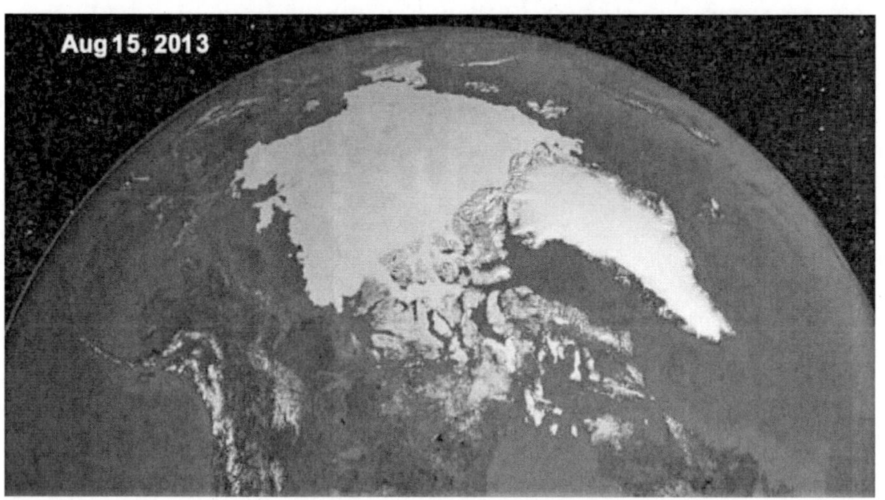

. . . And now, much bigger: The same Nasa image taken in 2013

alone could not explain all of the temperature rise over the past 150 years.

Nonetheless, the belief that summer Arctic ice is about to disappear remains an IPCC tenet, frequently flung in the face of critics who point to the pause.

Yet there is mounting evidence that Arctic ice levels are

cyclical. Data uncovered by climate historians show that there was a massive melt in the 1920s and 1930s, followed by intense re-freezes that ended only in 1979 – the year the IPCC says that shrinking began.

Professor Curry said the ice's behaviour over the next five years would be crucial, both for understanding the climate and for future policy. 'Arctic sea ice is the indicator to watch,' she said.

HOW NSIDC GOT ITS FIGURES WRONG AND THEN KEPT QUIET

Since publication of the original version of this article, the US source of the figures – the NASA-funded National Snow and Ice Data Centre (NSIDC) - was discovered to have made a huge error and then quietly corrected the figure without mentioning it.

On September 4, NSIDC, based at the University of Colorado, stated on its website that in August 2013 the Arctic ice cover recovered by a record 2.38 million sq km – 919,000 sq miles – from its 2012 low.

News of this figure was widely reported – including by Mailonline - on September 8. But on September 10, the NSIDC quietly changed it to 1.38 million sq km (533,000 sq miles) – and replaced the original document so the old figure no longer shows up on a main Google search. It can now only be found on an old 'cached' page.

The figures in this article have now been corrected.

Prompted by an inquiry from 'green' blogger Bob Ward, the NSIDC's spokeswoman Natasha Vizcarra said the mistake was a 'typographical error', telling him: 'There are no plans to make a statement on the change because it was not an error in the data.'

UPDATED: OCTOBER 11, 2014

Philippe Verdier

Top French Weatherman Fired For Denying Global Warming

By **Steve Birr**
Daily Caller
November 3, 2015

Top French weatherman Philippe Verdier was fired Saturday for publishing a book critical of the climate change narrative.

Verdier's story first gained traction in early October following reports that he was forced to take a vacation after his new book Climate Investigation was published. In the book, Verdier accuses global warming scientists of misleading the public and using scare tactics to force conformity on the issue, reports France 24. He specifically goes after the U.N.'s Intergovernmental Panel on Climate Change (IPCC), alleging that they have "politicized" climate change and intentionally published false data.

"I am being punished for exercising my freedom of expression," said Verdier. He was reportedly summoned two weeks ago to a meeting with top executives from French news channel France Televisions and received his official notice of termination on Saturday.

Verdier said he was inspired to write the book following a meeting he had with the French Foreign Minister Laurent Fabius. Fabius met with the country's top meteorologists to tell them to start pushing the global warming narrative by highlighting stories about the impact of climate change, according to France 24.

"I was horrified by this speech," said Verdier, who then set out to rebuke the climate change status quo by exposing the corruption within the movement. Verdier says there is a lot of pressure within the system to silence any dissent on this issue, especially with the upcoming COP21 climate summit in Paris this December.

"I put myself in the path of COP21, which is a bulldozer, and this is the result," said Verdier. He also notes that there could be many positive effects of global warming for France including a boost in tourism, cheaper energy prices and better health.

COP 21: Heads of Delegations

John Coleman, Weather Channel Founder

Weather Channel Founder: Man-Made Global Warming is 'Baloney'

By **Patrick Goodenough** | November 2, 2014
Published on CNS News (http://cnsnews.com)

On the same day that the U.N. Intergovernmental Panel on Climate Change issued a major new global warming report, John Coleman, a founder of the Weather Channel, appeared on CNN Sunday to reiterate his stance that **"climate change is not happening."**

The Weather Channel

Describing himself as a "skeptic," not a denier – "that is a word meant to put me down" – the veteran weather forecaster told CNN's "Reliable Sources" that the news network was promoting an inaccurate view on the issue.

"CNN has taken a very strong position on global warming, that it is a consensus," he said. "Well, there is no consensus in science.

Science isn't a vote, science is about facts."

"And if you get down to the hard, cold facts, there's no question about it: Climate change is not happening, there is no significant, man-made global warming now, there hasn't been any in the past, and there's no reason to expect any in the future. There's a whole lot of baloney."

Eyewitness News team, 1972. Back, from left: anchor John Drury, anchor Joel Daly. Front, from left: weatherman John Coleman, anchor Fahey Flynn, sportscaster Bill Frink.

Coleman said climate change has become part of the Democratic Party platform, adding that he regretted that the issue has become "political instead of scientific."

"But the science is on my side," he declared.

Challenged on the assertion that "97 percent of climate

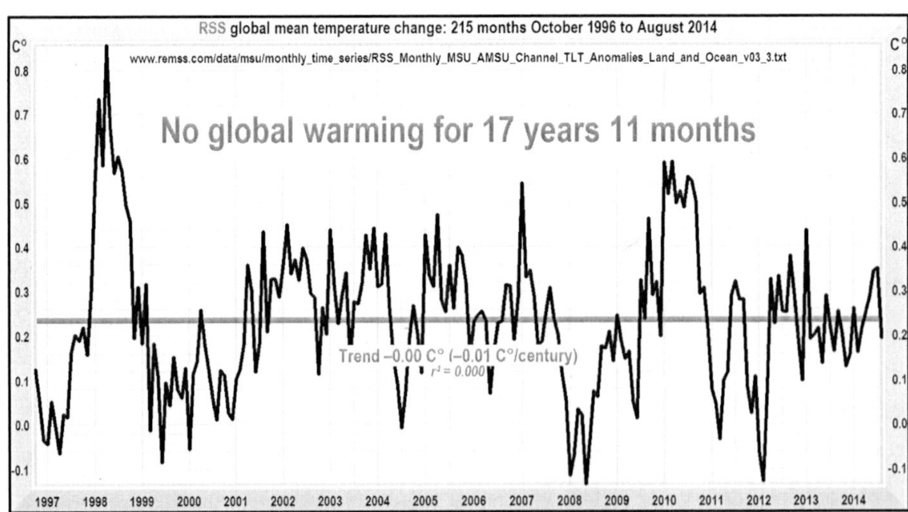

RSS (Remote Sensing System) monthly global mean lower-troposphere temperature anomalies (black) and trend (thick grey line), October 1996 to August 2014, showing no trend for 17 years 11 months. | HTTP://WWW.CLIMATEDEPOT.COM

David Kenny, *C.E.O. of the Weather Company, parent of the Weather Channel and Weather Underground.*

scientists" are in agreement on the issue, Coleman charged that the figure was "manipulated."

Since the government only funds scientists who put out results "supporting the global warming hypothesis," he claimed, "they don't have any choice."

"If you're going to get the money, you've got to support their position. Therefore 97 percent of the scientific reports published support global warming. Why? Because those are the ones the government pays for and that's where the money is."

Weather Channel CEO David Kenny also appeared on the show, and distanced himself from Coleman's views.

"We're grateful that he got it [the channel] started 32 years ago, but he hasn't been with us in 31 years, so he's not really speaking for the Weather Channel in any way today," he said.

"Our position is really clear, it's scientifically-based and we've been unwavering on it for quite some time now."

Last week the Weather Channel reissued a 2007 statement giving its position on climate change.

"More than a century's worth of detailed climate observations shows a sharp increase in both carbon dioxide and temperature," the statement says.

"These observations, together with computer model simulations and historical climate reconstructions from ice cores, ocean sediments and tree rings all provide strong evidence that the majority of the warming over the past century is a result of human activities. This is also the conclusion drawn, nearly unanimously, by climate scientists."

CUSHMAN
CUNNINGHAM

The Autobiography of a Real American Hero

On Tuesday, May 5, 2015, Chuck Ballard, freelance writer for the Breeze Newspapers, a publication in Florida, wrote an article titled, "World War II Veteran Recalls Battle for Bastogne." The photo above shows Earl B. Wilson giving his extemporaneous twenty minute speech before the awed members and guests during that weekly veteran's luncheon at the Southwest Florida Military Library and Museum in downtown Cape Coral. He spoke of the many incidents he witnessed through his battle for survival during World War II.

This is the true story of Earl B. Wilson, my hero!

Publisher, Jon Larsen Shudlick

AUTOBIOGRAPHY:

Earl B. Wilson

October, 2011

When I was 13-14 I went away to Kent School, in the Berkshires in western Connecticut. My main objection to life at Kent School was that in those years there were no girls at Kent School. I did not graduate from Kent, because in June of 1942 (at the end of what would have been my Junior year at Kent), I volunteered into the US Army and immediately volunteered into the Parachute troops. In January-February of that year I had taken and passed the entrance exams for the US Military Academy at West Point. But I had taken the exam on a 1st Alternate

Kent School

Aerial view of chapel and barracks, looking northeast – U.S. Military Academy, West Point, Orange County, NY. | SOURCE: LIBRARY OF CONGRESS

Earl B. Wilson

appointment. The Principal Appointment holder also passed the exam, so he got the appointment. Having passed the exam, that made me exempt from the draft. But I decided not to wait while all the young men my age were going into the armed military services. I had my own plan: I would go into the army and get some combat experience, and then go to West Point. That would give me a prestige advantage over my West Point classmates and hopefully faster promotions after I graduated and joined the army as an officer. I had read Charles de Gaulle's book "La Guerre Moderne" and was fascinated by his proposal for "vertical envelopment" by airborne forces. Combat experience in airborne warfare, I figured, would give me an additional competitive career advantage later. I had always, since very young, expected to make my career in the US Army, probably as a result of my Dad's tales of his life in the cavalry on the Mexican border in 1916-1920. He wrote and printed up a little booklet (titled: "Echoes of the Past"), which is the inspiration for this present autobiography ... which I am writing at my two sister's insistence, and that of my wife and others.

Charles de Gaulle

However, during my year and a half in Europe with the US Army some things happened (or in some cases I learned about them from others) which decided me against a career in the army. Canadian soldiers told me about how the British had intentionally sacrificed two Canadian regiments at Dieppe on the northern coast of France for some unrevealed political purpose. Free French paratroopers we were together with on a joint operation told me how the

British and Americans had not even told General de Gaulle and his Free French that they were going to invade French North Africa without them, had broken their promises to Admiral Darlan and French General Giraud (because of which promises Darlan and Giraud had allowed the Brits and Yanks to land unopposed in Algeria) and they had then murdered Admiral Darlan.

French General Henri Honoré Giraud

French Admiral Jean-Francois Darlan

Then there was the incredible case of how Eisenhower's London HQ had cut off Patton's ammo and supplies at Metz and had forbidden him to take his Third Army across the Rhine in Germany, as the German Generals in charge of the Middle Rhine were inviting him to do. All of that was written up in the "Stars and Stripes" (the Army's newspaper published in Europe for the US Army troops) and I personally was involved in those events, which were further confirmed to me personally afterwards by one of Patton's top staff officers. All this convinced me that it would be foolish for me to risk sacrificing my life in a politically-motivated war, initiated by politicians I despise, for purposes I disagreed with. So I never requested admission to West Point after the war.

General Dwight D. Eisenhower with Lieutenant General Mark W. Clark in Italy shortly before Eisenhower left for London to command the OVERLORD invasion forces.

Senior American commanders of World War II. Seated are (from left to right) Gens. William H. Simpson, George S. Patton, Carl A. Spaatz, Dwight D. Eisenhower, Omar Bradley, Courtney H. Hodges, and Leonard T. Gerow; standing are (from left to right) Gens. Ralph F. Stearley, Hoyt Vandenberg, Walter Bedell Smith, Otto P. Weyland, and Richard E. Nugent.

◄ *Major General George S. Patton Jr. (center) studies a map during World War II with General Lesley J. McNair (left), chief of staff of General Headquarters and later commanding general of U.S. Army Ground Forces.*

Harvard Yard as seen from Holyoke Center.

Instead I went to Harvard and graduated in 1949.

Back to the war. We were stationed at Camp Forrest, Tenn., in the spring of 1944, when I had a chance to volunteer to become a "Pathfinder" for parachute combat operations. Several crack men from our company had been selected and left for Camp McCall, NC, where pathfinder training was set up. But I had not been selected, much to my disappointment. All of those selected were older men (late 20s) and I was too young (still in my teens).

Suddenly one of the guys who had gone to McCall for pathfinder training returned to our company looking for me. That was Jim Foley. He told me that he had talked with the officer in charge of

◀ *The airfield at Camp Mackall located in eastern Richmond County and northern Scotland County, North Carolina, south of the town of Southern Pines.*

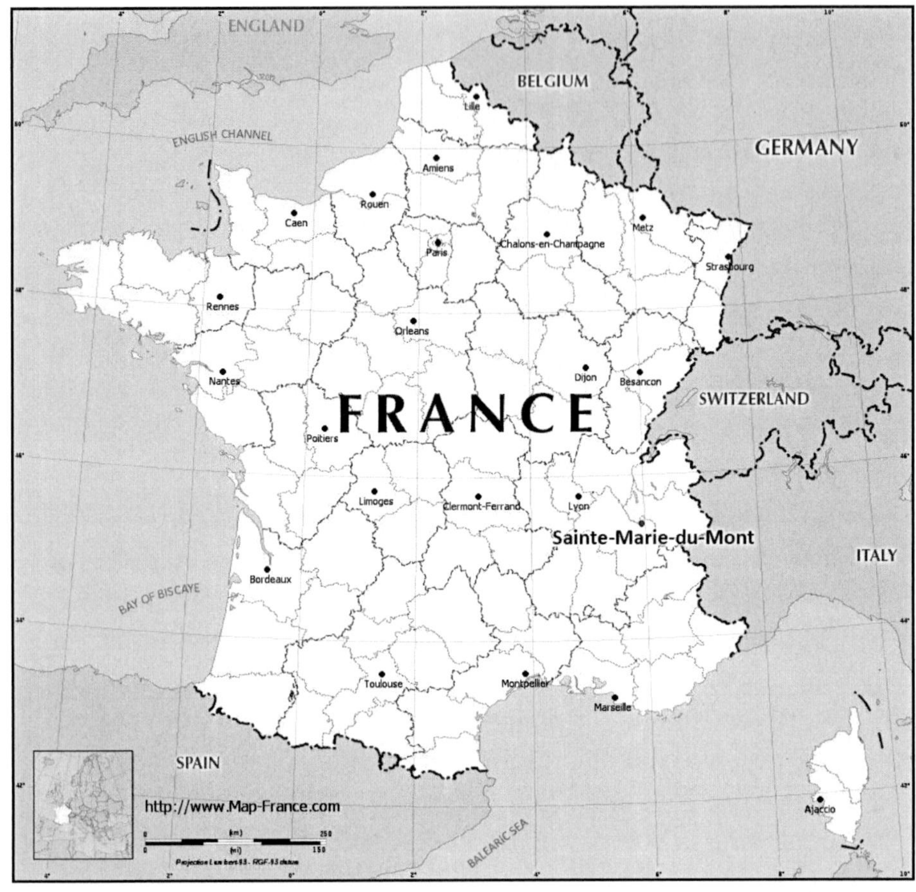

the pathfinder training at McCall and convinced him that I was a great candidate for pathfinder training. The officer had agreed to accept me, but only if I could be there on that next Monday. We quickly went down to the company orderly room and talked to "Pop" Collins, the First Sergeant. "Pop" agreed to forward my records to Camp McCall and to tell the "C" company commander, Captain Kendricks, that I had gone. "Pop" promised me "Cap" would be delighted at my good luck. We caught a C-47 to McCall that afternoon.

After Pathfinder training I ended up flying to England, arriving only a week or ten days before D-Day. I was assigned to a 3-man pathfinder team who would guide the 2nd battalion of the 506 in to their assigned "drop-zone" on D-Day. The 2nd battalion drop zone was around and including the town of Sainte-Marie-du-Mont, several miles inland behind the invasion beaches and a hundred feet or so higher than the beachheads.

There are normally 3-4 pathfinders assigned to jump into the battalion area a few hours before the planes fly the battalion into the "drop zone". Beforehand they get intensive orientation on the area around the "D-Z", its landmarks, rivers, roads, buildings and all physical characteristics. The expectation is that at least one of those pathfinders will find his way to the "D-Z". Then he should check it to make sure it is not occupied by enemy troops. If it is clear, he should position himself in the middle of a field or cleared area, towards the end where the planes will approach it. As the time approaches when the planes should arrive, he will start cranking the handle of his Ajax unit. This unit generates a radio signal beacon on which the lead planes will follow to the D-Z. When the lead planes pass over the radio beacon, the pilot switches on the green light over the open door in the cabin behind, and the paratroopers, who are waiting jammed together back from the door, all jump out as though pushed by a compressed spring.

The Ajax unit is about 8-9 inches long, by 3-4 inches wide and 2½-3 inches thick. It has a folding handle on one side which folds into a recess. The pathfinder is equipped with a heavy sheath knife. If he sees that he is about to be captured by enemy troops, he puts the point of the sheath knife into the recess on his Ajax unit and slams the handle of the knife hard. That destroys the Ajax unit, so enemy troops cannot activate it to lead the incoming paratroopers into a trap.

This SCR-536, hand-held radio transceiver is slightly larger than the pathfinder's AJAX unit of WW II.

The D-Z for the 2nd battalion, 506, was centered on the tiny village of Sainte-Marie-du-Mont. I expected to land near the village, so I was surprised, shocked (physically, as well as mentally) and horrified to splash down into shoulder-deep cold water in the dark.

On D-Day before dawn in our area (St. Mere Eglise - Sainte-Marie-du-Mont) a small allied plane flew east-to-west across the area dropping a few flares to signal to the pathfinders below that the paratroop planes were 5-10 minutes off (signaling us to "start cranking our Ajax units within 2-3 minutes, if you are in position".)

I was astounded to drop into such deep water, because during my long, intensive orientation in the marshaling area in England just before D-Day, I had not seen any lake, pond or river anywhere near Sainte-Marie-du-Mont on the aerial photos. I had not paid any attention to the brook, or small stream flowing eastward (ENE approx.) far to the south of Sainte-Marie-du-Mont. It was named the Douve, though on the maps and aerial photos it did not appear large enough to be dignified with a name. What had happened was that the German troops had closed the weirs downstream on the Douve, going towards the coast, and opened them upstream, so that the water rose and overflowed its banks, flooding adjacent low spots, such as the one where I had landed.

Weir – Le Bugue, France

I stood there chest-deep in cold water that shouldn't have been there, totally puzzled. Where was I? Which direction should I go to get to the nearest dry land? Would my carbine fire, if I ran into Germans? I knew it had been soaked, and in the dark I could not tell if perhaps it had also gotten full of mud too. As I stood there I heard a noise ... sort of a snuffling sound ... something like the sound a dog makes pulling on a leash. It was getting closer. Then I heard another sound, unmistakably the sound of boots walking on wood. I strained my eyes in the direction of the sounds, but it was too dark to distinguish more than a hint of something moving. I knew that German soldiers often patrol at night with guard dogs, because the dog's superior senses of smell, hearing and night vision can alert the soldier to dangers he cannot himself see or sense. Great! All I needed to complete my unhappy situation was to have a guard dog start yowling in my direction, and the German soldier turn his flashlight on me.

But the boots on the wooden planks and the snuffling dog continued on past and faded into the distance. I thought: … he was headed somewhere on a board walkway … probably headed towards dry land. If I waded on a course parallel to the way he was headed, I should reach dry land too. For lack of other better clues, I waded northwest and soon came up on shore. There were explosions and sounds of distant firing all around me, aircraft everywhere overhead. But I still had no idea where I was. Rather than walk into a minefield, or into a nest of trigger-happy Germans, I decided to sit down and think things over. I soon woke with a start, shivering in the first dim light of dawn. What a pathfinder I had turned out to be.

It turned out that I had been southwest of the village of Sainte-Marie-du-Mont near a wide place in the road called St. Come du Mont. By dawn the 506 paratroopers had taken the whole area and some had already crossed over the wooden bridge to Caretan … where the US forces would soon break out of the Normandy hedgerows and start their drive eastward across France.

M-60 Patton tanks.

The Allied armies, spearheaded by Patton's Third Army armored units raced across France to Metz during June and July. There at Metz Patton was met by two German Colonels coming to him under a flag of truce. They said they had been sent by the German Generals in charge of the Middle

The Ludendorff Bridge over the Rhine at Remagen after it was captured by U.S. troops.

Rhine defenses. Their mission was to offer Patton a bridge across the Rhine, so he could drive for Berlin before the Soviet armies arrived there. They asked him to order an American parachute regiment to be dropped at the east end of the Rhine bridge to hold it against any possible attack by SS or other fanatical German troops who might try to stop the American troops from crossing.

Patton immediately radioed to London that he was taking his Third Army across the bridge to run for Berlin, and explained the German offer. He requested that all Allied combat troops in France be ordered to head for Metz and follow the Third Army across the bridge into Germany. He also requested that a parachute regiment be dropped immediately off the east end of the bridge to defend it while the US troops were crossing it.

Parachutes open overhead as waves of paratroops land in Holland during operations by the 1st Allied Airborne Army. September 1944.

Meanwhile we parachute troops (and all airborne) had returned to England after D-Day. Our regiment was suddenly ordered into a marshaling area camp on a nearby British airfield. Contrary to all previous and later airborne operations, we were not told where we were going, nor given any orientation at all. The next morning we loaded up all our combat gear and went out to sit in the planes all morning without any further clues as to where we were bound. Finally in mid-afternoon the order came to de-plane and return to the marshaling area barracks. The second morning we again went out to the planes, loaded up and sat, still totally uninformed, until afternoon. Then we de-planed again and returned to barracks: The third morning we went out to the airfield again, but didn't board the planes. After 2-3 hours we loaded up on trucks and left the marshaling area, returning to our previous old barracks near Nottingham. We still had no clue as to what had been going on.

Later we read in the "Stars and Stripes" about how the Allied Headquarters in London had canceled Patton's plan to cross the Rhine, had ordered him not to cross. He had replied that he was going to take the Third Army across anyway and go for Berlin. Let them court martial him! Then London ordered the supply depots in Cherbourg not to issue another gallon of gasoline, not one more round of ammo, nor another artillery shell to anyone. They ordered the "Red Ball Express" (the continuous line of supply trucks which carried supplies across France to the armored spearheads at Metz) not to move a single truck anywhere. Patton was stopped at Metz by his own High Command, his fuel, ammo and supplies cut off. Because of that, the war with Germany would go on for another nine months, (instead of ending in August 1944) and thousands of young Brits, Americans and other Allied troops would lose their lives unnecessarily.

Stacks of war matériel in open storage near Antwerp.

Only later did we learn that more than a month before Patton was stopped at Metz, that on July 20, 1944, a conspiracy of

German Generals had attempted to kill Hitler by setting off a bomb during a staff meeting at Hitler's "Wulfschnauz" Eastern Front Headquarters at Rastenburg in East Prussia. Hitler miraculously survived the explosion, but emerged furious at the "traitors". He ordered the summary execution of everyone and anyone even suspected of being involved in the conspiracy. The Gestapo, SS and military intelligence executed dozens of high German Army officers over the next week or two. That was the blood bath going on inside the German army when the Generals of the Middle Rhine sent the two Colonels to offer Patton a bridge across the Rhine.

Hitler in July 1944 – The photograph shows Hitler, second from the right, shortly after the assassination attempt had failed. He is accompanied by, left to right, Wilhelm Keitel, chief of the supreme high command of German armed forces; Hermann Göring, commander of the German air force; and Martin Bormann, Hitler's secretary.

A few weeks later, on September 17, 1944, we participated in "Operation Market Garden", General Bernard Montgomery's complicated, three-stage Airborne offensive across Holland to the Rhine at Arnhem. As Allied troops were already on the west bank of the Rhine from Holland to Switzerland, it seemed unnecessary to waste military resources swinging around north through Holland to arrive at the Rhine at Arnhem. **But that was what Montgomery ordered**

General Bernard L. Montgomery watches his tanks move up.

us to do. He was the worst General on the Allied side. But the British kept praising him and insisting on putting him in charge. His "great victories" were all pointless, empty exercises, wasting men and resources. The battle of El Alamein in 1942 in North Africa was preceded by a gigantic days-long WWI-style artillery barrage. But the German Africa Corps had already left the battlefield and gone west, leaving their tanks and armored vehicles dug in and abandoned for lack of gasoline. Rommel, the "Desert Fox", had already flown back to Germany (on Hitler's orders) before the so-called "battle". In the Allied invasion of Sicily (May 1943) Montgomery had fought Patton and the Americans for commands and priorities, but after the British army under Montgomery landed at the east end of the Bay of Gela, they just sat there on the defensive for weeks, while Patton pushed the US troops hundreds of miles, northwest to Palermo, then east to Messina, ready to invade the Italian mainland. The same thing on D-Day: Montgomery's British troops landed successfully at Caen on the Normandy coast, but pretty much just stayed on the defensive for weeks while Patton's Americans fought their way out from Caretan to Argentan, thence across France to Metz and the Rhine.

Following D-Day, Field Marshall Erwin Rommel urged Hitler to bring the war to an end as soon as possible, which sent Hitler into a further rage.

But here we were now under Montgomery on "Operation Market Garden". Our battalion was assigned to jump at Eindhoven, to secure the bridges over the canals; other American airborne would land northeast of Eindhoven at Nijmegen at the same time, while the British Red Devils Parachute Regiment would jump at Arnhem on the Rhine. The intention was to clear a path for Allied armored columns to drive across Holland to the Rhine at Arnhem.

THE STARS AND STRIPES

Vital Rhine Bridge Seized in Holland

Scribe Chutes to Holland--and Scoop

S. & S. Reporter, 'Too Old' for Pacific, Is First in Eindhoven

U.S., British Forces Drive to Split Nazis; 1st Army Attacks

The choice of terrain to get to the Rhine was the worst possible, being as this part of Holland is criss-crossed every few miles with canals (being the lower Rhine delta) any one of which could have been made into a heavy defense line by German troops. As it turned out for us, the drop at Eindhoven was a breeze, as all the German troops had been pulled back to defend the Rhine. The Red Devil Brits at Arnhem had a rough time. German troops held on to the Rhine bridge and most of adjoining Arnhem.

After the operation in Holland we airborne troops returned to England, as we had after every airborne operation on the Continent so far.

Port of Antwerp, Belgium.

But in mid-December Hitler launched a heavy surprise attack against the western allies in the Ardennes, using his best remaining Wehrmacht troops, Waffen SS and German parachute troops, driving west through the forests just north of Luxemburg, to surprise and destroy the American 24th Infantry Division, which had been assigned there for rest to a "quiet sector" of the front. **Hitler's intention was to surprise**

the Allies and take the port of Antwerp from the Allies, then to turn west to drive for Paris.

We were hustled on to planes in England and flown to Rheims, France, in terrible stormy winter weather. Many paratroopers were sick to their stomachs on that terrible flight. We were then taken by truck from Rheims north across the Meuse to a small cross-roads village in Belgium called Bastogne. We arrived there in a snow storm to find that some Germans in a scout car were already there. We took them prisoner, killing one and wounding

Panzer VI Tiger of Schwere Panzer-Abteilung 503, tank number 311 1943

another in the process. We soon came under shell fire as we were digging in. Then came German tanks and armored infantry. We were able to stop them, destroying several tanks with assembly-packs for making the new "Gammon" grenades (throwing the whole pack of C2 explosive up on the back deck of the tank after it passed our foxhole, after having mowed down the infantry coming behind the tank) the tremendous explosion would blow a hole in the back deck, and even at times blow the gun turret completely off. More heavy shelling. (It turned out they were using American 75mm field guns with American shells they had captured from the 24 Infantry and an American ammo dump.) **They had to take that crossroad village of Bastogne to get to the roads west to Antwerp. And they tried, attacking ferociously and continuously. We killed them by the thousands. But we suffered 70-80% casualties ourselves. But we held them ... until in January, when they retreated back into Germany.**

Until late December the battle for Bastogne raged in snow and stormy darkness; we didn't have enough men to defend the whole perimeter around Bastogne. We could tell when the Germans were gathering their forces for an attack on our sector, because we could hear the growl of the heavy diesel engines of the Tiger tanks and mobile gun carriers moving into position the night before out there in the dark beyond our defense lines. We would then call in to battalion HQ to rush us troop reinforcements well before dawn, so they would have time to dig in.

Other times we had to leave our foxholes and dugouts to go to support another section of the perimeter, to reinforce the defense lines which were about to be attacked. That left temporarily undefended gaps in the American defense lines. In between we did a lot of patrol work to try to determine German positions and intentions. I was frequently called to go on patrol with battation intelligence patrols. When in defense positions we cut down pine trees back inside the woods to use the tree trunks to make a cover over our two-man foxholes, which we would then cover with dirt to stop shrapnel from tree bursts of incoming German artillery. The cover of the foxhole would have a hole about l'-1½' long in the end towards the enemy, where one man would stand to keep watch while the other slept. The German "Nebelwerfer" rockets made a gigantic explosion and left a huge hole, but seldom hit a foxhole.

Two soldiers in a foxhole Battle of the Bulge in Belgium December 1944.

Starting in early January the battle began to change in our favor. The skies cleared and American bombers and fighters came out by the thousands, leaving long lines of burned out German vehicles along the roads leading to Bastogne. Patton's Third Army broke through to Bastogne and American heavy artillery, 120 mm and 155 mm, began shelling German infantry attackers with the new proximity fuse artillery shells ... with deadly effect.

Tiger destroyed.

When they caught a German infantry attack in the open, the proximity-fuse shells killed them all. I saw a miles-long field filled with thousands of Germany infantry bodies. They had evidently been caught by the artillery while advancing towards our company positions. Shortly thereafter the German army retreated back into Germany. What the US called "The Battle of the Bulge" was over.

After "The Bulge" we did not go back to England, but instead went to a tent camp outside Chalons-sur-Marne. I joined my old outfit there (Company C, 513 PIR) returning from the hospital in Metz from "The Bulge" via the Repo Depot in Thionville, France (south of Luxemburg).

Funny story: while in the Repo Depot at Thionville, which was an old French barracks, stone buildings 4-5 stories high with wide stone entrances (6-8 stone steps) on which we would sit while eating out of our canteen cups, the food being served out of big "ashcans" in the middle of the cobblestone courtyard. As the Repo Depot was flooded with wounded casualties returning to their units after the "Bulge", they had run out of food, except for plenty of green pea soup. So we were all enjoying pea soup out of our mess cups, sitting on the stone steps, when suddenly a German ME-109 swept down on us from over the top of a barracks, letting off a burst of machine-gun fire. The machine gun fire only hit the top of the barracks building opposite, but all of us were so surprised and conditioned to dive for cover when fired on, that all of us tried to run for cover, dropping our cups of pea soup in the process. Suddenly everybody was slipping and falling on pea-soup-covered stone steps and cobblestones and trying to get up again to run, which was impossible on pea-soup-covered cobblestones and steps. Soon everybody was just sitting in pea soup laughing.

After a couple of months at the airborne camp at Chalons-sur-Marne, we were again sent into a marshaling area on an air strip in eastern France for the jump across the Rhine at Wesel. We flew this time in C-46 transports, which had come to us after being rejected by the pilots flying the "Hump" between India and China. It was a beautiful day as we flew towards the Rhine across the smiling face of "La Belle France". **As we stood up, hooked up and closed up in a line back from the exit door, all of a sudden the sun was blotted out by thick clouds of smoke. The Brits were operating smoke generators to cover the pontoon bridges their engineers were putting across the Rhine. Simultaneously with the smoke our planes were hit with blasts of German anti-aircraft fire, which literally blew our planes apart. I saw holes appear all over the cabin floor, pieces of plane aluminum flying every where, the wings outside the windows breaking up. We jumped (I think perhaps even before the green light came on.) Four of the five planes that carried our company that day went down in minutes. But most of the men in our company got out of their plane before it went down. My chute opened and instantly machine-gun fire from below made patterns of holes in the canopy above my head. I frantically pulled my BAR from its case, to be ready to return fire, but I couldn't see where the fire was coming from Then I hit the ground. The barrel of my BAR plowed into the earth, leaving me unarmed and helpless.**

BAR gunner 1944.

Flak 18 – 88 mm anti aircraft gun ready to fire.

If I had tried to fire it, the barrel surely would have blown up. Whoever had been firing on me while I was dropping was surely somewhere nearby. So I frantically began disassembling my BAR to clean the barrel out ... the only thing I could do to arm myself to protect myself. "'Allow, Yank", said a British voice. There were two British paratroopers walking towards me. They stood there and chatted while I finished cleaning my BAR. "Good job", said one as I finished up, "But a curious place to do it." They ambled off together.

I started looking for some of my company. I came across a dead American paratroop lieutenant still in his chute harness hanging from a tree. I thought: the same kraut that fired his machine gun at me may have gotten him. Eventually I found some Company C men gathering.

During Operation Market-Garden, Waco gliders are lined up on an English airfield in preparation for the next lift to the Netherlands.

We all knew what our big job was now ... the reason we had been parachuted in here. We had to find and destroy the "hedgehogs" before the gliders came in carrying the bulk of our airborne army. We had seen the "hedgehogs" on the aerial photos and maps in

Members 325e RIF loaded into a WACO glider in preparation for the invasion of Holland. Note the GI front left door two packages, one mounted on his M-1936 suspenders, and another under his helmet net.

the marshaling area before this jump. We knew what they meant. Bad, bad news. It meant that the Germans knew exactly where we were going to jump ... and they had prepared for us. Those "hedgehogs" were anti-airborne installations protecting anti-aircraft batteries. The anti-aircraft guns and heavy anti-aircraft machine-guns were dug-in in the center of each "hedgehog", which were each surrounded by a double circle of trenches with a parapet of earth thrown up on the outside of each ring of trenches. The parapet ringing the outside ring of trenches had a slot for a machine gun cut in it every 15-20 feet all the way around. So the hedgehog could not be directly assaulted from any side by troops rushing it, because of the many machine-guns. The only way they could be taken was by using small infantry trench mortars (60mm + 81mm) and by troopers

Overhead view of a hedgehog with the outside ring of trenches and several machine gun defensive positions. A nightmare for ground troops to assault.

crawling at the same time forward on their bellies and heaving hand grenades into the hedgehogs.

Unfortunately the German military often knew more about what the Allied military was planning than we Allied soldiers did. The "hedgehogs" now indicated that it was true again. The classic example which we all knew in 1944-45 had been that nightly radio broadcast of the "Berlin Bitch" the night before D-Day. That afternoon, which had been in June of the previous year 1944, they had taken away our winter extra blanket. We still carried our usual sleeping bag.

When the "Berlin Bitch" came on the air that night of June 5, 1944, we were dismayed to hear her say, "You airborne boys will miss that extra blanket tomorrow night, the blanket they took away from you this afternoon, because we are having an unusual cold snap right now on the coasts of Northern France." If they new about that blanket, they must know everything else about our D-Day landings the following day. Not at all good for our morale.

American soldiers taking up defensive positions in the Ardennes during the Battle of the Bulge

The first "hedgehog" our group of paratroopers found was warned that we were coming by German scouts in fox holes some 100 feet out from that "hedgehog". Some nervous machine-gunner squeezed off an ineffective burst in our direction, not hitting any of us. Our one crew of mortar men set up their 60mm mortar behind a low rise. The rest of us started crawling towards the "hedgehog". We all had plenty of grenades … as after we had seen the hedgehogs on the aerial photos, we had begged, threatened and finally persuaded the supply sergeant to give us more grenades. We were each carrying 3-4 times as many grenades as on a normal jump. After a few minutes we heard one, then two, grenades explode in or near the hedgehog. But then we heard the low distant roar of many airplanes approaching; we froze, horror-stricken. The German machine-gunners in the hedgehog also stopped firing. Both German soldiers in the hedgehog and American paratroopers outside waited as the masses of planes towing their gliders passed overhead and released their gliders. Gliders can't descend steeply and quickly, but must glide down in gentle-angled circles. The German anti-aircraft guns and heavy machine-guns opened up on them, blowing whole gliders-full of men-out of the sky. Shattered gliders rained men, field guns, jeeps and more men out of the sky. We paratroops just lay on our backs and watched the slaughter above us, helpless to do anything about it. The German machine guns inside the hedgehog were also silent. The gliders which made it down to ground smashed into stone walls, houses, barns and other buildings, most of them breaking up and killing many of the troops inside them. Gliders should only be used to land in very open fields, not places occupied by enemy troops.

101st Airborne inspecting broken glider in Holland.

Another horror remaining in my memory from that day of horrors, was the wounded paratrooper propped up against the trunk of a tree, who begged me to get a medic for him, but then asked me to first check if he still had his balls undamaged. He said he was newly married and still hoped to have children. When I checked, I saw his lower abdomen was all blown apart. I lied and told him “yes”, his balls were okay, then went off to find him a medic. With his terrible wounds he surely died soon after.

1 have cursed Montgomery in my mind every time I remember that terrible day. Any half-way intelligent commander would have changed the drop zone to a few miles further inland from the Rhine, once he saw the hedgehogs there on the photos. But that was not Montgomery's way. Once he had made a plan, it had to be carried out just that way, no matter how ridiculous subsequent events had made it. Just like the farce of El Alamein.

Once most of the Germans had surrendered across the area, we gathered up as many Company C strays as we could find and moved out eastward. We had not gone many miles before we ran into German defenses along the new "autobahn", which was still in early construction stages. There were 6-8 foot high piles of dirt along each side of the highway construction, with open intervals between the piles of dirt every 30-40 feet. A German machine gun crew was behind the dirt piles on the other side of the highway in construction, firing occasional bursts through the opening between two piles of dirt, firing diagonally across, so it was dangerous to cross just there. The obvious thing to do was to cross a few dozen feet beyond the zone under fire, circle behind the machine gun nest and flip a grenade into it. Having crossed without a problem, I was suddenly surrounded by several friendly civilians, men and women, offering me a cup of acorn tea. They had emerged from a dugout under one of the piles of dirt, evidently they were foreign construction workers. While I was trying to explain to them that I had an urgent date to offer the machine-gun crew next door a hand-grenade treatment, a Company C paratrooper (a new replacement after the Bulge) appeared at my side and said that "the lieutenant" (a "90-day wonder", fresh out of Officers Training School (OCS) who was now the officer in charge of Company C (now the only officer in Company "C", after we had lost all 8-9 Company C officers in the Bulge) had sent him to "order" me to immediately come back across the autobahn and report to him … to stop whatever I was up to and come back to him. That was an order.

At that time I was still thinking and acting on my own volition, as a paratrooper must do when dropped behind enemy lines, not as a soldier in a stateside camp, where he is under the control of his company officers. However an order is an order, so I crossed back over the autobahn and reported to the lieutenant. **He ordered me to stay with him. He was obviously much impressed with his now being an officer, which he had become only a few weeks before. Not only did he not have even a day of combat experience, but he had no idea of how war is fought and how to handle troops in combat. This made him very dangerous for his men. He never asked for advice from the experienced combat veterans under him, but seemed to take offense any time one mentioned a possible danger or a better alternative. He nearly got me killed twice that day.**

That night I was assigned to an outpost about 50 yards on the other side of the autobahn, to watch for possible German attacks. Well into the next morning I briefly came back in to the company perimeter to see why no one had come out to check on me. I discovered that the company had left the area without telling me. I never found out how that had happened, because the "lieutenant" had been replaced before I could locate them and rejoin them. He was replaced by a combat-experienced Captain who was very able and intelligent in combat.

After a nice cup of acorn tea, I struck out by myself to try to find Company C, or another 513th company: I crossed the Lippe river on a downed steel bridge, walking along the girders still above water. Before long I found a group of British Churchill tanks. It turned out that

Two men of the 107th Regiment Royal Armoured Corps, The King's Own in front of a Churchill tank, "Able".

they were Coldstream Guard tankers. They offered me a ride. They already had several lost American paratroopers riding atop their tanks. When I considered the alternative of continuing to wander by myself around the German countryside and possibly bumping into some hostile German troops, I accepted their invitation. Besides, they had food, which they were willing to share. They told me they were headed for Bremen. That didn't increase my enthusiasm for the trip. But I didn't see any American troops around, so there wasn't much alternative.

2 Squadron, Coldstream Guards - taken in a farmyard in Germany.

We rode on the Coldstream Guard tanks several more days up to Munster, which we took, an assault by a few dozen homeless American paratroopers with British Coldstream Guard tanks. We put up in the Hermann Goering barracks on the north side of Munster for a few days, while our Coldstream Guard friends continued on the road to Bremen.

One of the things I will always remember about the British army in combat, was how they always stopped and had tea at tea time. When tea time arrived, the war stopped, out came the teakettle and cups and everyone climbed out of their tanks and had tea. After tea, back to business.

While we were relaxing at the Hermann Goering barracks in Munster we got word that the US Army was sending some trucks up to Munster to pick us up and take us back to the Ruhr, where they said some Nazi SS troops were holding out. We were to round up those Nazi SS troops. We knew that there were no SS troops in the Ruhr, because the SS were all east of Berlin fighting the oncoming Soviet armies. And we had just come from Wesel, which is just north of the Ruhr, where we would have heard about any SS troops nearby. We marched around the Ruhr for a few days. (We had no idea why we were doing that … just to entertain us, I guess.) Of course there were no SS troops there, as we had known all along.

We finally settled down in a Ruhr town named Bottrop, a few miles northwest of Essen, the main industrial city of the industrial Ruhr. We lived in private houses (commandeered) and had frequent passes to nearby Oberhausen, where the US army had set up recreation facilities for US troops in NW Germany. But life in Bottrop wasn't bad either, as the local brewery delivered a case of beer to us at our house every day and a bierstube-open-air dance pavilion opened in a park nearby. Those German girls loved to dance. They were very friendly. The official reason for keeping us in Bottrop was to guard a nearby work camp full of Russians who had been working as prisoners in the Ruhr coal mines at Bottrop. I spent a lot of time at the Russian camp, as I was curious about the Russian people. A professor from the University of Kiev became a good friend of mine. I drank their homemade vodka in the lager, danced with the Russian girls and ate their homemade hamburger-like food. The young Russian ex-soldiers were friendly too. Some tried to interest me in having sex with my choice of the Russian girls in the lager. In order to facilitate my choosing one, they brought me into the girls shower room, where half a

dozen naked girls were showering, to allow me to inspect them to decide which one(s) I wanted to take to bed. I had many interesting experiences in the Russian lager.

When the word came that we were going to be shipped off for the invasion of Japan, about the same time the Russians in the lager were shipped back to East Germany to Soviet army authorities there. None of them wanted to go. We heard later that Stalin had them all shot.

I heard later that other US Army units which crossed the Rhine into Germany about the same time as we did (mid-March, 1945) had all been sent on wild-goose chases around Germany, north and south and back to the Rhine, everywhere but east to Berlin, just as we had been. **The reason for this was apparently to let the Soviets take Berlin, rather than have it fall to the Western Allies. This fits nicely with the common theory later that several earlier delays of the Allied campaign against Germany had been created by Roosevelt and Churchill to allow the Soviets to take as much of Europe as possible: the phony Dieppe invasion of France in 1942, which was used as an excuse to send Allied armies around through the "soft-underbelly" of Europe in November 1942, rather than by a frontal assault (as at Normandy in 1944) ... Patton being stopped at Metz ... the "surprise" Nazi attack in the Ardennes in December 1944, which should have been known before hand and prepared for, because Captain Max Weibel of Swiss intelligence had given a full report of Nazi plans for the Ardennes attack to Allen Dulles in Bern (the "Lucy" agent report) months before, in the summer of 1944. Many other intentional delays.**

We were offered a choice of going to Berlin on guard duty (against marauding Soviet troops from East Berlin) or going to Manila to participate in the invasion of Japan. But I was told that they especially wanted me to go to Manila because of my pathfinder experience in Europe. As inducement they told me that I would be flown to the US for 2 weeks home-leave with other pathfinders from Europe before being flown to Manila. The 11th

Airborne division in Manila had never participated in a large-scale invasion, and therefore had no pathfinders.

But instead of being flown back to the US we spent several months more in Europe. This change (or delay, then change) I later realized coincided exactly with the successful test explosion of the first nuclear device at White Sands, New Mexico. I imagine that at that moment the US military realized they had the means in their hands of bringing Japan to its knees. Therefore, no invasion of Japan was going to be needed.

So we were sent on furlough to the French Riviera, then we were taken to Paris for a performance of the Broadway show "Oklahoma", then we spent weeks on a canal east of Lyons, playing water polo and drinking the local "Mirabelle".

Finally we were taken to Marsailles, where we spent a couple of weeks in the "Callais" area above Marsailles in the mountains. Finally we were put on a transport ship (the old "Del Argentine") a former grain ship, bound for Manila via Panama. But in mid-Atlantic while we were all playing chess (which the Red Cross had provided) on the open decks, the ship's loudspeaker came on to announce:

"We are happy to announce that the Empire of Japan has just surrendered. So we are now ordered to change course to Newport News, Virginia."

We watched the wake of the ship swing around to a course more northeasterly. Then all pandemonium broke loose. Chess boards flew in the air. Booze appeared from nowhere. Then the ship's loudspeaker came on again:

"You are all invited to attend a celebration gathering in the main lounge. There will be a special performance".

We assembled in the main lounge, a beautiful two-level seating area with big curved staircases on either side with finely-carved wooden railings leading up to the second level. Opposite the 2nd level was a stage with a podium. We sat on the stairs and anywhere we could. The lounge was crowded to capacity. The officer in charge said a few words of thanksgiving and then he introduced a paratroop captain who was the leading baritone from the Metropolitan opera. None of us (at least not I) knew that he had been with the paratroops in Europe. He sang "The Lord's Prayer" beautifully followed by a long respectful silence. Many a tough, battle-hardened paratrooper had glistening eyes.

We learned later that if the invasion of Japan had taken place we would have jumped 11 miles inland on the main plain of southern Kyushu the night before the invasion, with the Japanese planning to dig in 1½ million troops immediately behind the beachheads for a suicide-type defense. Am I glad we missed that one.

My parents were still living in Washington then. I was given one furlough after another, until I was given my discharge from the army just before Christmas 1945 at Ft. Meade just outside Washington, D.C.

Main Barracks, Ft. Meade, Maryland

This is the true autobiography of Earl B. Wilson written with no political correctness in mind. This autobiography was edited by author and publisher Jon Larsen Shudlick hoping that the visuals and captions included will further educate our readers. Graphics and formatting of photos, maps, etc. were inserted by Linda Leppert.

Knocked-out US Medium Tanks. During the last few days of Dec 1944 the main effort in Third Army zone was concentrated in the vicinity of Bastogne.

Bastogne

By **Earl B. Wilson**

Recently a friend who had read my little "Autobiography" dated October 2011, asked me why I had skipped so quickly through the description of the battle for Bastogne, one of the most famous and critical battles of World War II. Didn't I have some other remarkable experiences there, he asked, which would interest my grand children years from now?

Earl B. Wilson, author
Army Pathfinder
World War II

Yes, indeed, I replied, lots of them, including the time when during the battle for the crossroads at Mandy, just north of Bastogne, I was hit in the head by an 88 and left for dead

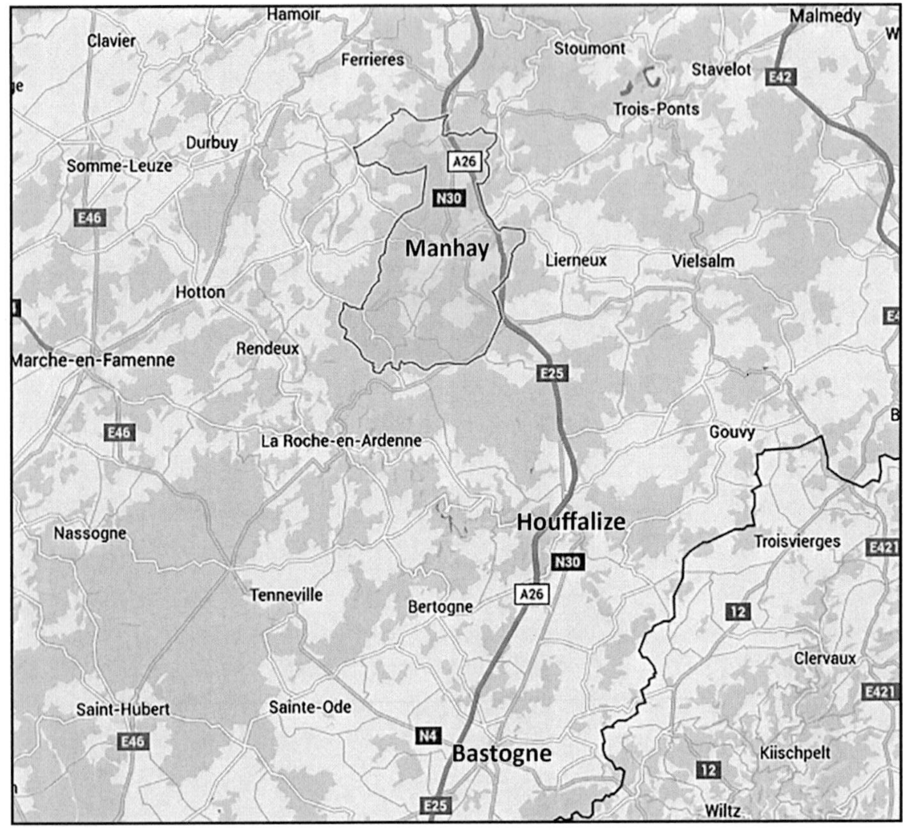

in the snow, while all my paratroop companions in Mandy were wiped out.

So I now will describe my experiences in the battle for Bastogne in more detail, starting from our arrival in Bastogne shortly before Christmas in 1944. The German army had sent its best remaining troops: Waffen SS, paratroops and some veteran panzer battalions from the Russian front, to clear the way for their panzer divisions following them intending to crash through to Antwerp, the main British invasion port and then on to Paris. That was their plan. But first they had to capture the crossroads at Bastogne, in order to give their panzers access to the only well-built and well-paved road leading to Antwerp, a road which could stand up to the passage of so many heavy tanks and mobile armored artillery.

As we arrived on trucks from Rheims at the village of Bastogne, the first German troops had already been arriving there, and our

Paratroopers on the way to their positions in order to keep the Germans from Bastogne.

troopers were already fighting them out along the roads just east of Bastogne. We were instructed to defend the road coming into Bastogne from the north. We drove a mile or two northwards and then dismounted from the trucks and continued north on foot on a back road through heavy forests. Occasional artillery fire hit the treetops near us and above us . . . "searching fire" commented Lt. Grady casually. Eventually the road came out of the trees with open fields in front of us. We moved east along the edge of the woods a few hundred yards and then dug in just inside the line of woods. (The ground inside the woods was soft enough to dig in, which would have been impossible out in the frozen fields.) It was soon dark. An hour or two after dark I heard someone (perhaps 2-3 persons) moving eastward further back in the woods behind us. I could hear the fallen leaves rustling as they walked cautiously along. I told Captain Kendricks, but none of us made any attempt to catch them. After what happened the next day I realized later that they had been a German patrol heading back to report where we were.

US troops pinned down in the Ardennes.

As daylight began to dawn several

more rounds of artillery hit our line of woods . . . while we were getting ready to attack northwards across the open fields. As we moved out, Captain Kendricks went down, hit by shrapnel in the back of his legs. We moved on in line of skirmishers towards a farmhouse and barns slightly to our right. It was a crossroads called "Mandy". A German soldier was flushed out of a foxhole and escorted to our rear. Some (a very few) of our men were hit by mortar fire or by rifle fire from the farmhouse. We took the farmhouse and its attached barn. Lt. O'Rear and Lt. O'Malley were killed crossing the cut where the N-S highway cut through an E-W ridge next to the farmhouse: Lt. Grady was wounded and evacuated back to Bastogne. Some US paratroopers appeared from the other side of the farmhouse yard. It turned out they were from Company B, and one of them was my good friend, Ronnie Clark. This farmhouse was at a place called "Mandy", only a few miles north of Bastogne. It sat in a low spot just to the east of the main road from Bastogne north to Houffalize (10-12 miles). Just N of the farmhouse was an E-W ridge, through which the road was cut. This ridge ran 50-60 ft East from the cut, then angled south. Someone yelled "German troops attacking!" We troopers then saw lines of German infantry attacking towards us from the north and more coming west towards us from the east. Sheltered just behind the ridge, we opened fire on them. But they were coming on in short rushes, then hitting the ground. And they wore white snow capes, which made them hard to see in the snow.

German King Tiger tank near La Gleize covered in snow German Tigers, La Gleizes, December 1944.

Suddenly from the road coming from Bastogne there was a

Infantry and tanks near Bastogne.

roar of engines and four American tanks came roaring up on our left, in the field on the other side of the road to our west. They pulled up four abreast behind the ridge, in full defilade, their guns pointing north over the crest of the ridge. But almost immediately all four tanks exploded and went up in flames.

As we watched, stunned, I suddenly realized that as the first tank blew up, two or three of the others had thrown their gears into reverse and backed down a dozen or so feet before they too exploded in flames.

I realized: those two or three had not been hit from in front, but from the rear . . . the German tank which had hit them all was behind us, to our south. And the German infantry in snow capes were now coming up only dozens of yards away on our north and east We were surrounded. The trap was about to close.

I shouted to Ronnie: "We're trapped. The only way out is toward those burning tanks, then back the way we came this morning. Follow me!" I ran to the farmhouse and shouted the same thing to some of our guys holed up in the barn. Then I ran up the bank of the highway and dashed across it intending to dive off the other side into the deep snow down below.

But I didn't remember diving off the road when I woke up laying in the snow below the road some time later. My helmet was next to me, split in half. Dazed, I looked around, then crawled back up to the edge of the road and looked back to where Ronnie and the others had been. Dead American paratroopers were laying everywhere, and some dead Germans too. All was silent.

Then I noticed that it was late in the day, nearing sunset. It had been late morning or early afternoon when we had taken Mandy and watched the tanks blown up. I must have been unconscious for hours. I learned later from Company C survivors that the German tank had moved down from its hiding place inside a barn on a hill a few hundred feet to our south, with its escorting infantry, just as the German infantry from the north and east closed in, taking our boys from three sides at once. Only a few survived to be wounded and taken prisoners, as the Germans then all moved out northwards towards Houffalize, taking a few of our wounded paratroopers with them.

Two American soldiers inspect a destroyed German Tiger tank, Belgium 1944.

Dazed and confused, I started walking back up towards the woods from which we had attacked that morning. I saw Lt. Kosner standing back up there, looking down towards Mandy.

Years later one of the Company C survivors told me that the German commander in the Tiger tank had coordinated all the German troops by radio to surround our boys in Mandy and wipe them out.

The German commander of that operation had been an experienced, battle-hardened veteran of the Russian front. We Americans were amateur beginners by comparison. I trudged slowly uphill to Lt. Kosner. "Wilson," he said slowly. "Is there anyone left down there?" "Nobody" I replied, and trudged on past him towards the woods.

* * *

We dug in again along the line of trees where we had been the night before, but a couple of hundred feet further to the west.

There were only a half-dozen or so Company C boys now. We had been 150-180 men when we first arrived in Bastogne.

The next evening we were attacked by two German tanks supported by less than a hundred German infantry. The tanks were a Mark IV and a Tiger tank. We couldn't stop the tanks, but we wiped out the infantry with them. The two tanks crashed past us on through the pine forest. The Tiger tank was disabled by Gammon grenades and its crew killed and the crew of the Mark IV surrendered after losing treads on one side.

The evening after that we heard the rumble of German heavy tanks back in the woods to our left. I thought since we had no antitank weapons, perhaps there were some on that knocked out American tank which was sitting nearby at the corner of the woods. So I climbed up on it.

Looking down inside the open hatch I could see the hashed remains of what had been the tank crew. I couldn't bring myself to climb down through that mess to try to get to the tank gun controls. But then I realized that even if I did, I had no idea of how to operate them. They probably didn't work anyway, the tank's electrical system being all blown up.

So then I began to fiddle with the 50-caliber machine gun mounted on the outside of the turret. It was designed much like the infantry 30-caliber machine gun with which I was familiar and it seemed to be undamaged. By then it was quite dark, and so I had to explore the 50-caliber gun by feel. I wasn't sure whether the safety was "on" or "off", not being familiar with the safety on a 50-caliber gun. As I cautiously explored the gun by feel, I evidently touched the wrong thing and the gun fired off two rounds. The noise sounded like cannon shots in the silence. And out ahead in the darkness of the woods opposite there was a tremendous explosion. The diesel engine rumbles stopped. I had no idea what I had hit. It could have been an ammunition truck loading up the German tanks or a light armored vehicle. A tank wouldn't be damaged like that by a 50-caliber gun. Some hours later the engine rumbles started up again, but then they receded off into the woods. We could finally get some sleep. No attack that night.

An old company C veteran told me in the 1990s that he had recently gone back to Bastogne, and he found our foxholes along the front of the woods above Mandy were still visible there. We had dug two-man foxholes some 5-7' long, and 1½' to 2' wide, by about 4' deep. An opening about 1½' x 1½' was left open at the end towards the open fields, where one man would stand watch all night while the other man slept . . . watching and sleeping in shifts. Often we didn't have enough men to man all the foxholes, and there were long gaps left unmanned in our defense lines. But we covered the avenues of most probable attack. And often we had to leave our usual part of the lines to reinforce some other parts of the lines then coming under attack.

4th Armored Division tanks.

From time to time a few new men dribbled in as replacements. I remember one who came to share my foxhole, who was named Tony Reinwald. He told me that he had two brothers, one of whom had just written him that their third brother had been killed in the Pacific war. He had predicted that none of them would survive the war. Sure enough, Tony was killed a few days later when we attacked a ridge a couple of miles to the north. We advanced on this attack in a northward direction, but well to the west of Mandy. The Germans withdrew as we advanced and we only had a few light casualties, mostly caused by mortar fire.

We moved into German-dug foxholes they had abandoned on that ridge that afternoon. We saw several American artillery observers move into the forward side of the ridge. They each carried gigantic binocular field glasses. The next morning we started hearing big artillery shells passing overhead northbound.

A day or two later we got out on the road near Mandy and

marched north towards Houffalize. As we got beyond the ridges west of Mandy, we saw extensive open fields on the west of the road, filled with German army bodies, hundreds or even thousands of them. They had evidently been advancing towards the ridge where we had been, when the American heavy artillery caught them in the open fields and slaughtered them. That was demonstration of the deadly efficiency of the new American proximity fuses for heavy artillery, which explodes the incoming shell at a set height above the ground, say 20 or 30 feet, and kills everyone below within almost 100 feet. We encountered no German resistance on our way north to Houffalize, though there were plenty of signs that they had passed that way. They had all withdrawn back into Germany from Houffalize. We dug in east of Houffalize and sent out patrols along the banks of the Oerthe river but had no further contact with German troops.

More than 70 years later, World War II foxholes remain in the forests of the Belgian Ardennes.

I really regretted Ronnie Clark's death in Mandy, though I don't know what more I could have done to warn him about the trap we were in. I myself just barely escaped.

Perhaps the thing that puzzled me most during our battle for Bastogne, was how I could have been knocked unconscious and had my helmet split in half while escaping from Mandy, but not been killed. I have never figured out how that could have happened. I assume I was narrowly hit by an 88 round from the same Tiger tank which had destroyed the four American tanks minutes before it fired at me. But I had no wound on my head. Strange!

Shah Mohammad Abdoreza Pahlavi, in the 1950's.

The Lowell House (Harvard University)

My Meeting with the Shah of Iran

I lived in the Lowell House dormitory during my later years as a student at Harvard. In addition to student dormitories, Lowell House also housed a large student dining room providing three meals a day for its student-residents. It also had a larger, more elegant apartment for distinguished visitors to the university and their entourages. This "distinguished visitor" apartment was next to and above the main entrance to Lowell House, opposite the dining hall on the other side of the large interior courtyard.

One day a Norwegian (foreign student) Erling Lorenzen, who was a friend of mine, had a group of friends visiting from Norway. He had taken them to lunch in Lowell House. After lunch they stood together talking outside the dining hall. As I came out I said "hello" to Erling in passing. Erling turned towards me and thrust out his hand to me. I took his hand and shook hands, thinking perhaps he wanted to introduce me to his friends. But instead he gave me a mighty yank to throw me (a schoolboy-sort-of-trick). My automatic reflex (from years of rough-and-tumble training in the army paratroops in World War II) responded automatically by exploiting the power of his yank to yank him back even harder. He flew through the air, landing on his back with me sitting on his chest. I was as surprised as he was. Erling and I had often horsed around together, wrestling and playing tricks (like on that day) on each other. We drank beer and dated girls together. Good friends.

Unbeknownst to me, an aide to the Shah of Iran had observed this little episode from across the courtyard. I didn't even know that the Shah had just arrived and was then in the guest apartment. The aide was evidently impressed by the little episode and had told the Shah about it.

Shortly thereafter a student I had met, but hardly knew, Russ Hunter, arrived at my apartment asking for me. He asked me if I would like to meet the Shah of Iran. The Shah had been much in the news in those days. The opportunity to meet him personally was flattering.

So we went up to meet the Shah in his apartment. He was very pleasant and friendly, as he asked me a few questions about myself.

Then much to my surprise he asked if I would like to work for him as one of his personal escorts.

Harvard University campus, Cambridge, MA

I was so surprised that for a moment I didn't know what to say. Later I learned that the Shah had wanted to find a Harvard student as an escort to show him around without a lot of fuss … as though he was just another new student. But he also wanted a competent bodyguard. If the student escort could also protect him, so much the better. And his aide had told him that the student who had flipped Erling was a small, slight fellow. Being unobtrusive as a bodyguard was a definite asset in such an escort, the Shah was thinking.

After recovering somewhat from this surprise, I told the Shah that I felt highly honored by his offer and would like nothing better than to escort him around for a few days anyway, but that I already had made a commitment to work for my family company after I graduated.

The Shah wanted to accompany me to a couple of my classes the next day. So we went together to a couple of lectures up in the "Yard". I tried (at his request) to avoid introducing him to too many fellow students at the lectures. When it was unavoidable I introduced him simply as my friend "Dore", as if that was his first name. (His real full name was Mohammad Abdoreza Pahlavi, but he was called "Dore" by his close friends.)

He didn't want to stir up a lot of attention by letting everyone know he was the Shah of Iran. And he was already tired of official ceremonies. So he was happy to go around "incognito" with me.

US President Dwight Eisenhower and Shah of Iran Mohammad Abdoreza Pahlavi, Tehran, Iran, 1959

His aide reminded him that he had an important meeting elsewhere at the end of the week, so the day after our trip to the lectures in the Yard would be his last day in Cambridge (at Harvard). He was pleasant company. I was sorry to see him go.

Earl B. Wilson standing with his back to the village of Schwyz. Towering against the sky behind, is the rock called Hoch Ybrig on which is the alp contested with the abbot by Schwyz. Hoch Ybrig is a meadow ("alp") atop the rock (the "Mitten") between Eiseideln and Schwyz.

THE FREE SWISS

By **Earl Wilson**

Americans are proud of their Constitutional self-government, but few are aware of our debt to the Swiss for its inspiration and example.

When the colonial Americans first began to think about the possibility of freeing themselves from British authority, many critics branded them as crazy: "To think of opposing the mighty British Empire, whose fleet ruled the seas, which could muster many regiments of redoubtable British Regulars. That was crazy. No gang of confused and disorganized civilians had ever successfully opposed a great empire!"

William Penn

No? The Swiss people had produced some patriot leaders. Long before, when William Penn had gone to Europe to recruit settlers for his new colony, Pennsylvania, he had gone to the upper Rhine valley to recruit Swabians and Swiss, as people with good values and the fighting spirit needed to populate a frontier region full of savages.

Maximian

The Swiss people, when not yet a nation, governed themselves in a series of independent "cantons" at first. Most "cantons" occupied a separate valley, or a cluster of high alps (mountain pastures). They were often called (and called themselves) "the Free Swiss"...which status they claimed had been granted them by a Roman Emperor. If true, that could well have been the Roman Emperor Maximian, at a time when he was leading his legions

Image Courtesy of Boston Tea Party Ships & Museum, Historic Tours of America, Inc.

down the lower Rhone valley en route to suppress a rebellion in Gaul. He did not want his rear to be attacked by fierce mountaineers from the upper Rhone, so he sent an envoy to offer them good will from Rome.

In any case, when the Americans began to react against British "injustices" (the Stamp Act and unauthorized taxes provoking the "Boston Tea Party") and the high-handed methods of noble British governors sent by the British crown, some "Founding Fathers" began to whisper to sympathizers how the Swiss peasants had totally defeated the Austrian Empire a few centuries earlier. "If they could do it, so can we!" they whispered.

We are all familiar with the story of William Tell reacting against the Austrian governor Gessler, when Gessler put his hat with a plume of Austrian colors on a pole in the village square of the Village of Altdorf and ordered all Swiss passing by to take off their hats and salute his hat as a gesture of submission. When Tell refused to do so, Gessler had his guards seize Tell, and ordered him to shoot an apple off Tell's son's head. William Tell was known as the best crossbowman in

Gessler

Willam Tell

William Tell shooting the apple off his son's head.

those parts. So he took careful aim and fired at the apple. He hit it squarely and an audible sigh of relief was heard from the crowd.

But Gessler was still frowning at Tell. "When you drew out the bolt from your belt, you drew out two bolts, what was the other bolt for?" Gessler asked Tell.

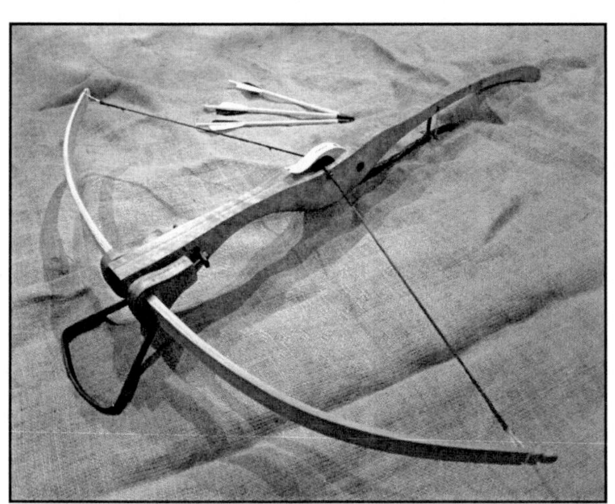

Crossbow with steel trigger.

"In case I missed the apple, and killed my boy, the second bolt would have been for you, tyrant!" replied Tell.

Gessler, red faced with anger, ordered his men-at-arms to seize Tell. Then they took him with them down to their boat on the lakeshore to row back to Gessler's castle.

But shortly after they started out onto the lake the wind came up. Soon whitecap waves appeared, and the water became rougher and rougher. The helmsman cried out to Gessler that he could hardly control the boat. If it got even a bit rougher, they would surely capsize he shouted. One of Gessler's men shouted: "Tell is known as the best boatman around here, let him take over the rudder!"

Tell's escape from Gessler.

So Gessler took off Tell's chains and ordered him to take over the rudder.

Tell steered the boat downwind towards the shore. Gessler stayed silent, thinking: "He is planning to beach the boat! That is a good idea! He must be heading for some little sloped piece of beach that he knows!"

But as they approached the rocky shore, Tell suddenly threw the tiller hard over, turning the boat directly towards a big, flat rock. As they almost hit the rock sideways, Tell leaped onto the rock, while pushing the boat back out into the lake with his leap. Those in the boat scrambled to control the boat, while Tell disappeared into the underbrush.

"Hohle Gasse" (the Holloway of Kussnacht)

Gessler and his men were very lucky to get back to Gessler's castle that day.

A few days later Gessler rode out again with his bodyguards. He was leading his little troop along a shady trail known as the "Hohle Gasse" ("the Holloway of

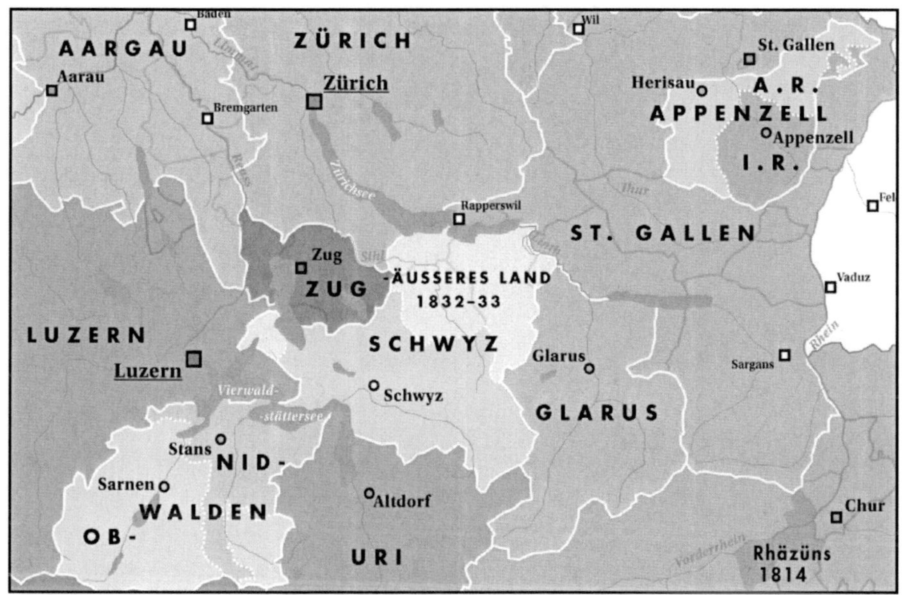

Switzerland

Kussnacht) when suddenly Tell popped up out of the brush aiming his crossbow at Gessler.

"This is Tell's reply to Gessler!" he shouted, as he shot Gessler in the chest. Gessler fell from his horse dead. His men milled around over Gessler's body, but none of them wanted to try to pursue "Deadshot" Tell into the brush.

This was a period when the Swiss people were turning rebellious against Austrian authority, and in some cases had infiltrated Austrian castles and fortresses and burned them down.

The Einsiedeln Abbey at Einsiedeln, Switzerland

This situation came to a head when the Abbot of the monastery of Einsiedeln at Goldingen, appealed to his "overlord" the Hapsburg Emperor in Vienna to discipline the people of the nearby village of Schwyz. The abbot had earlier ordered his rangers (in charge of the monastery's forests, farmlands

Cattle in the Hoch-Ybrig

and rural properties) to stop the people of Schwyz from pasturing their cattle during the summer on the high alp (summer meadow) atop the "Mitten" (the mountain just behind the monastery, on the other side of which was the village of Schwyz). It had always been the custom of the village farmers (as all over Switzerland) to drive their cattle up to the nearby alp where the snow melted only in late spring, and where the summer grass grew luxuriously, thick and unusually nutritious. There, some village boys would pass the summer milking the cows and making cheese from the milk. No one ever had had legal title to any of the high Aps. So the villagers were indignant over the Abbot's claim of authority over the Alp Hoch Ybrig.

The abbot's rangers set out to enforce the abbot's order. But the village boys turned up with baskets of bottled beer which they shared with the rangers. Then the rangers were invited to come to a beer party in the inn down in Schwyz. There they were served by pretty village girls, who also were very friendly. The rangers totally forgot the abbot's orders.

When the abbot learned that his rangers were not enforcing his order about the alp, he was furious. He gave them a good lecture. But the same thing happened the next summer. The abbot was so furious that he wrote a letter to his overlord down in Vienna, the Hapsburgs, asking them to please send an impressive delegation with armed guards up to Schwyn to order the villagers to obey the Abbot's order. But somehow the "impressive" Hapsburg delegation went back to Vienna, without much impressing the villagers. Blame it on beer and pretty girls again.

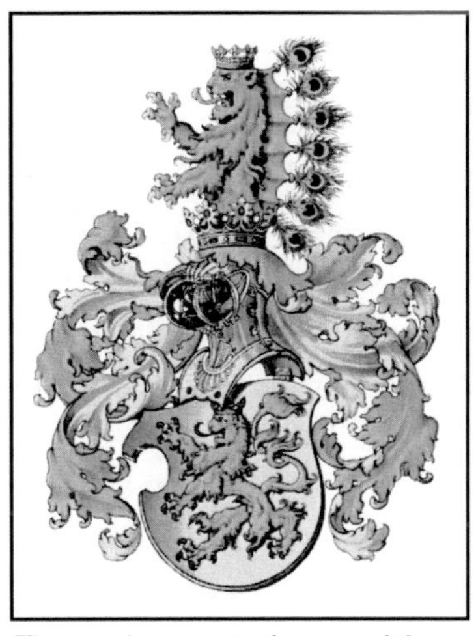

The ancient coat of arms of the Counts of Habsburg

Of course the Abbot's authority was not so acceptable to the Schwyz villagers (not to his rangers) because he was not Swiss. He was from Vienna, appointed abbot because of family connections to friends of Hapsburg officials. Relations continued to sour. And Swiss anti-Hapsburg actions elsewhere in the Swiss mountains were infuriating the Hapsburgs against all Swiss. The Hapsburgs had originated in Switzerland near Brugg, centuries earlier, before they became so powerful (mainly through noble marriages) and moved to Vienna.

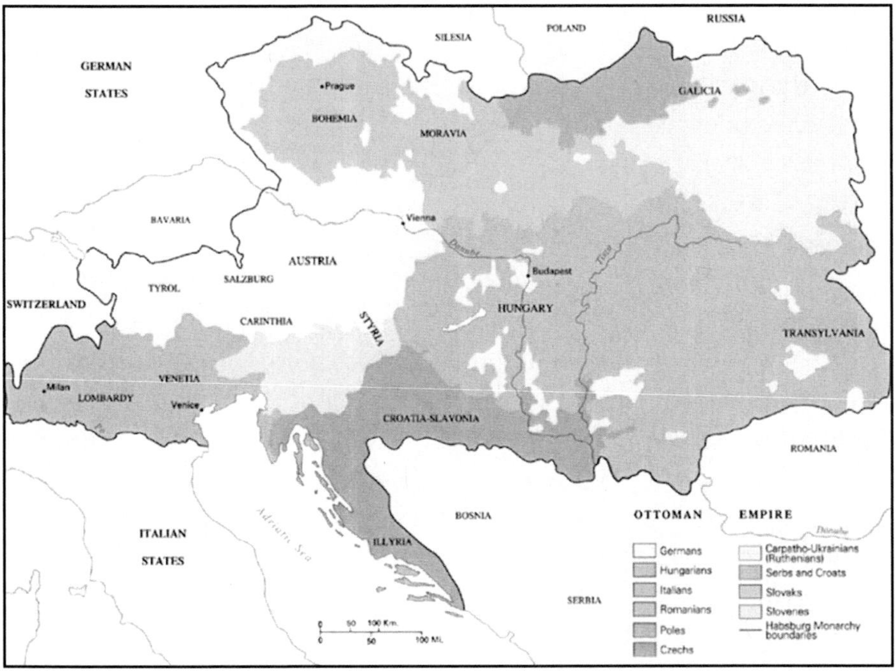

As Swiss relations with the Austrian Hapsburgs continued to deteriorate, rumors began to circulate amongst the Swiss that the Hapsburgs were assembling a huge army in Vienna from all over the Hapsburg Empire…from Hungary, the Balkans, Italy, France, Burgundy and the Lowlands. The apprehensive Swiss guessed that they were probably the "enemy" the Hapsburgs were preparing to attack. How could they defend themselves against such a huge army? Though their apprehensions mounted, they never even considered surrendering to them.

That was during the "Feudal" era in Europe, the times when the "divine right of Kings" (and their nobles) ruled European societies. Every common man was expected to identify himself by identifying his noble master. If he could not, he could be killed by anyone, because he had no noble protector, and was therefore an "outlaw".

This imposing monument shows the three legendary founding fathers of the Old Confederacy Werner Stauffacher, Walter Fürst, and Arnold von Melchtal based on the legendary Rütliwiese on Lake Lucerne in 1291.

But this had one advantage for the Swiss as well as it being their most awful danger: as inevitably occurred elsewhere in Europe at times, some hot-blooded young commander would react to the high-handed arrogance of his local lord and do something to offend him. That would earn him an arrest warrant. So he had to flee for his life. But where could this young "outlaw" find safe refuge? There was one place known throughout feudal Europe as a refuge; Switzerland, the land of the Free Swiss. Thousands of young "outlaws" from feudal Europe had crossed into Swiss territories. So then when the threat of Austrian invasion of Switzerland arose, the young "outlaws" hiding out in Switzerland all volunteered to fight Austria, the epitome of the feudal system. They were young, strong and brave.

The other great strength on the Swiss side was the dedication of most of the independent Swiss cantons against any foreign attacker.

The figures of the three oath takers or Eidgenossen during the 16th century merged with the legend of William Tell and became known as "the Three Tells". Impersonations of the Three Tells in historical costume played a role during the Swiss peasant war of 1653.

While all this Austrian threat was developing, the Swiss in other cantons decided to make a stand with Schwyz against the Austrians. William Tell, Arnold of Melchtal, Werner Staffacher and Walter Furst, all of whom had personally tangled with some Austrian officials earlier, agreed to meet at a meadow on the north shore of the Lake of Lucerne, known as the Rutli Meadow. Each brought ten good respected men of their canton with them. There they swore to come with an army of volunteers to fight any foreign attacker. The men of the four forest cantons all swore to come with all their fighting men.

The showdown battle occurred in a steep v-shaped valley called the "Morgarten", which led up towards Schwyz. At the lower end the Morgarten emptied into a lake when rain water flowed down it. As the Austrian army, 20,000 strong, advanced up from Zug towards Schwyz, they heard the deep bass sound of Alpen horns from the mountains above them and saw bonfires on the mountain tops above at night. Surely the Austrian troops understood from that, that the Swiss were preparing a welcome for them. But where? Today we call that "psychological warfare".

The Swiss prepared their "welcome" at the steep, v-shaped Morgarten. They had always cleared their fields for cultivation by rolling stones and boulders out of their fields to the sides of the fields. Now they rolled all the boulders towards the slope leading down into the Morgarten, ready for a final push to send them rolling down the Morgarten.

Rudolph von Habsburg

As the Austrian army reached a point a little more than halfway up the Morgarten, the Swiss blew a trumpet to signal their attack. Down came waves of boulders, crushing men and horses like bugs. Right behind the boulders came the Swiss, their scythes straightened into sharpened pikes, the Swiss charging down one sloped side of the valley and the "outlaws" charging down the other side. The Austrian army dissolved into masses of terrified men fleeing downhill. Many of their cavalry and mounted knights, unable to control their terrified horses plunged into the lake below and were drowned. Their elegant armor only served to take them to the bottom. Only a tiny remnant of the once proud Austrian army struggled back into Zug.

The Hapsburgs brooded over their Swiss defeat for decades, until they finally convinced themselves that it must have been some nearly-impossible freak accident. It wasn't really possible for a bunch of ragged peasants to defeat an imperial, professional army. So against common sense and harsh educational experience, they decided to try again.

This time natural Hapsburg arrogance was greatly inflated by pride of title: their march to victory would be led by the

Emperor of the Holy Roman Empire, the recently elected titular overlord of all of central Europe, Rudolph von Hapsburg. And they decided that their big mistake leading to the Morgarten had been that someone had chosen the wrong route. So this time they marched west across lowland Switzerland, intending then to turn south to take Berne, the Swiss capital. But the Swiss anticipated their every move and defeated them in a series of battles, killing Rudolph von Hapsburg in the process.

Rogier van der Weyden painted Charles the Bold/ the Rash as a young man in about 1460, wearing the Order of the Golden Fleece.

Of course, the Hapsburgs were not the only misguided and overly-ambitious royal rulers in Feudal Europe. Charles the Rash of Burgundy decided to punish the Swiss for a detachment of Swiss mercenaries disagreeing with him and abandoning his victorious army in Paris to return on their own to Switzerland. He marched his army into Savoy and paraded it for his cousin, the Duchess of Savoy, shortly before the Swiss destroyed it and made him flee west for his life. Savoy also disappeared shortly after when the Swiss expressed their displeasure.

We should mention the Swiss system of government, which is still used today. It is based on the canton, which makes the Swiss federal government respond to the voters out in the Cantons as the will of the Swiss people.

Periodically, when foreign and national issue require it, the central government in Berne will ask the cantons to each call a meeting (a "Landsgeminde") in a village square in each Canton to inform the opinion of their citizens on a specified list of issues back to Berne. The heads of each family in the Canton meet together in the village square. Each family head carries the family sword, as a sign that he will not be intimidated in voting on the issues on the list. The issues on the list are read one-by-one, with a vote by show of hands being counted on each issue. When the meeting is over a delegate of the canton personally carries the results to Berne and the result of the total of votes from all Cantons is announced in Berne as the policy of the Swiss National Government.

Any citizen of the Canton can appear at a Landsgeminde and ask for a vote by show of hands on whatever public issue he feels needs to be addressed. Such a vote can be ignored by neither the Canton nor the Berne national governments.

The Landsgemeinde is an old form of direct democracy. It is still practised in two cantons.

New Governor General of Philippines. Washington, D.C., July 27, 1939. Francis B. Sayre, Assistant Secretary of State, appointed by President Roosevelt to succeed Paul V. McNutt as Governor General of the Philippines.

FRANCIS B. SAYRE

The Great Conspiracy Continues

By **Cushman Cunningham**

To those of us who served in combat with patriotic enthusiasm in WWII and saw our friends die at our side, it was particularly painful to realize later that we had been tricked and deceived into WWII. We learned that President Franklin Roosevelt goaded and insulted the Japanese into attacking Pearl Harbor, only after having failed to goad Germany into war by acts of war against Germany during the previous decade before Pearl Harbor.

Roosevelt knew that if Japan attacked the US in the Pacific, Germany would be obliged to also declare war on the US, because of the Tripartite Treaty between Germany, Italy and Japan (the "Axis Pact") which those three powers

signed in 1940, the year before Pearl Harbor. FDR's purpose was to draw Nazi Germany into war with the USA, so as to be able to destroy Hitler, the Nazis and Germany.

But Roosevelt did not act alone in maneuvering us into war. He was helped by numbers of important co-conspirators on the top levels of government, one of whom was Alger Hiss, the only traitor (of many) who eventually was convicted and sent to jail. Later during the 1940s, '50s and '60s, as this conspiracy was investigated in Congress, these traitors were denounced as "Communists". But the truth is that this conspiracy was not simply "Communist", though they did give tremendous support to Soviet Russia during and after WW II, but the conspirators had their own separate agenda ... to take over control of the US government and eventually control of the whole Western world. **Later these same traitors and their associates became leaders of the Committee on Foreign Relations, the Trilateral Commission and the Bilderbergers.**

Alger Hiss

Franklin Delano Roosevelt

Because it is difficult to classify this conspiracy under any conventional label, such as "communist", "liberal" or "fascist", we are calling it "The Secret Empire" in recognition that it is a worldwide, organized and powerful conspiratorial force, capable of influencing the policies and direction of several major nations.

The story of how FDR goaded and insulted the Japanese into attacking Pearl Harbor is now well-known. But another major event occurring at the same time on December 7, 1941, has remained a mystery. How General Douglas MacArthur's well-prepared defense of the Philippines mysteriously failed on that December 7th has never been revealed.

Douglas MacArthur

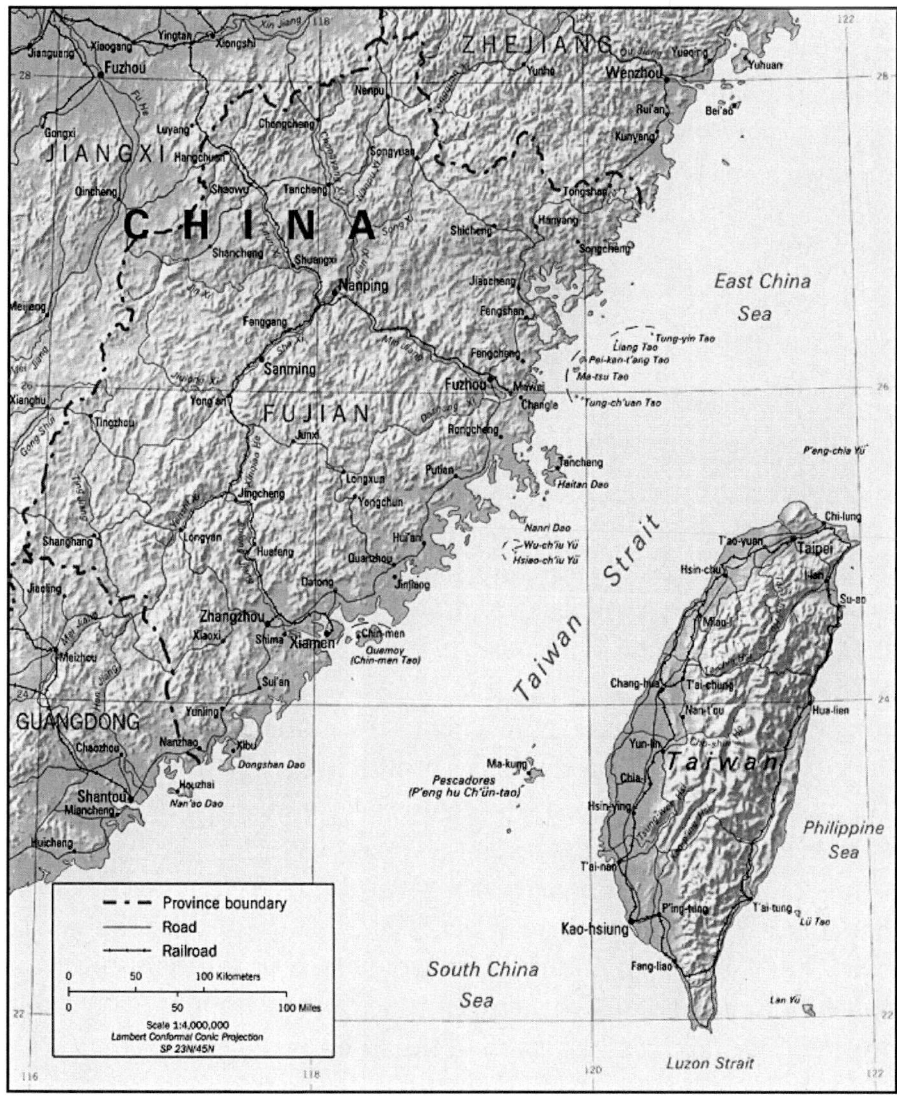

The Taiwan Strait or Formosa Strait

General MacArthur had feared (and expected) that the Japanese might soon attack US forces in the Pacific. He knew that the Japanese had been assembling troops and troopships on Formosa to the north of the Philippines and assumed correctly that they were intended for an invasion of the Philippines. They also had assembled fleets of Japanese warplanes on Formosan airfields to support their invasion of the Philippines.

MacArthur's proposed defense of the Philippines centered on attacking and destroying the Japanese warplanes on Formosa the moment a Japanese attack on US forces anywhere in the Pacific took place (Pearl Harbor was the obvious prime target). For this purpose he had assembled an impressive number of the latest model "Airacobra" fighters at Clark Field north of Manila. These fast fighters had a 40 mm cannon firing through the propeller shaft, in addition to four 50 caliber machine-guns mounted on the wings. At the first word of a Japanese attack MacArthur planned to order the Airacobras into the air with orders already drawn up for their attack on the Japanese airfields on Formosa. He reasoned that without control of the air over the Formosa Straits ... with US warplanes in control over the straits ... the Japanese would not dare to launch their fleet of troopships down the straits to invade the Philippines. The Airacobra pilots were waiting to receive MacArthur's orders to attack the Formosa airfields.

P-39 Aircobra fighter in flight.

But somehow when Pearl Harbor was attacked the morning of December 7, 1941, the order was never given to the Airocobras at Clark Field, and many hours later Japanese warplanes swept in on Clark Field and destroyed every one of the Airacobras on the ground. The Japanese invasion of the Philippines followed.

MacArthur's headquarters knew that he was planning to order the Airacobras at Clark Field to attack the Formosan airfields, but when the Pearl Harbor attack came, they were unable to contact him to get him to give the order. They tried frantically all day December 7, 1941, but could not contact him.

The evening before, the evening of December 6th, MacArthur had been urgently summoned to the American Governor's mansion, by Philippine High Commissioner Francis B. Sayre. Sayre had sent the High Commissioner's limousine to bring him to

Dramatic photograph of the opening moments of the attack on Pearl Harbor. Water can be seen rising from the battleship Oklahoma. Note aircraft above Battleship Row.
PHOTO BY THE JAPANESE NAVY. | USS ARIZONA MEMORIAL

the Governor's mansion. Somehow MacArthur had been detained there until after the Japanese had destroyed the Airacobras at Clark Field. MacArthur never explained what had happened to him over those critical 48 hours. The rumor was around Manila Army Headquarters that somehow Eisenhower had had something to do with it.

Eisenhower had been reprimanded in Manila for something some weeks earlier by MacArthur and sent back to Washington in disgrace. But soon after arriving back in Washington, Eisenhower had been promoted to top Army command, in command over MacArthur. Apparently (according to unconfirmable rumors) when MacArthur arrived at the Governor's mansion the evening of December 6th, he had a long-distance phone conversation with

Pearl Harbor aerial view of Honolulu, Hawaii before the Japanese attack on Pearl Harbor on December 7, 1941. In the foreground is the Honolulu harbor area, the Aloha tower, the tallest building, is at left in the foreground. | HANDOUT AP

◀ *Ford Island, seen on 10 October 1941 from much the same angle as Japanese bomber pilots viewed it on 7 December.*

Pearl Harbor ▶
Navy Yard
Oct. 1941

Southeast Loch of Peal Harbor Naval Base, Oahu, Hawaii, Oct 13 1941. The Submarine Base finger piers (right), Supply Depot (center), last 2 berths of Battleship Row (upper left), and East Loch anchorage (upper right).

HAWAIIAN AVIATION ARCHIVES

◀ *Aerial photograph taken by a Japanese pilot of the attack on Pearl Harbor a Japanese bomber in lower right foreground.* LIBRARY OF CONGRESS

The USS Arizona burning after the Japanese attack on Pearl Harbor.

USS Shaw ▶ *exploding, Pearl Harbor.*

Sailors stand among wrecked airplanes at Ford Island Naval Air Station as they watch the explosion of the USS Shaw in the background, during the Japanese surprise attack on Pearl Harbor, Hawaii, on December 7, 1941. | ASSOCIATED PRESS

Three U.S. battleships are hit from the air during the Japanese attack on Pearl Harbor on Dec. 7, 1941. Japan's bombing of U.S. military bases at Pearl Harbor brings the U.S. into World War II. From left are: USS West Virginia, severely damaged; USS Tennessee, damaged; and USS Arizona, sunk. | AP

◀ *In this image provided by the U.S. Navy, U.S.S. Nevada beached at Hospital Point at Pearl Harbor, Hawaii in December 1941.* Anonymous / AP

◀ *In this photo provided by the Department of Defense, U.S. aircraft destroyed as a result of the Japanese bombing on Pearl Harbor is shown, Dec. 7, 1941.* | Huffington Post

Black smoke rises from the burning wrecks of several U.S. Navy battleships after they had been bombed during the Japanese surprise attack on Pearl Harbor, Hawaii, on December 7, 1941. | AP ▶

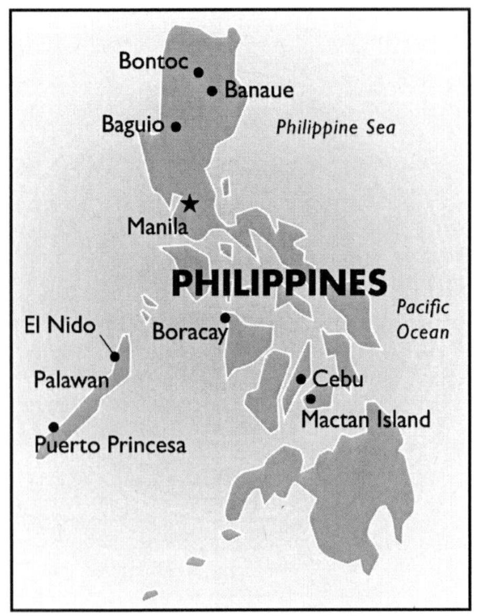

Eisenhower in Washington. Whatever else occurred is unknown. MacArthur, who was never shy about expressing his critical opinions, has never told anyone, to your author's knowledge.

The Philippine High Commissioner Francis B. Sayre, had been appointed Assistant Secretary of State in the 1930s and put in charge of the Trade Agreements Division of the State Department. He had selected as his top assistant Alger Hiss, who later went to jail as a Communist agent. Sayre associated in Washington with other high officials accused of Communist associations, such as Harry

Harry Dexter White

Adolph Berle

Noel Field

Labor Secretary Madame Frances Perkins

Supreme Court Justice, William O. Douglas

Dexter White, Adolph Berle, Noel Field, Labor Secretary Madame Frances Perkins and Supreme Court Justice William O. Douglas.

When the scandal broke after World War II about how the Roosevelt administration had shipped all the secrets for making the atom bomb to Soviet Russia in 1942-1944 through the secret Air Force field at Great Falls, Montana, Francis Sayre was again apparently involved in doing that. Major George Racy Jordan, an Army inspector at Albert Gore Field (the secret Montana airbase) reported his experience there after the war in his book "Major Jordan's Diary" and was extensively interviewed about it by Fulton Lewis, Jr., on his radio program. Otherwise it was ignored by our press and media.

Major George Racy Jordan

Fulton Lewis Jr.

Major Jordan had opened case after case of secret nuclear information, samples of uranium and other nuclear instruments and samples being sent by air to Russia through the secret airfield at Great Falls. Some boxes included notes from the senders in Washington. Amongst these were notes from a State Department person, who signed the note "Sayre". At that time Francis B. Sayre was back in Washington as a top official in the State Department, the only one in the State Department with the name "Sayre"

Francis B. Sayre had married President Woodrow Wilson's daughter in the 1920s. He was high-up in the Conspiracy.

As we now see the Conspiracy deployed in US invasions of the Middle East (in Israeli interests, rather than US interests) we must recognize that we cannot explain their purposes simply as "Communist". The conspiracy continues to dominate Washington, D.C.

"Money power denounces, as public enemies, all who question its methods or throw light upon its crimes."

William Jennings Bryan

"Of all the contrivances for cheating the laboring classes of mankind, none has more effect than that which deludes them with paper money."

Daniel Webster

"In free governments, the rulers are the servants, and the people their superiors and sovereigns."

Benjamin Franklin

After Kennedy was declared dead at Parkland Memorial Hospital, LBJ returned to Love Field airport with his body. Onboard Air Force One, Johnson was sworn in as the thirty-sixth president of the United States.

LYNDON BAINES JOHNSON

Evil Lurks in the Minds of Men

> *"Power tends to corrupt, and absolute power corrupts absolutely."*
>
> **John Dalberg-Acton, Lord Acton 1834-1902**

LBJ became president when John F. Kennedy was assassinated in Dallas on November 22, 1963. There were always questions as to whether LBJ had a hand in the JFK assassination. A brief review of the shady influences behind LBJ's rise to power suggests that he probably did have an important hand in it. From the beginning of his political career LBJ was supported by organized crime. In every election most of LBJ's campaign funds came from mafia chieftains belonging to the Bronfman Jewish

Edgar M. Bronfman Sr.

mafia all across the USA. When LBJ ran for the U.S. Senate against the popular Texas favorite son, Ralph Yarborough, the election was decided by the four South Texas counties controlled by political boss George Parr nicknamed "The Duke of Duval" (Duval being one of the four counties controlled by Parr).

George Parr, "The Duke of Duval"

Parr ran all the rackets in those South Texas counties ... drugs, prostitution, protection, etc. ... through the offices of his corrupted county sheriffs. LBJ won the election because in all four South Texas counties, ballot boxes were burned or disappeared, voter lists were falsified and witnesses mysteriously disappeared or ran off to California, or elsewhere, in fear.

How did LBJ facilitate the Kennedy assassination? LBJ became Vice-President by tricking the Kennedy's (JFK and Bobby) into believing that he did not want the V.P. job

At the 1960 Democratic National Convention in Los Angeles, campaign manager Robert F. Kennedy watches as his brother, presidential nominee John F. Kennedy, talks with his choice for vice president, Lyndon B. Johnson.

because he vastly preferred his present job as the powerful leader of the Senate. His southern agent who had cleverly infiltrated his way into the confidence of the two Kennedy brothers, told the Kennedy brothers that LBJ much preferred his powerful job as Senate Leader, but if the Kennedys wanted LBJ's help in the Senate with some vital legislation then pending, it would help to flatter him and win his cooperation, if they made the gesture of offering him the V.P. job, even though (he assured them) LBJ would never accept the offer. ***(The Vice-President's office had no authority whatsoever and was entirely dependent on the President for everything until the President died or resigned).***

Bobby Kennedy was assigned the job of calling LBJ at his Senate office and making the gesture of offering him the VEEP job. Both brothers were aghast when LBJ promptly accepted it.

It was at LBJ's pleading to him that JFK went to Dallas in late November 1963. LBJ said that there was a dangerous split in the Texas Democratic Party which needed the prestige of a Presidential intervention to heal it. But instead, of course, a team of assassins was awaiting JFK in Dallas.

First, LBJ tricked his way into the Vice Presidential slot, then he lured JFK to come to Dallas to be assassinated. How can anyone not be suspicious that LBJ's intention in taking the VP slot was to become President? We all remember John Nance Garner's joke about the old widow-woman down in Texas who had three sons … one ran away to sea, a second joined the French Foreign Legion, and the third became Vice-President; and none of the three were ever heard from again.

Franklin D. Roosevelt and John Nance Garner in Uvalde, Texas

Cord Meyer Jr. *(1920-2001) - CIA Officer*

Why would LBJ want the V.P. slot? (John Nance Garner was FDR's VEEP).

There is also a credible story that LBJ assigned Cord Meyer the job of arranging the JFK assassination. This has credibility because Cord Meyer's wife (Mary Pinchot Meyer) was JFK's mistress for several years (starting while she was still married to Cord Meyer). We can all understand why Cord Meyer may have had profound animosity toward JFK.

Mary Pinchot Meyer

LBJ had spies and allies all over Washington. It is highly probable that he had learned of the ongoing JFK-MPM (Mary Pinchot Meyer) affair. **Cord Meyer was in the CIA and therefore could well have worked in cooperation with James Jesus Angleton to arrange the JFK assassination.**

CIA Kim Philby, Donald Maclean, Guy Burgess and James Jesus Angleton. *Kim Philby was instrumental in setting up the American CIA. Philby along with Donald Maclean and Guy Burgess were all members of the* ***Cambridge Five*** *(University of Cambridge in the 1930's) a ring of spies recruited by Soviet scout Arnold Deutsch in the United Kingdom for the Office of Strategic Services (OSS) (British intelligence). In the early summer of 1951, Burgess and Maclean defected to the Soviet Union followed by Kim Philby in 1963. James Jesus Angleton former OSS member and companion of Philby was head of counter intelligence for the CIA from 1954 until he was ousted in 1973 by Richard Helms. We all remember JFK's statement, "I want to splinter the CIA in a thousand pieces and scatter it to the winds."*

Cord Meyer was not only a high CIA official but was also the son of Eugene Meyer, the owner of *The Washington Post. The Washington Post* was the top political newspaper in our nation's capital, read daily by everyone of importance in Washington, D.C. Eugene Meyer was a political power in "D.C.", a real political king-maker. His son, Cord Meyer, was also an insider-pal with the club of powerful Jewish-lesbian women in D.C. who had a formidable hand in feminist and student groups nation-wide.

Also, the Meyer family was Jewish. This could have been another link to the Israeli plotters who intended to have JFK assassinated to shut him up about their building atomic bombs at their secret facility at Dimona in the Negev Desert. J.J. Angleton was in charge of the Israeli desk of the CIA and headed the CIA assassination team, together with CIA agents E. Howard Hunt and Clay Shaw. Cord Meyer could well have collaborated with them ... under LBJ's protection.

Clay Shaw

E. Howard Hunt

Israel's Dimona nuclear power plant, in the Negev desert, started the country's nuclear program when it was built in the 1950s with French help.

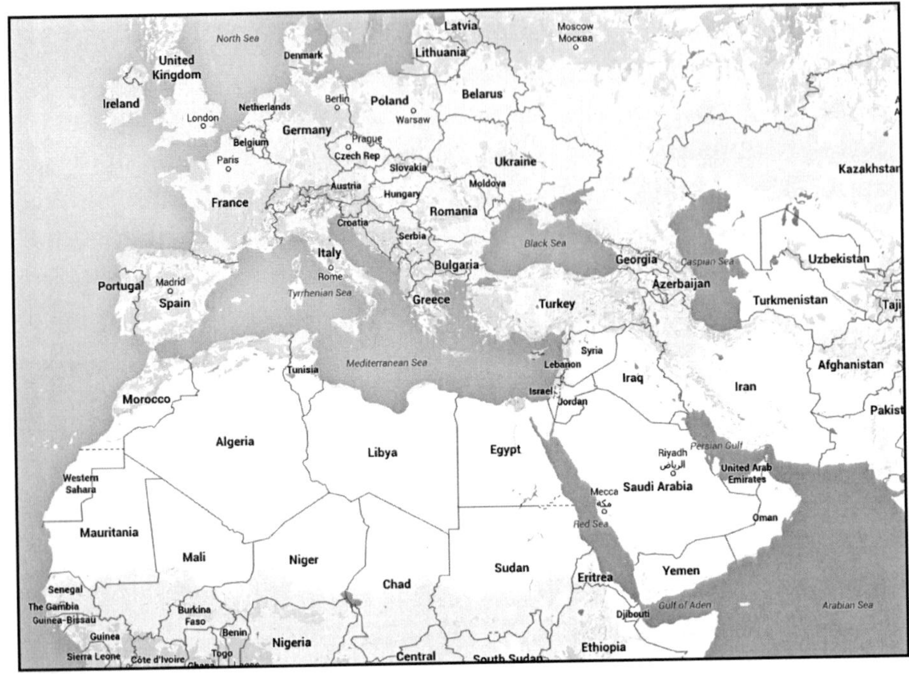

During LBJ's term in the White House he was also Commander-in-Chief of the U.S. Army and Navy. It was he who ordered the USS Liberty to the Eastern Mediterranean while the war between Israel and Egypt was underway in the Sinai. He also ordered three U.S. carrier groups into the same Eastern Mediterranean area. (Normally there is only one carrier group in the Mediterranean posted between Malaga (Spain) and Naples (Italy).

The plan was that Israel would sink the USS Liberty, LBJ would blame it on the Egyptians, and the three carriers would launch all their planes to blast Egyptian military and air bases, which at that time were loaded with Soviet troops, armor, aircraft and artillery; because the Soviets were then helping Egypt in the war against Israel. When the carrier planes attacked Egyptian bases, many Soviet soldiers and airmen would be killed. So then the Soviets would be obliged to declare war against the U.S. (and Israel). But before the surprised Soviets could decide on war and plan, prepare and launch any retaliatory action,

U.S. bombers and intercontinental missiles would atom-bomb the U.S.S.R. into oblivion. Nuclear World War III would be lightning fast, but the world-wide loss of life would be staggering.

That was the plan.

But unexpectedly a hitch occurred ... the USS Liberty refused to sink, despite repeated Israeli bombings, strafing and torpedo boat attacks. The Liberty just would not sink. The nearby U.S. carriers launched planes to beat off the Israeli attackers. But LBJ personally called from the White House and ordered the carrier commanders to call back their planes ... **and he prohibited them from aiding the *Liberty* as it was being attacked by Israeli planes and torpedo boats.**

Still the *Liberty* remained afloat.

Finally, the Israeli command faced revolt amongst their pilots, who were protesting that it was an American ship that they were being ordered to attack. The whole American fleet in the Mediterranean was up in arms against the orders to allow the attack on the Liberty to continue. Ships were approaching the Liberty to tow it into Malta. LBJ could no longer control the situation in the Med.

Of course this meant the whole original plan had to be abandoned, because the surviving crewmen on the *Liberty* would be able to testify that it had been the Israelis, not the Egyptians who had attacked the *Liberty*. The High command (as ordered by LBJ) ordered the crewmen of the *Liberty* <u>not</u> to talk to <u>anyone</u> about the attack, <u>not even</u> to talk amongst themselves about it. The Navy brass was fuming in indignation. The scandal was spreading to the Army and Air Corps brass, and then beginning to be rumored amongst civilian circles, despite frantic efforts by the Administration to keep it under wraps. It had been LBJ along with the Israeli government who steered the United States military into disgrace.

USS Liberty receives assistance from 6th Fleet after she was attacked, June 1967.

USS LIBERTY

By Victor Thorn

History speaks, and despite attempts to suppress and overtly censor it, those who've lived through particularly traumatic events can never be silenced as long as they continue to speak out.

There exist few, if any, more courageous men than those who were aboard the *USS Liberty* on June 8, 1967 ... men who endured a two-hour assault by torpedo boats and gunner ships belonging to the Israeli Defense Force (IDF). Some of these crewmembers survived. 34 others perished that tragic day as the Israeli Defense Force deliberately attempted to sink this ship that clearly displayed an enormous American flag on its mast.

Because history speaks, attempts have been made by the U.S. and Israeli governments, not to mention Congressmen such as John McCain (now U.S. Senator from Arizona and 2008

Republican presidential candidate) to cover up this murderous attack. None of these treasonous individuals or government officials wanted the world to hear the damning truths that history could provide. **So, they've compensated by engaging in an ongoing disinformation campaign that includes slander, threats, and the most egregious of lies.**

Still, although their deceptions may fill history books, other voices can never be diminished. These are the voices which call out directly from that ominous date of June 8, 1967. **Their demands for justice may be banished from nightly newscasts or military ceremonies, but their words won't be erased like inconvenient historical facts that were flushed down a Memory Hole in George Orwell's *1984*.**

The reason why is evident: those that crawl on their bellies and speak with forked tongues can never triumph over the bravest among us who stand proudly on their feet and speak with absolutely nothing whatsoever to hide.

Fortunately, over the past decade this writer has had the honor to personally interview eight surviving *Liberty* crewmembers, some of them on multiple occasions. Not only have these men relayed their harrowing tales in a book I co-authored entitled *Ship Without a Country: Eyewitness Accounts of the Attack on the USS Liberty*, but I've also been privileged to contact them for updates that appeared in the pages of *American Free Press*.

For all those with ears to hear, history — untainted by the hidden hands of treachery — still rings out loud and clear in the voices of the following men:

Larry Weaver

21-year-old crewman Larry Weaver's first impressions of the Israeli Defense Force's onslaught were suddenly vanquished when a rocket blast shattered his body. Blown five feet in the air, he landed back on the deck, blood surrounding him everywhere. Critically wounded, he laid down, hoping to find safety. That's when the fallen seaman helplessly watched as an Israeli pilot saw him and deliberately dive-bombed in his direction.

The horrors continued, and despite his injuries, Weaver pushed a fellow crewman out of the line of fire in hopes of saving his life. Another man wasn't so lucky. Weaver looked on as the sailor's body was cut in half by the strafe.

In Weaver's opinion, these attacks were undoubtedly calculated (and not accidental or a case of mistaken identity). First, jet fighters with rockets and cannon fire riddled the ship with armor piercing munitions. Next, torrents of napalm burned the *Liberty* from within. Finally, gunboats unleashed volleys of torpedo fire.

Captain *(future Rear Admiral)* **Isaac C. Kidd**, *USN in a picture taken while he was Chief of Staff to the Commander, Base Force, U.S. Fleet.*

Afterward, when Weaver got out of intensive care in Philadelphia, officials summoned him to a small room, whereupon he met three-star Admiral Isaac Kidd. The admiral sat alongside Weaver, removed his stars, and then wanted to be told everything that the young crewman had encountered. Upon hearing his story, Kidd threatened Weaver with imprisonment and said he'd lose the key if he ever mentioned these events to anyone. Disillusioned by the interrogation techniques directed against him, Weaver said, "I was treated like a criminal by the U.S. government and told that I'd be abandoned in a federal prison if I ever spoke out. Further, all records pertaining to my duty aboard the USS Liberty were expunged."

Jim Ennes

Amid all the chaos of this murderous attack, *Assault on the Liberty* author Jim Ennes recounted how lifeboats that could have been used to save injured crewmen were intentionally machine-gunned by those aboard Israeli Defense Force torpedo boats who had examined them at close range. Later, one of the life rafts marked "U.S. Navy" was pulled from an Israeli vessel. Unconscionably, Israeli Defense Force pilots and boatmen fired on anything that moved. **Their machine-gunning of life rafts constituted a clear war crimes violation.** Ennes also described another gruesome element of this attack: how the Israeli Defense Force doused the *Liberty* with toxic napalm. "The military purpose of napalm, which is jellied flaming gasoline, is to destroy personnel. It assures the destruction of troops, is lethal to ships, and turned the *Liberty* into an inferno."

Speaking of President Lyndon Baines Johnson, Admiral Kidd, and Defense Secretary Robert McNamara, Ennes lamented, "We weren't defended at all. We were abandoned when we needed their help the most."

Dave Lewis

An officer in charge of the *Liberty's* research department, Dave Lewis experienced an excruciating amount of physical pain. Burnt paint was thrust into his eyes, and the resulting damage was so severe that doctors lanced his eyelids and scraped the burnt paint off his eyeballs. Temporarily blinded, he also suffered severe damage to his eardrums, while a piece of concrete pierced his lip as shrapnel wracked all parts of his body.

Obviously traumatized by this unexpected onslaught, years later Lewis told an amusing story of what happened next. When help finally arrived many hours later, the most severely wounded were hoisted from the *Liberty* onto a helicopter which flew them to the *USS America*. Wrapped in bandages from head-to-toe, Lewis was strapped into a basket and lifted aboard the helicopter. However, during this frantic emergency flight, a crewman couldn't differentiate Lewis' head from his toes, so he sat directly on his head. Still able to maintain his sense of humor, Lewis laughed, "What an ignominious way that would have been to die, especially after surviving a torpedo attack."

Ernie Gallo

Electrical technician Ernie Gallo will never forget his fallen brothers. **"34 men were murdered by the Israelis, and we're not going to let them die for nothing. Even if the media won't tell you the truth about it, we will. You don't spend two hours strafing and bombing a ship that you didn't intend to sink."**

Gallo further confided, "It was incredible to see what our ship had gone through: holes in the walls like peeled paper. It's a miracle that anyone survived. It's hard to imagine the amount of damage and destruction. The helm was completely blown away and there was incredible carnage . . . bodies everywhere. The scene was horrific. You can't imagine what it looked like."

Joe Lentini

During Israel's murderous rampage, crewman Joe Lentini suffered a four-inch gash in his leg, a collapsed lung, broken ribs, a broken left leg, in addition to being knocked unconscious.

Lentini insisted, **"Anyone who was on that ship will tell you it wasn't a mistake. The Israelis blew out our topside hatches, hit our only gas tank, machine-gunned the life rafts, and took out our antennas. For the Israeli Defense Force to hit these targets, each pilot**

would have had to be pre-briefed before the attack with photographs of the targets."

Gary Brummett

Following this onslaught where their ship miraculously still managed to float with over 800 holes in it, the U.S. Navy didn't allow them to dock at a port that was only two days away. **Rather, the *Liberty* was forced to travel another 1,200 miles to a destination that took them an additional three days. Eventually resting in Malta, third class petty officer Gary Brummett confessed, "I was afraid to sleep in my rack because our ship had taken such a beating."**

Years later during an *American Free Press* interview, Brummett told this writer that he noticed an alarming number of similarities to the Sept. 11, 2012 attack on a U.S. consulate in Benghazi, Libya. Brummett unequivocally stated, **"Benghazi smells just like the *USS Liberty* because Barack Obama denied reinforcements to our men. I heard the fighter jets could have reached Benghazi in 30 minutes."**

Of course, authentic historians know full-well that Pres. Lyndon Johnson called back fighter jets en route to save the *Liberty* on two different occasions. His rationale was spine-tingling, not to mention cold-blooded in an unimaginably inhuman way. Johnson said, **"I don't care how many Americans are attacked. I will not attack our friend and ally, Israel."**

Phil Tourney

Petty Officer Phil Tourney volunteered a similar observation when contacted in 2013. **"Obama left our men out there to die in Benghazi just like Johnson did with the *Liberty*. Benghazi and the *Liberty* are very**

similar because both presidents called back air fighters who were already in flight. You don't let fellow countrymen out there to die." It's hard to picture a more cowardly act than when a president turns his back on those placed under his command.

A year earlier during a 2012 interview, Tourney described how he'd been brushed off by government officials for the past 30 years. Once, at a 2003 State Dept. conference, Tourney rose to address the speakers during a Q&A session. But instead of hearing him out, organizers cut off Tourney's microphone. **"It was one of the biggest disappointments of my life," Tourney said sadly. He added, "The naval investigation that followed was a sham. In essence, our crewmen were left out there to die in order to protect Israel."**

Merlin Staring

This corrupt investigation left a bitter taste in the mouths of every surviving crewmember, especially Rear Admiral Merlin Staring. As a former Judge Advocate General in the U.S. Navy, as well as Treasurer of the USS Liberty Association, Staring complained, "If the true facts of this attack in 1967—plus the nature and quality of the investigation were widely known—any reasonable person would know this is not the way to treat sailors and men from the armed forces who were serving their country. The report was terribly flawed. I was shocked and chagrined to cosmetically find it a poor piece of work. There were typographical errors, incorrect citations, and it lacked credibility."

Indeed, history speaks, and those of us who seek justice will forever carry a torch of truth for those righteous men of the *USS Liberty* that so bravely served their country, yet received nothing in return but betrayal.

Damaged USS Liberty arrives at Malta, June 1967.

Torpedo hole viewed toward stern.

Torpedo hole viewed toward bow.

Framing Assange

By **Cushman Cunningham**

Julian Assange

To most thinking patriotic Americans Julian Assange and Bradley Manning are patriots and heroes for exposing the secretiveness and police-state mentality of the US government (especially the US Intelligence and Military).

The Swedish and British governments should be buried in shame for their cooperation with their obvious framing of Assange by pressing the ridiculous claims of two loose Swedish sluts, who had Assange over for an elaborate breakfast the morning after the night on which they later claimed he had raped them. One of them had thrown a big party for Assange the same evening she later claimed he had raped her.

Ever since the Bush government purged the US military's top Generals (and Colonels) in late 2001 and early 2002 because of their opposition to the wars in Afghanistan and Iraq, the US military have slavishly obeyed the will of the Neo-Cons and the Israeli Lobby.

Our Constitution assumed our self-government would function with the cooperation of transparency about Federal activities.

***

Our controlled press and media continues to screech about the Syrian government's killing of "rebels", always ignoring the fact that the attacks against the Syrian regime are almost all happening along the borders of Syria, clearly invasions coming from outside Syria. The most-probable perpetrator, "Israel", is never mentioned in connection with this war.

* * *

U.S. Army Private Bradley Manning is escorted as he leaves a military court in June 2012. Bradley Manning, the Army private accused of leaking a massive cache of classified information to WikiLeaks.

> **"The material that Bradley Manning is alleged to have leaked has highlighted astonishing examples of U.S. subversion of the democratic process around the world, systematic evasion of accountability for atrocities and killings, and many other abuses."**

JULIAN ASSANGE

THE WORLD POST | NOVEMBER 29, 2012

Israel Lies.

By **Cushman Cunningham**

Benjamin Netanyahu

The recent release of official Israeli government documents by a South African source reveals what many of us have suspected for years: that the Israeli government does not believe that Iran is trying to make a nuclear bomb. The same documents also reveal that "Bibi" Netanyahu intentionally lied to the UN when he spoke to the UN describing just how Iran was planning to make its nuclear bomb. We all knew Bibi was a swaggering liar, but this is official Israeli proof of that.

Syria

By **Cushman Cunningham**

The UN and the Security Council talk continuously against the legally elected Syrian government. But the principal Syrian peoples, the Alawites and the Druse, still hold over 90% of Syrian territory, while the Israeli-recruited and paid "rebels" have only succeeded in tearing up border communities along the Syrian borders.

All the Middle East communities, Christians as well as Arabs and others, know that it is the Israelis (and other Jews) who have created, recruited and paid the so-called "rebels", in the hope that after the legitimate Middle Eastern governments are overthrown, Israel will take over the whole area as "Eretz Israel". That has been the publicly-declared aim of the Jews for over a century.

The so-called "rebels" are seldom really Syrians, but are human trash recruited out of the jails, the streets and alleys of Africa, the Middle East and everywhere else, recruited, paid and transported by the Jews to Syria to overthrow President Assad's government. That is why the "rebels" don't fight very determinedly, but principally just "stick around" waiting for payday.

How Cremation Works

By **Robert Bouchard**

Before cremation of a dead human body can take place, it must be placed in a casket or container which has been approved for cremation. This means the casket or container must be made of a combustible material such as wood, fiberboard, or cardboard. Steel caskets cannot be used for cremation.

The container is then placed in the cremation chamber at which time the cremation process begins. The heat and flames produced by the cremation chamber can reach temperatures as high as 1800 degrees Fahrenheit. At this extreme temperature, everything in the cremation chamber is consumed except for the bone fragments of the deceased.

The total amount of time required to cremate the body is approximately one and a half to three hours. Factors such as the size of the deceased and the type of container used determine the amount of time required for the complete process. Once the actual burn time has been completed, it is necessary to have a cooling period time before the bone fragments are removed from the cremation chamber. To achieve this cooling process, the door to the cremation chamber is partially opened so that heat can escape from the enclosed chamber.

When the remains, or bone fragments, are removed from the chamber, they are separated from any noncombustible materials that may remain in the chamber. Noncombustible materials could be metal objects such as nails or screws used in the construction of a wood casket.

The bone fragments removed from the chamber must be further reduced in size in order to be returned to the family in a respectful and proper manner. To achieve this goal, the crematory operator transfers the bone fragments to a pulverizer which reduces the bone fragments to a finer, more uniform substance.

At this point, the cremated remains are packaged in a container for presentation to the family. In many cases, the cremated remains are placed in an urn which has already been selected by the family. If, for any reason, the family has not selected an urn, the crematory places the remains in a temporary container.

Urns can be constructed of many different materials such as wood, marble, steel, porcelain, or plastic. Stylish urns are normally chosen when the surviving family plans to have the cremated remains present for funeral services or for display in a niche at a columbarium. Temporary containers are often used when the cremated remains will be spread over land or water.

One of the protocols of the treaty that ended World War II was the fact that the Allies being victorious were allowed to write the history of the war years and those events leading up to the Second World War.

"History is nothing but a pack of tricks the living play upon the dead."

VOLTAIRE (1694–1778)

Often there is a reference to the figure that six million Jews were killed during World War II allegedly gassed in a Jewish genocide. One of the anomalies is that the number of Jews in Germany in 1939 was approximately six hundred thousand - by some estimations considerably less—and of these many came to the United States, some went to Palestine and some stayed in

Germany. For the historical truth about the Jews before, during and after World War II the best documentation comes from the book, The Holocaust Never Happened & The CIA Killed JFK by Jorgen Lars Rasmussen.

According to worldbookonline.com the Second World War started on September 1, 1939 and the United States joined the war on December 7, 1941. According to wolframalpha.com the Second World War ran for 2,193 days. If you take 24 hours in a day and multiply it by 2,193 days the number of hours involved in World War II is 52,632. Now if you multiply that previous figure 52,632 by 60, which of course is the number of minutes in an hour, the total minutes come to 3,157,920 minutes in World War II.

With reference to the article How Cremation Works by Robert Bouchard; when the news media and talk show hosts bring up the six million figure of Jewish people allegedly gassed during World War II, I suggest they are paid substantial amounts to undercut the truth knowing full well that the idea of a Jewish holocaust during that time frame was the hoax of the Twentieth Century.

RICE LAKE CONNECTION

Lake Buena Vista, Florida

The Great Speech

Given by **Jon Larsen Shudlick**
Before The American Bar Association
Lake Buena Vista, FL

December, 1992

You have given me, among several others, the opportunity to have ten minutes to speak to the American Bar Association. I should thank you for the opportunity, but, if you ignore what I have to say, I will have wasted my time and funds in coming here. However, even should you ignore what I have to say, which is what I expect, I do not plan to request another opportunity to speak to you. The reason being that I am hereby as an American citizen saying "Farewell" to the American Bar Association.

You might think that that means that I am about to move to another country or go into retirement, but that is not the case. I am saying "Farewell" to an organization I believe will someday become as extinct as the dinosaur. I say this out of the belief that every attempt at serious reform that your group has made has been one that has been only cosmetic at best. You were given the opportunity to repair the damage done to society through the personal injury system several years ago and you came up with "tort reform" that included various features all of which increased your bureaucratic control on injury victims, insurance companies and vastly increased your profits. Reforms in the criminal law system have only seen the procedures simplified which inject

hordes of criminals back into society before the ink on their arrest warrants has even dried. It is for this reason that I am saying “Good-bye” to you. You are the next dinosaur.

I believe that the day is coming when your monopoly on law in America will be broken. Instead of coming to a lawyer to draw a will, we will just walk up to a renovated Register of Wills office, ask for the proper form, fill it out in front of a video camera, pay the fee and file it in the office along with the video tape which will prove competency as a matter of fact. No more will you and your word processors be able to charge people vast amounts to complicate and delay the transfer of their estates on their death. No more will you be able to profit by encouraging litigation to contest validly drawn wills. Titles to real and personal property will go directly to heirs upon proof of death. **In short, the parasitic role that lawyers have carved for themselves over the centuries preying upon decedent’s estates will be over.**

Those of you who have made a living seeing that criminals are better treated in America than I am should also start looking for new work. For example, in return for what you have done to the land by making it a lengthy and expensive ordeal for society to put away criminals, you are someday going to face unemployment. We are going to redo the criminal justice system from top to bottom one day. A call to the police is going to result in the arrival of the police with a squad car plus the arrival of an evidence van from a separate branch of the police. **The complaint and the resulting arrests will be on video tapes and so will all stories from witnesses. They will be interrogated by the finest law enforcement officials in the land and those tapes will be shown to a jury in the presence of the defendant within three weeks of every crime.** Should there be questions, live testimony will be taken from the proper witnesses, but never again will lawyers be allowed to meet in private with witnesses and do like you

Criminal Justice students take part in mock trial with the help of local district attorney presiding as "judge". On the witness stand, one student describes evidence while playing a "law enforcement officer", as the "prosecutor" and "court reporter", recording testimony, look on.

have done for centuries ... **arrange for people to lie under oath without the slightest twinge of conscience. You call it euphemistically "sandpapering witnesses" but it is suborning perjury nevertheless.**

Some of you have friends called psychologists and psychiatrists whom you have made rich by arranging for them to testify that certain defendants cannot be held responsible for their actions because of mental deficiencies. **We will someday drive these soothsayers out of business as well and never again will criminal acts be judged by the likes of these twentieth century sophists. They have made millions with your help lying about your clients and they have unleashed a vast wave of irresponsibility on the land, also with your help.** So you might want to start looking for work for them and with them because you are both going to need to get into honest work one of these days.

There will be courtrooms, but truth will prevail. Anyone who commits perjury or suborns perjury will get the **ancient penalty**. If they lie in a murder case, they get the same penalty as the murderer. If they set up an innocent man, they get the same penalty for their perjury and deceit that the innocent man would have gotten if wrongfully convicted of the false charge. **I can see you really squirming out there because many of you have committed horrendous crimes against your innocent countrymen.** You are tallying up how many life sentences you would have earned under such a system.

St. Mary's Law School, San Antonio, Texas

There will be law schools as well, but justice will be taught. Instead of turning young leaders into the deceitful, gold digging type which law schools have made of you, they will be transformed into individuals who serve only the needs of justice. They will be selected only from men who have already proven before law school or judge's school that they are men with a passion for justice. There is hardly a man on the bench today who will be acceptable to those who someday pick the new type of judge and lawyer.

When it comes to lawsuits over torts or divorce or contracts or property rights, most all disputes will be subject to rapid determination in courts of conciliation. **Arbitration will be the key manner of disposing of most litigation. It will be rapid, just, and inexpensive.** No rewards will be given to the chronic litigators who will have to pay increasing costs to enter the system after a series of clear losses showing the individual to be a social crank rather than a genuinely aggrieved citizen.

I have read in the past few months that litigation has almost become the largest, if not the largest, industry in the United States. In short, we are totally wrapped up in suing each other and in committing crimes against one another. Because of the system you have devised in drafting the laws, in enacting them, in enforcing them and in interpreting them, you are a monopoly that benefits mightily from all this social and economic turmoil. You're the core of the problem! **You are enablers and allies of an increasingly hostile and criminal governmental system and when the people have had enough of you and them, you will all be swept away and disappear like the dinosaur!**

You fill your pockets with blood money as you send to "debtor's prison" those hard pressed middle income men, veterans, and solid citizens of all walks of life who now must support two families on a diminishing income. When those down-trodden men are led away, shackled and beaten, you smile in your wickedness and deceit as you proclaim "the Judge did it". **Yet by your tacit approval of this criminal JUST US System, you have become the defilers of wisdom, destroyers of the spirit and fornicators of the truth. Surely you will be swept away and disappear like the dinosaur.**

We honest taxpaying citizens demand the adversary relationship in family law (divorce court) be changed to a **mediation mandatory conclusion**. Otherwise, your children and heirs will end up spitting on your graves for the living hell you have left them. Yes, you will be swept away and disappear like the dinosaur.

My ten minutes are up. You surely have more time than that during which to plunder America and Americans. But mark my words well because time is running short. You will need every available moment to find cover in order to survive what is coming upon this land!

Presented Before the Florida Supreme Court

By **Jon Larsen Shudlick**
Monday, April 5th, 1993

In Opposition to the Anti-Discrimination Proposal of the Florida Bar Anti-Discrimination Hearing

Your FLORIDA BAR ASSOCIATION system now excludes litigants who choose to proceed in propria persona sui juris or pro-se. Your system is a RESPECTER OF PERSONS.

As the U.S. Supreme Court observed:

"Judges, having ears to hear, hear not;" the apparatus and machinery of civil government skulk away as if government and justice were crimes and feared detection.

Mitchum v Foster 92 S.Ct. 2151

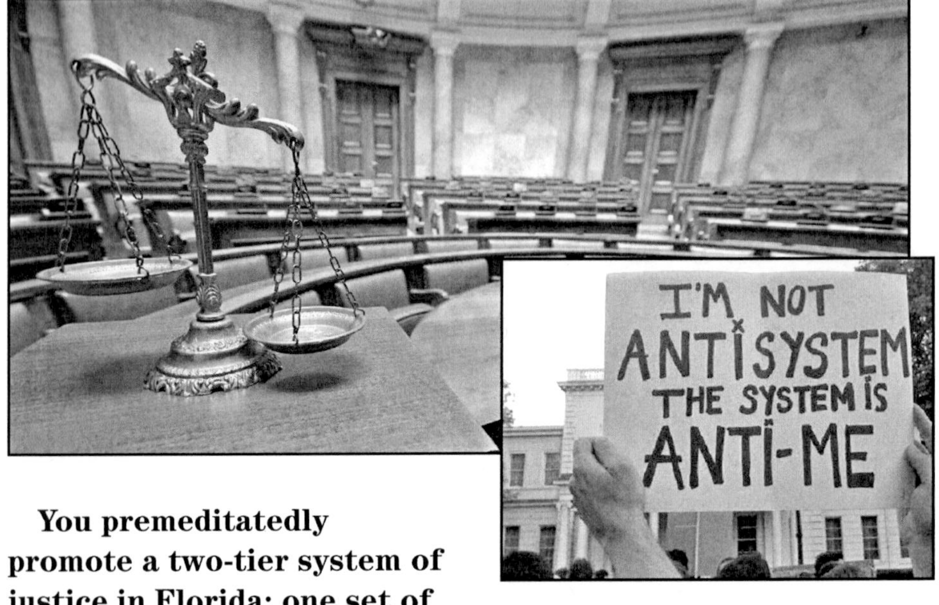

You premeditatedly promote a two-tier system of justice in Florida: one set of rules for you and your cronies in the BAR ASSOCIATION; another set of rules stacked squarely against the interests of the people you pretend to serve and in unambiguous violation of your sworn oaths as judges.

The DIVORCE INDUSTRY you oversee turns middle-class American housewives

into bag-ladies; their ex-husbands into non- productive vagrants. And it is your profession and its staff that profits handsomely from the misery of the families destroyed.

Your inaction identifies you Justices as being "OF COUNSEL" in the law-firm of LOOT, RAPE, PILLAGE, STEAL, DOUBLE-TALK, DRAWDOWN and RIP-OFF.

By your tacit approval of your JUST-US system, you have become the defilers of wisdom, the destroyers of the spirit and the fornicators of the truth. Like the dinosaur, you and your corrupt system stand at the precipice of extinction.

You are the board-of-directors of the NEW DESPOTISM. You profit handsomely from the destruction of our republic, our way of life, our principles of jurisprudence and our people.

You are the enablers and allies of an increasingly hostile and criminal governmental system. When the people have had enough, they will toss you and yours onto the scrap-heap of judicial history where you belong.

The deeper the keel of a sailing vessel, the more stable it will be in a hurricane. This "criminal JUST-US system" is steering a rudderless raft, leaking like a sieve with its destination hell.

Rice Lake Students Beat State and National Average for ACT Scores

Reprinted from

RICE LAKE, WI — The Chronotype — SEPT. 7, 2015

Rice Lake School District students who took the ACT college entrance exam this year scored above the state and national average.

Students here scored an average of 23.3 on the composite test, compared to the state average of 22.1, which was the second highest state average score in the nation. The local score also exceeded the 22.7 reached in Minnesota, which led the nation.

The 126 Rice Lake students who took the test recorded a higher average than nearly all of its neighboring or athletic conference

schools. Only Hudson, at 24.4 did better, with New Richmond students equalling the Rice Lake average.

The Rice Lake score was slightly below the 2014 average of 23.4.

About 73% of Wisconsin's 2015 public and private school graduates (**46,738** students) took the ACT during high school. Their average composite score was the same as in 2014.

Nationally, 59% of graduates, 1.9 million students, took the ACT. Their average composite score was 21.0, also the same as last year. The ACT is scored on a scale of 1 to 36.

"These college-bound students did a fine job on the ACT assessment, demonstrating their overall preparedness for the next steps in their education and careers," said State Superintendent Tony Evers.

Tony Evers, Wisconsin State Superintendent of Public Instruction

Tying student test results to postsecondary outcomes, ACT has established college-readiness benchmark scores. **Those scores for each subject area, such as 18 for English and 22 for mathematics, indicate a 75% chance of a student earning a "C" or better on credit-bearing coursework,**

reducing the likelihood that the student will need remedial coursework in college.

Rice Lake with an average English score of 22.2, had 82.7% of test takers college ready in that subject area. Wisconsin had 74%of ACT-taking students who earned the English benchmark score compared to 64% nationally.

In math, Rice Lake students achieved an average of 24.3, which translates to 70.9% college ready, according to the benchmark. That compares to 52% in Wisconsin, 42% nationally.

In reading the average score here was 22.9, equaling 55.5% college readiness, compared to 53% for Wisconsin and 46% nationally.

For science, Rice Lake students averaged a score of 23.3, resulting in a readiness level of 54.5%, Statewide test takers in science were 49% college ready and national just 38% met that benchmark.

"Our students, their families, and teachers will rise to the higher expectations we set," Evers said. "The research is clear, and business and industry tell us, that college-ready is career-ready. That is the goal for all of our graduates."

With virtually all of Wisconsin's public school 11th-graders having taken the ACT this past spring as part of statewide assessments, ACT participation will rise dramatically next year and scores are expected to decline. Those results for last year's 11th-graders will be reported later in fall.

By setting a new course and administering the ACT to all high school juniors, we're helping way more students consider further education after high school."

2015 composite ACT Averages

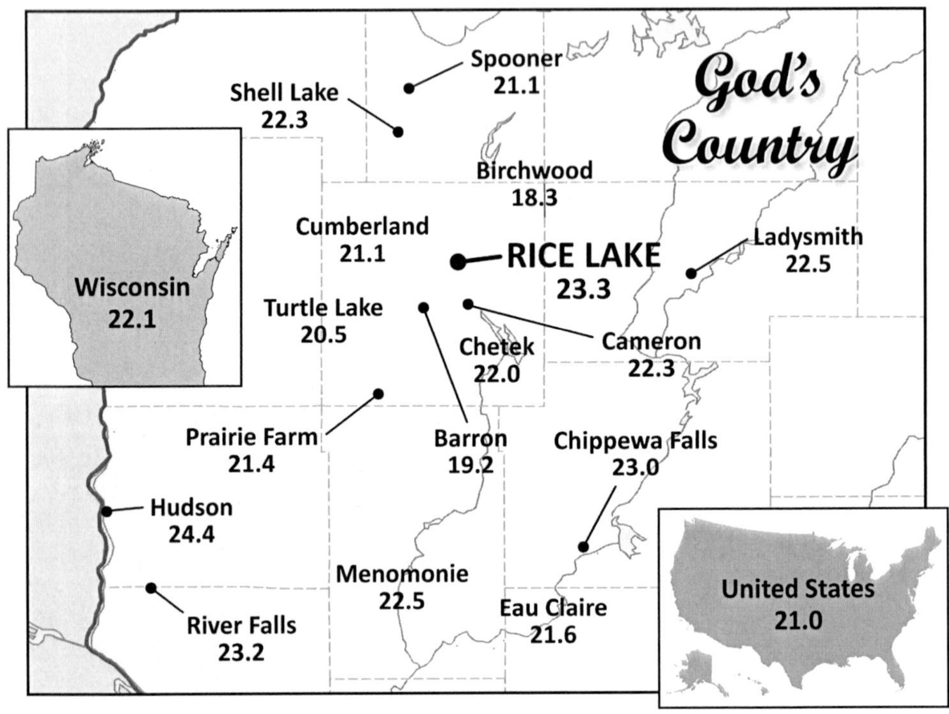

Florence Shudlick

My mother, Florence Alfreda Irene (Nee Larsen) Shudlick, was a dedicated one room eight grade country school teacher for 34 years in Barron County, Wisconsin. She and my dad met at Normal School (two year teachers' college) and raised five vibrant children starting when a teacher's salary was $40.00 a month. My dad also taught for one year at an eight grade one room country school. Only one person in a family could receive a check from the government in those days so my parents drove to Duluth, Minnesota and eloped. Their best friends Gwen and Clyde Magett witnessed for them.

My mother, with her beautiful Norwegian-Danish soprano voice ably enhanced the family income by singing at weddings, funerals and a variety of ceremonial events. It is funny how when you are a child and someone praises one of your parents you don't seem to think a whole lot about it, however, the older you get you realize how lucky you were just to be able say she was my mother or he was my dad.

Weather Modification

Cloudseeding

By **Diane MacMillan**

Diane and Thumper

I remember riding with my Dad as he tired of my many questions. There was that familiar sigh.

I think at the time it was called "a curious mind". And these days, it is now called "Critical Thinking". Maybe it came from my Grandfather who was trying to stop Senator Humphrey from allowing Taconite tailings being dumped into Lake Superior or my mother stopping snowmobiles on BlueberryRun, an old railroad spur, past our house on the St. Croix River. More than likely it also had something to do with the way that we were taught in our Lincoln Grade School, Junior High and our High School many years ago in Rice Lake, Wisconsin. Our teachers then required us to "wonder".

Senator Hubert H. Humphrey

PHOTO COURTESY OF THE MINNESOTA HISTORICAL SOCIETY

For every ton of iron ore produced, 2 tons of waste material has to be disposed. The Reserve Mining Company dumped the waste material, called tailings, into Lake Superior, with permits approved by the state of Minnesota.

Cloud seeding can be done by ground generators, plane, or rocket. | WIKIPEDIA

In the early 1990's, I was standing along one of our Colorado mountain highways, watching another one of our horrific wildfires. We used to call them forest fires that burned a few acres and was out. But in the 1990's something was different. As I talked to myself, **"What is this fire all about?"** A man standing beside me, answered my question. He said, **"They are cloudseeding"**. From there the questions proliferated. **What cloudseeding? What's that got to do with it? Where are they cloudseeding? I thought that they didn't cloudseed anymore.**

Then there was the Hayman Fire. 130,000 acres running from the Colorado Springs area along the Platte River all the way to the south end of Denver, Colorado. And the 2012 North Fork Fire in Conifer burning over 4,000 acres, 27 homes and 3 people died,

Denver, Colorado

Silver iodide is an inorganic compound with the formula AgI. The compound is a bright yellow solid, but samples almost always contain impurities of metallic silver that give a gray coloration. The silver contamination arises because AgI is highly photosensitive. This property is exploited in silver-based photography. Silver iodide is also used as an antiseptic and in cloud seeding.

The crystalline structure of AgI is similar to that of ice, allowing it to induce freezing by the process known as heterogeneous nucleation. Approximately 50,000 kg are used for cloud seeding annually, each seeding experiment consuming 10–50 grams.

with 80 mile per hour winds in a little over two hours. I was listening to a scanner on the internet, there were firefighters in their truck, they were surrounded by flames. They were told to stay in their truck and let the fire roll over them. It worked, they survived.

The fires started in the '90's and have continued every Spring until this year when we had several heavy downpours. Also, starting in the '90's, were major cloudseeding programs during the Winter months. At this same time, the forests further east of the cloudseeding programs stopped receiving their usual amount of snowpack during the winter months. They said it was a "drought". The cloudseeding contractors and weather specialists said there was no correlation, same said by the ski areas and cities spokesman. Yet the City of Denver was spending as much as $1,000,000 per season for cloudseeding, same for Pueblo and

The U.S. Army Corps of Engineers gave the state of Colorado the green light to expand Chatfield Reservoir on the southwest side of Denver to store more water for the growing population along the Front Range and northeastern Colorado.

Fort Collins. The water has to come from somewhere.

This only raises more questions. Then where does the moisture come from? These fires are east of the cloudseeding programs.

Our storms come from the west, southwest and northwest. It's a proverbial bucket dipped in the Pacific and moisture from that bucket is dropped as it moves east across the western states.

Mountain pine beetle.

Enter – the Departments of Weather Modification. They issue contracts to cloudseeding contractors to set up their cloudseeding generators in specific areas. **As the weather clouds pass over these generators, just west of the ski areas, silver iodide is sent up into the clouds and 25 minutes later, the clouds drop snow *from the proverbial bucket*, into the target areas, the ski areas and drainage areas. The area east of and beyond the target area does not receive any snow. The snow melts in the Spring and drains into reservoirs on the west side of the continental divide, owned by the cities. This water is then transported via several tunnels under the continental divide into other reservoirs owned by these same cities, to be used for future growth/development. There is no water left in the bucket for the mountains east of the ski areas, front range or metro area, east of the continental divide.**

Our forests also, go without their usual winter snowfall. A ponderosa tree has been long known to not burn if they have their winter snows and are well hydrated. Our trees no longer have the water needed to fight the pine beetle explosion. The amount of dead trees remain at a minimum because the hydrated trees were able to fight off the beetle larva. **The snow/moisture that would have historically been dropped in the areas**

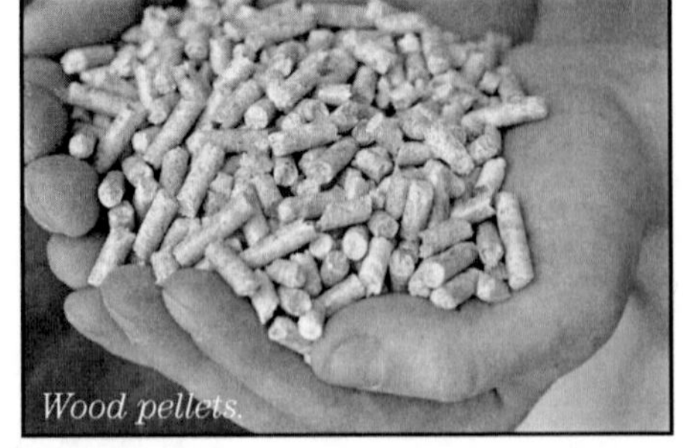

Wood pellets.

A map of the principal hydrological divides of North America. The Continental Divide is highlighted. There are three closed drainage areas along the divide, which appear as loops. From north to south they are the Great Divide Basin, the Guzmán Basin, and the Bolsón de Mapimí.

The Continental Divide of the Americas (also known as the Continental Gulf of Division, the Great Divide, or merely the Continental Divide) is the principal, and largely mountainous, hydrological divide of the Americas. The Continental Divide extends from the Bering Strait to the Strait of Magellan, and separates the watersheds that drain into the Pacific Ocean from (1) those river systems that drain into the Atlantic Ocean (including those that drain into the Gulf of Mexico and the Caribbean Sea), and (2) along the northernmost reaches of the Divide, those river systems that drain into the Arctic Ocean.

Though there are many other hydrological divides in the Americas, the Great Divide is by far the most prominent of these because it tends to follow a line of high peaks along the main ranges of the Rocky Mountains and Andes, at a generally much higher elevation than the other hydrological divisions.

was prematurely dropped into the cloudseeding target area instead.

Now our wildfires begin in March, costing millions of our tax dollars and insurance claims, loss of homes and lives. Prior to the cloudseeding programs, there were snowstorms from Labor Day in September all the way into July of the next year sometimes. Mountain residents kept their snowtires on all year. And snow every seven days was common. When the weather forecasters predicted snow, we received snow, lots of it. You could see a wall of clouds coming over the continental divide and there was little time to get ready for another two feet of snow.

Now when the snow is forecasted, the roads are covered with magnesium-cloride and reports of all the snow up at the ski areas are broadcast across the country, to attract skiers from everywhere, but no snow arrives on the front range, and our snow shovels remain in storage.

The list of the effects of the cloudseeding continues. Black Forest fire in 2013, near the Air Force Academy, Colorado Springs lost 14,280 Acres, 486 homes, 2 people died. The heat from these fires cause the soil to melt into a impermeable crust where seed and moisture cannot penetrate. **It takes 80 years to bring back the burn areas with vegetation.** There is nothing to hold the moisture, thus the rains continue to flood our communities, the silt, ash from previous fires, magnesium chloride and sewage end up in the reservoirs providing the city water. **To top all this, these fires provide a massive amount of heat into our atmosphere, which moves eastward. Would this have any effect on the record setting tornadoes in Texas, Oklahoma, Alabama, and Missouri a few days after these wildfires?**

This not only effects the immediate front range with the wildfires, crops were planted east of the Metro area, our vegetable crops end up diseased because there was no snow cover to kill the diseases left in the soil. The hay crops, once known for their high quality, purchased nationwide are non-existent. The cattle have been sold long ago. There now is a plant in Greeley, Colorado, manufacturing wood

This fire restarted. Some prisoners were doing some burning of slag[1] *and didn't properly put out all the ashes. A high wind came up and 4,000 acres burned in 4 hours.*

This is the fire that I was listening to the fire dept monitor when a call came in from a fire truck that was in a field with fire surrounding the truck. The dispatcher told them to stay in their truck and let the fire roll over them. Seem to work. Never heard any more.

The fire area next to this fire burned a few years earlier and burned 130,000 acres, it later turned into a flash flood area and this water ended up in Cheesman Reservoir – Ash Water for Denver.

These are homes that burned and were rebuilt on the same site.

pellets from the beetle kill trees to feed the cattle.

And I am still learning answers to my many other questions. Not only does Colorado have a winter cloudseeding program, but so do most of the the states west of the continental divide from Wyoming down to Arizona and New Mexico and over along the Pacific Ocean coast, California, Oregon and Washington. And the fires burn millions of acres, thousands of homes are lost and people, their pets and ranch animals, wildlife die every year. Experts and our local weather men still call it a drought.

So we can build more houses, Denver is needing water for a million more people. Not sure what they are going to eat, now that they have taken all the farmers water rights away from them. Maybe some cucumbers from Mexico, who knows.

Is it really necessary to have prime ski conditions from November to June, water parks and other water features in cities built on the prairie? Denver is now drilling down 30,000 feet for water for their new communities, because two of their four aquifers are now dry.

Is it right to take the snows needed for the farmers raising our food or the ranchers raising hay for their cattle, or the

This photo of a wheat field shows the level of devastation from the extreme, multi-year drought. Most wheat fields in this region were abandoned due to drought. Thin wheat stands can leave some fields vulnerable to blowing sand and wind erosion.

vegetable farmers needing the winter snow to kill the disease in their soil. What about the families that wanted to raise their children in the mountains that have lost not just their homes but everything around where their home used to be, just a barren crust of ground. Their insurance went to pay off their balance on their homes. Few have rebuilt in these burn areas. President Hoovers memoirs were lost in the North Fork fire. Does all this justify the cloudseeding programs. **Is it right to ask 19 Arizona "Hot Shot" firefighters to give their lives to fighting these fires? Or is the burning of the historic Sequoias in Yosemite National Park right? Not to mention the billions of taxpayer's dollars to cover the many costs of this quandary. Now Colorado is considering burn-zone homes to increase taxes and insurance in the mountain areas.** Many of these residences were here long before the cloudseeding programs,maybe these fire costs should be the burden of the ski areas and developers promoting growth. They are the ones profiting. **Economic development should not be at the costs of the taxpayers. whether they are living in the mountains, making a living on their ranches and farms or living in the areas hit by the tornadoes.**

Yet the cloudseeding continues. Where are the critical thinkers. What have they to gain to allow the cloud seeding programs to continue. Why aren't they asking these same questions.

Another way of visualizing would be to take a map, locate all your cloudseeding programs - generators, which will be to the west of your wildfires. This information can be found in your Division of Weather Modification

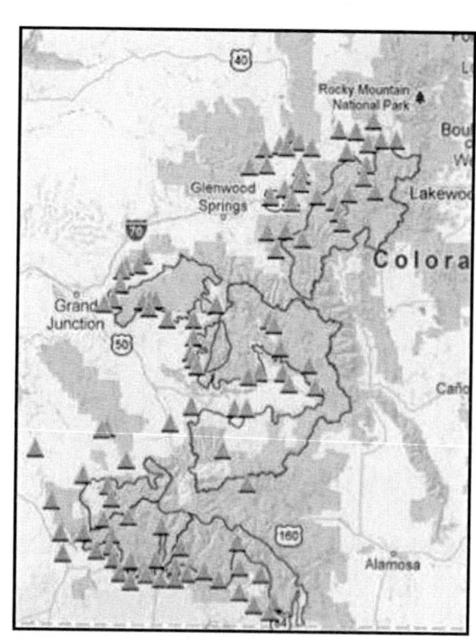

Example: Sites of cloud-seeding generators in Colorado during the 2012-2013 winter.

in your state government or on the internet.

It amazes me that they call their regulatory agency the Division of Weather Modification, yet will tell you that they are not modifying the weather.

Some time ago I read an article from Organic Gardening, saying that each chicken in the chicken house needed one square foot of space, when designing this house. Or they would peck each other to death. Now Denver is building 500 square foot apartments downtown. We not only will be pecking each other, but we won't have any water either.

Ground-based Cloud Seeding Generators

A plume generator blasts ▶ silver iodide into clouds over the Sierra Nevada Mountains in California.

▲ *A typical cloud seeding generator.*

◀ *This automated high output seeding system allows flares to be ignited from remote locations, using customized software and cell phone communications. Each flare burns for approximately 5 minutes, releasing a significant amount of seeding material. Pourous metal cylinders called spark arrestors cover the flares.*

1) Slag – stony waste matter separated from metals during the smelting or refining of ore.

California Statewide Fire Summary

Wednesday, September 23, 2015
www.fire.ca.gov

Nearly 9,000 firefighters are on the frontlines of 9 large fires in California. Containment continues to increase on all the fires as firefighters are making progress.

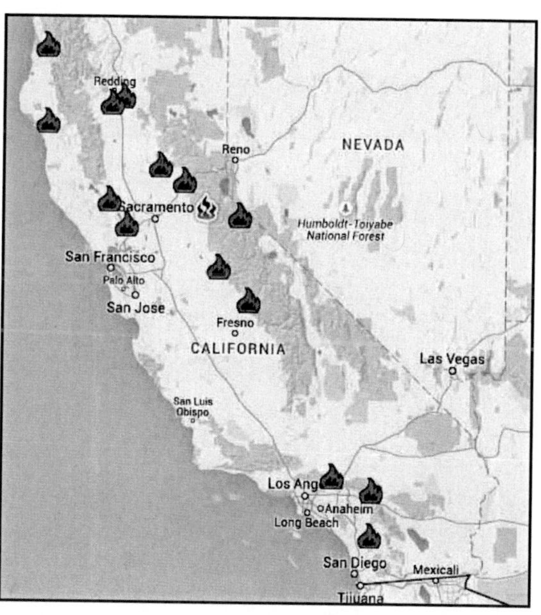

14 large fires burned in California, July 30, 2015.

Weather conditions in California continue to lead to high fire danger. While temperatures in Northern California are expected to cool down slightly for the next couple of days, they are likely to increase towards the end of the week. In Southern California temperatures will continue to be hot and will even reach triple digits by the weekend.

As drought conditions continue to have a strong hold on California, bark beetle attacks are killing millions of trees in California's forests. While bark beetles are mainly native, during drought conditions all trees are susceptible to their attacks. It's estimated that 25 million trees have died due to the drought including those killed by bark beetle. CAL FIRE is asking residents in areas impacted by tree mortality to ensure they have removed dead trees from around their homes. Learn more at www.PrepareforBarkBeetle.org.

◀ *Flames from the Rocky Fire approach a house on July 31 in Lower Lake, California.* JUSTIN SULLIVAN / GETTY IMAGES

A firefighter ▶ *scrambles down an embankment while battling the Butte fire near San Andreas, California*

Nearly 2,000 firefighters and support personnel were battling a 25-square-mile wildfire in California's San Bernardino National Forest on Sunday, officials said, and high temperatures and westerly winds were expected to push smoke from the blaze east toward residents. | NBCNEWS.COM JUN 22 2015

About Diane...

I was the one that fell out of the tree house and/or went to the fairgrounds up the street to help with the harness racing horses in grade school. I finally got my own horse in the 6th grade and then went to showing Appaloosas (that is a horse) in high school and received a National Championship before moving to Colorado. I continued showing horses and in later years, showed our horses with my two sons.

I also became a certified ski instructor and taught skiing in the Colorado mountains for 20 years. At the same time, I sold real estate in the Colorado mountains for almost 30 years.

I currently have my own business, assisting Internet Technology businesses, doing the business end of their business so they can spend their time programming new technology.

My grandfather had a cabin on the north shore of Lake Superior and spent a lot of time in the woods picking wild blueberries. I became well aware of forest fires and the destruction during my young years. In the 1990's our Colorado fires began, and I, with my curious mind, began to wonder why now, when there had been minimal fires, an acre or two, before that time. This story was the result of what I have learned through years of critical observation.

Grade three Lincoln Elementary School: Miss Lucille Cain was our teacher. Publisher, Jon Larsen Shudlick, was seated up front surrounded by girls possibly for disciplinary reasons. The author of Weather Modification and fellow co-conspirator, Diane MacMillan, is on Jon's left.

Redskins vs. Cultural Communism

Where does the word Redskin come from? Is Redskin a derogatory term?

The name Redskin developed from the Indian Nations themselves who did not want to be identified or associated with the designation White man or Negro (understandably). Smithsonian Linguist Emeritus, Ives Goddard, is the person who researched the origin of the word Redskins and its authenticity. The Indian Nations had many hundreds of individual tribes all with their own customs and uniqueness.

Now, to answer the next question, is Redskin a derogatory term? The term Redskin is not a derogatory term as proven in the following history of local events in Rice Lake, Wisconsin. On December 8, 2002, I was at the Rice Lake Sports Hall of Fame second annual induction ceremony at Lehman's Supper Club in Rice Lake, where Warren Leary, Charles Currier, Dave Crotteau, Harold Shudlick (my brother) and William Henry (Lone Star) Dietz whose great-grand-niece, Diane Dietz, along with the other inductees or their representatives accepted a plaque and a certificate of achievement for life-long recognition of sports success. After the ceremony I met Dr. Tom Benjey, a gifted author and national expert on Indian history and folklore who wrote the book, Keep A-goin' The Life of Lone Star Dietz (ForeWord Magazine's 2006 Book of

the Year Award Finalist). More information on "Lone Star" Dietz and our nation's Indian heritage is available by going to www.tombenjey.com. Email: tom@tuxedo-press.com.

Eighty years ago in 1933, George Preston Marshall, who had purchased the *Boston Braves* football team in 1932, changed the name of the team to the *Boston Redskins* in honor of its first coach William Henry (Lone Star) Dietz who coached the *Boston Redskins* during the 1933 and the 1934 seasons. "Lone Star" Dietz was born in Rice Lake, Wisconsin on August 17, 1884. In 1937 the *Boston Redskins* football team of the National Football Conference moved to Washington, D.C. and became what is known today as the *Washington Redskins* football team. In the year, 2013, the *Detroit Lions* defeated the *Washington Redskins* football team at the new FEDEX stadium in Washington, D.C. The major media including sports network ESPN noted it was the first time in 80 years that the *Detroit Lions* had defeated the *Redskins* on their home turf. That was when the *Washington Redskins* were actually named the *Boston Redskin*s and played football at the Fenway Park baseball field in Boston, Massachusetts. According to *Forbes* magazine the *Redskins* are the third most valuable franchise in the NFL, behind the *Dallas Cowboys* and the *New England Patriots* and were valued at approximately $1.6 billion as of 2013. They have also broken the NFL's mark for single-season attendance nine years in a row.

W.S.C. Coach, "Lonestar" Dietz, Dazzle's Portland's Dressy Avenue

"Lone Star" Dietz was formerly the coach of the *Washington State Cougars* from 1915-1917. It was during his tenure as coach that they played the *Brown University Bruins* in the second Rose Bowl game held in Pasadena, California on New Year's Day in 1916 after a hiatus of fifteen years. The *Washington State Cougars*

Coach William 'Lone Star' Dietz, with cane, and his Cougar football team that defeated Brown 14-0 in the 1916 Rose Bowl game.

2-1 underdogs won the game 14-0. This was the first time a team from the west coast had been victorious over the eastern football establishment in a game of major significance. "That was the game (1916) which was to change the face of New Year's Day in the years to come. That game provided the stimulus which turned the holiday from the day after the night before (of celebrating) into a day of football in many parts of the United States — yeah, even the world — as bowl games sprung up without number." – Rube Samuelsen, Rose Bowl historian.

As mentioned Rice Lake, Wisconsin native "Lone Star" Dietz, the *Washington State Cougars'* coach in 1916, was the same "Lone Star" Dietz who was honored to have the word "Redskins" attributed to him as the first coach of the *Boston Redskins* in both 1933 and 1934. Not only this honor but the famous fight song, "Hail to the Redskins" and even a 110 piece marching band with Indian uniforms and headdresses promoted a college like atmosphere in professional football when the Boston Redskins were moved to Washington, D.C. in 1937.

The impact of that college football game, the Rose Bowl in 1916, was comparable to quarterback Joe Namath's *New York Jets* 16-7 victory over the *Baltimore Colts* in Super Bowl III in 1969. That game led to the present alignment of the American Football Conference and the National Football Conference in today's National Football League. In both instances there was a paradigm shift in the way the sport of football was accepted.

! ! ! BREAKING NEWS ! ! !

In a bold move the Redskins have dropped "Washington" from their official team name citing embarrassment as the chief motivator in this landmark decision.

The *Redskins* were the first team in the NFL with an official marching band and the second team in the National Football League to have a fight song, "Hail to the Redskins" written by renowned band leader Barnee Breeskin with lyrics by Corinne Griffith, wife of owner George Preston Marshall. The first team to have a fight song was the *Green Bay Packers* with, "Go! You Packers! Go!" composed in 1931. The *Packers* were my childhood favorites as they are today. Below are the lyrics to the famous *Redskins* fight song:

DAVID LEEDS / ALLSPORT

Hail to the Redskins!
Hail Victory!
Braves on the Warpath!
Fight for old D.C.!
Run or pass and score –
we want a lot more!
Beat 'em, Swamp 'em,
Touchdown! –
Let the points soar!
Fight on, fight on
'Til you have won
Sons of Wash-ing-ton.
Rah! Rah!, Rah!

Death Valley Summer

A park ranger recalls the hitch he served in hell

By Don Carney

The sign said "Hell's Gate." As I stood at this Death Valley overlook, I was stunned and awed by the vast expanse of rock and sand below me. It looked like a gigantic unfinished construction project with spots here and there embellished by the devil. I wondered why I had ever agreed to come here and… should I turn back? Fortunately for me, it was the relatively mild month of January that my employer, the National Park Service, had asked me to move from Mammoth Cave National Park to Death Valley National Monument.

It was just after New Year's Day that Superintendent John Aubuchon of Mammoth Cave had called me into his office to say, "Carney, you rascal! Some people have all the luck. You are headed out west to the real God's Country." For the next few minutes, I listened as he enthusiastically described the subtle beauty of places like Dante's View and Badwater.

Then he handed me a sheet of weather statistics "Don't be scared by the numbers," he said. "You'll get used to it."

Old west entrance marker to Death Valley National Monument, dating back to the CCC era. ▶

◀ *Badwater Basin in Death Valley National Park is the lowest point in North America, with an elevation of 282 ft below sea level.*

Dante's View to North ▶

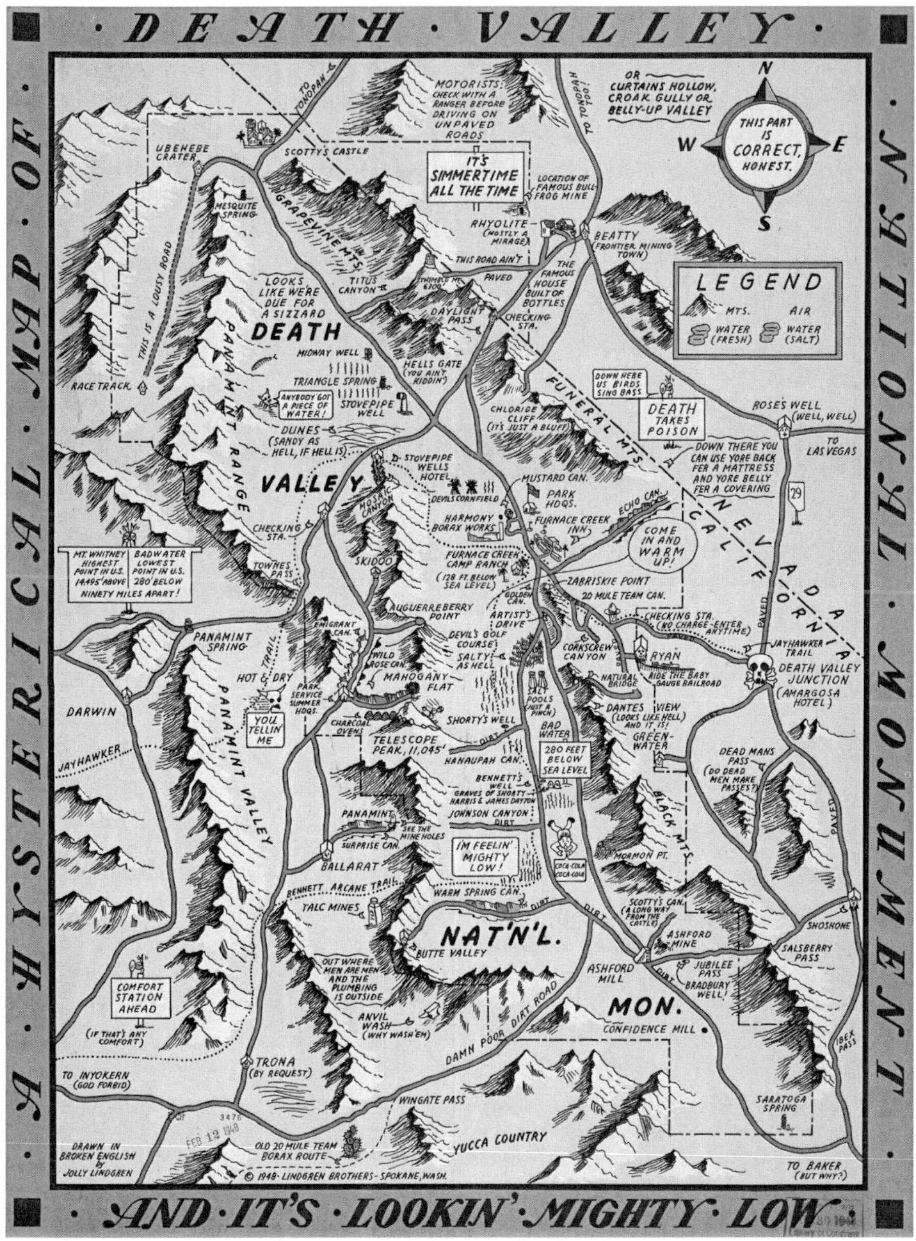

A hysterical map of Death Valley National Monument : and it's lookin' mighty low / drawn in broken English by Jolly Lindgren.

Spokane, Wash. : Lindgren Brothers, 1948.

LIBRARY OF CONGRESS GEOGRAPHY AND MAP DIVISION WASHINGTON, D.C. 20540-4650 USA DCU

One line in the mass of temperature data stood out from the rest. It said: July average high 116 degrees, average low 88 degrees, and extreme high 134 degrees. How could that be possible and could I stand it? How hot was hot? I would soon find that places like the Devil's Corn Field, the Funeral Mountains, Coffin Peak and Desolation Canyon deserved their names.

Desolation Cayon

Within a few weeks, I was on patrol as a district ranger. My 450,000-acre Grapevine District covered the northern one-quarter of the monument, straddled the California-Nevada state line and varied in elevation from below sea level to almost 9,000 feet. Hints about how hot and dry it would be came from one of the first people I met, Basil Wickett.

Wickett, on-site manager at Scotty's Castle, was my nearest neighbor, three miles to the east. He casually remarked that matches were not needed in the valley during summer, "Just puff on a cigarette and it'll light," he said.

On Coffin Peak; Death Valley National Park, CA. The Death Valley Salt Pan is visible in the distance. It is almost 5500' lower than this vantage point.

Devil's Cornfield in Death Valley National Park is an array of unusual bushes.

Death Valley Dunes & Funeral Mountains | GARY E. RICHARDSON PHOTO ©1972

SCOTTY'S CASTLE

Construction began on Scotty's Castle in 1922, and cost between $1.5 and $2.5 million. Prospector, performer, and con man Walter Scott, born in Cynthiana, Kentucky, also known as "Death Valley Scotty," convinced Chicago millionaire Albert Mussey Johnson to invest in his gold mine in the Death Valley area. Though initially angered when the mine turned out to be fraudulent, Johnson was fascinated with the colorful Scott and the two men struck up an unlikely friendship. By 1937, Johnson had acquired more than 1,500 acres (610 ha) in Grapevine Canyon, where the ranch is located.

Johnson and his wife Bessie made several trips to the region it was Mrs. Johnson's idea to build something comfortable for their vacations in the area, and the villa eventually became a winter home.

Unknown to the Johnsons, the initial survey was incorrect, and the land they built Death Valley Ranch on was actually government land; their land was farther up Grapevine Canyon. Construction halted as they resolved this mistake, but before it could resume, the stock market crashed in 1929, making it difficult for Johnson to finish construction. Having lost a considerable amount of money, the Johnsons used the Death Valley Ranch to produce income by letting rooms out, upon the suggestion of Scott. The Johnsons died without heirs and had hoped that the National Park Service would purchase the property, and in 1970, the National Park Service purchased the villa for $850,000 from the Gospel Foundation (the socially-oriented charity Johnson founded in 1946), to which the Johnsons had left the property.

Walter Scott, who was taken care of by the Gospel Foundation after Johnson's passing, died in 1954 and was buried on the hill overlooking Scotty's Castle next to his beloved dog Windy. | WIKIPEDIA

In late May, the heat struck. I was patrolling higher, cooler terrain for most of that day but as I drove down into the valley in late afternoon, it was 115 degrees. Our park patrol cars were not air conditioned and with the window rolled down, I could feel the blast furnace air drying up my face like a prune. I put my hand out the window and it felt like someone was holding a match to my fingernails. It actually felt better with the window rolled up. I mentioned this to an old miner and he said, "When your fingernails bust completely out, you'll know it's 150."

Creosote bush.

The real fierce heat came in late June when the temperature held above 90 degrees all night and went over 120 degrees several days in a row. At about that time, a car with Georgia license plates stopped at the ranger station and the driver got out to ask for directions. From the station it was possible to see about 30 miles to the north and nearly 60 miles to the south with nothing in view but rocks and scattered creosote bushes. He looked both ways and turned to me with an incredulous look. "Holy Toledo! You here all summer? There's nothing here!" When I said I was, he thought for a moment and said, "Oh, well. If you eventually go to hell, at least you'll know how to be comfortable there."

Cigarette plant.

I seemed to be drinking water steadily but could never get enough. Some small plants had lost their leaves and had gone dormant for the summer. Many animals were estivating, which is really a summer hibernation. The cigarette plant had a special hollow bladder in order to store carbon dioxide so it would not have to open itself up on

Furnace Creek Visitor Center

hot days. And everywhere was a vast deep silence, a silence so all pervading, it rang in my ears. Nothing moved in the shimmering heat; no birds sang, no insect buzzed, the air had no smell. All signs of life had disappeared. Even the little pesky gnats were gone.

All visitors in summer entered the valley by motor vehicle, mostly cars. Each day a few would stop at our Furnace Creek Visitor Center and at Stovepipe Wells Village near the middle of the valley. Others would struggle northward through my district to Scotty's Castle. Their engines were almost always boiling and we maintained large water barrels for their radiators along the main roads. Some folks had to be rescued from the elements, usually due to cars with boiling engines, broken fan belts or flat tires. Gloves were needed for repair work, especially changing a tire. We often saw cars driven by desperate visitors – cars with no spare tires being run on the rims after a tire had gone flat and had worn away. On some, the rim was worn down to the brake pads. Other visitors ran out of water when their car engines boiled over.

Stovepipe Wells Village

Some kept right on driving until the water pump conked out and the engine block cracked, leaving the car useless.

The Indians called Death Valley "Tomesha" which means "ground afire." With ground temperatures often over 160 degrees, my tires always seemed to wear out in 6,000 miles. On July 15, 1972, the hottest ground temperature ever recorded anywhere in the world scorched Furnace Creek – an incredible 201 degrees. The air thermometer in the shade of the weather shelter read 128 degrees.

People were always needing treatment for heat exhaustion and sunburn. Some came without hats, some had no shirts and a few were barefoot. When their cars broke down, some were taught a painful and expensive lesson. These were the people we watched for while on our daily road patrols.

Some were in serious trouble. The California Highway Patrol had a crackerjack patrolman in Jim Pursell, who lived with our Furnace Creek staff. One day in early July, he was called to a one-car rollover near the top of Mud Canyon and just above the valley floor. Jim later related, "There were three people in the car and all survived the accident unhurt. But, by the time I got there, their feet were all blistered and burned from running up and down the hot asphalt road looking for help. All were barefoot – they had brought no shoes. They had to spend weeks in the hospital recovering from second-degree burns."

Mud Canyon.

We always carried five to 10 gallons of water on these daily patrols, and we covered the main roads and sometimes the side roads. As a result, very few monument visitors died. But some came close, like the unfortunate who was found naked and delirious in the last stage of dehydration. Taken to the hospital, he gained 24 pounds in 48 hours after being treated and given fluids.

The dean of all Death Valley field rangers was Matt Ryan, who spent 18 years there including some summers on the valley floor without electric power or any type of cooling device. Matt and his wife Rosemary treated scores of dehydrated visitors.

"Many of them had lost their ability to reason as the dehydration progressed," Matt said. "The odd thing was that they would become obsessed with saving the water they had rather than drinking it. I remember the time I found the bodies of two kids who died with a gallon of lemonade in their arms near Warm Springs. Another time, I found a man who had saved several cases of soda pop in his car while he wilted away and died in the heat near Daylight Pass."

Warm Springs

At the other extreme were many visitors who went through the valley untouched by the heat. This kind of visit was typified by an experience Furnace Creek District Ranger Al Schneider had on a fiercely hot day:

Daylight Pass

"I was picking up beer cans along the road in the Furnace Creek area on an early afternoon in July. A big air-conditioned, cream-colored Cadillac driven by a heavyset man pulled to a stop and the driver rolled the window down about six inches. As I walked up to him, he said, 'What is the temperature right now?' I told him it was about 127 degrees in the shade. He said the heat was not bothering him at all and that he could not understand all the fuss and publicity about the heat in Death Valley. I said 'Why not stop for awhile and see some sights and perhaps stretch your legs a bit?' It was windy that day and an old beer can was burning my hand. My face felt like it would peel away – I wanted to ask him if I could stick it through the window to cool off. Of course, I didn't!"

Hardest of all to get used to were the very hot and oppressive nights. Low and rocky deserts do not cool off during summer nights and usually the rocks were warm to the touch at 6 a.m. There were always some nights each summer with lows in the 100- to 104-degree range. Overnight lows of 110 have been recorded three times.

Dwight Warren, a park naturalist, told me how a skeleton park staff used to stay in the valley all summer without any cooling device except water. "Wetting down sheets or sprinkling water over yourself was fairly common when trying to get to sleep in those days and this would often bring on a peculiar type of summer pneumonia."

Some people slept outside in hammocks on a hillside with water barrels just above the sleeping area, according to another early resident. A tube from the barrels, with a cork stopper, was available to each hammock. The occupant would wet himself down, go to sleep, and wake two or three times each night to uncork the tube and drink without getting up.

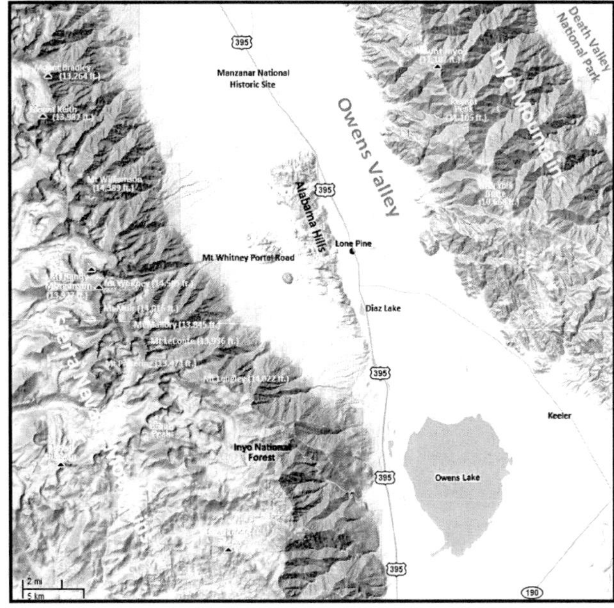

To escape the heat, I would drive 140 miles each weekend to the nearby Owens Valley at the base of the Sierra Nevada Mountains. There, the cool evening breezes were like a welcome balm to my spirit. Since

I would usually play a round of morning golf, I kept my golf clubs and bag in the car. One day in late July, I was amazed to find that all the balls had burst – the cork centers had popped right out through the covers. Then I remembered that I had left my car parked in the open sun at Furnace Creek the previous day. In the week following, I parked in the same place with the windows rolled up on a 120-degree day. Four hours later, I returned and stared in disbelief – the thermometer read 236 degrees!

On some days, the humidity was under 5 percent and my furniture started to warp.

In his book, Death Valley and Its Country, George Palmer Putnam put it all into words when he described Death Valley as "a reasonable facsimile of a first class "inferno in a state of suspended animation."

Putnam goes on to tell about a native son who sold shriveled and dried-up oranges to monument visitors. He explained to one lady that the oranges came from the hottest part of the valley. "It's so hot the water sometimes boils when we irrigate the grove," he assured her. "This fruit dehydrates right there on the trees. Instead of having all that waste pulp, the sweetness is concentrated. Cooked right in, you see? They don't weigh more than half of what a regular fat orange would (which was true), that's because all the water is dried out of 'em. Soak 'em and they swell up wonderfully. Natural dehydration, that's what it is."

DEATH VALLEY AND ITS COUNTRY

GEORGE PALMER PUTNAM

National Park Service training courses always stress the importance of getting along with people, especially the park visitor. By the end of that first summer, I had found, somewhat to my surprise, that getting along without people was also a challenge. At one point, a thunderstorm washed out all the roads and I only saw a handful of park visitors for six weeks. My nearest neighbor to the west was 125 miles distant by road and it was 50 miles north or south to the nearest permanent residence. The nearest telephone was 30 miles east. At night, I could see over 100 square miles from my front door, unbroken by a single light.

Grapevine Ranger Station

My residence at Grapevine Ranger Station was not in the hottest part of the valley so it was sort of like being one step up from purgatory. My daily patrols and everyday work kept me in close touch with the staff at Furnace Creek, where it was usually about 10 degrees hotter.

All of the park houses had "swamp coolers," or evaporation coolers rather than air conditioning. Temperatures inside were usually around 90 degrees on hot days and most of us were able to adjust to it to a certain extent, just as the body adjusts to cold air.

Still, several months of high heat were tough to take. Every aspect of one's personality was tested by heat and isolation. If there was anything wrong with you, the valley would find it and magnify it, sometimes all out of proportion. The thought of the next trip to the mountains or an eventual transfer to Yellowstone kept us going. On the other hand, people with certain respiratory or circulatory ailments usually felt better in the valley as did those with arthritis.

I was always partially dehydrated from April to October, and lost water by sweating faster than I could drink it. Even though I drank a gallon or so of water a day, it seemed like my kidneys never had to function. Often my whole being longed for rain. After a month or two without rain, I could smell it two or three hours before its arrival. Lucky for me. I was not there in 1929, for in that year there was no measurable precipitation.

The wildlife also had a tough time adapting, especially birds that were migrating through on hot spring days. Large birds such as egrets and herons were often seen close up at springs and crouched under water coolers. They seemed completely exhausted and so desperate for water that they seemed to throw all caution to the wind.

A turkey vulture once landed in the reflection pool within the visitor center patio. It was so thirsty that it drank more or less continuously for an hour even as people passed within a few feet.

Loons would mistake the salt flats for water and then could not take off after landing. This was always a fatal mistake.

John T. Medler, former professor of entomology at the University of Wisconsin.

Even the insects were dehydrated. John Medler, a former professor of entomology at the University of Wisconsin once told me, "Nobody has ever seen a bumblebee drink water in the wild state." Well, that may have been true when he said it, but I later saw a bumblebee queen eagerly lapping water at a mountain spring on the west side of the monument.

Las Vegas, Nevada

Only a few people lived in this bleak and hostile summer environment simply because they like it. Premier among them was Walter Scott, later known as Death Valley Scotty. He first saw the valley in 1884 and stayed there most of the next 60 years. I personally knew a few like Seldom Seen Slim, an old prospector who lived in a trailer without air conditioning. Still another was one of our park naturalists, Pete Sanchez. Pete suffered from what he called "urban phobia" and was not even able to stay overnight in Las Vegas, our main port-of-call. Others like Matt Ryan simply accepted the desert on its own terms. Matt drove a black Chevrolet sedan patrol car and was fond of entertaining visitors by frying eggs on the hood just above the radiator cap.

I was destined to spend a memorable five years at my station in the Grapevine District. When it was over, I had logged some 60,000 vehicle miles and 2,500 miles on foot over the mountain ridges and canyons of this huge valley. Those travels brought me in contact with a wide array of oddities: winds strong enough to roll brick-sized rocks, homosexual burros, tiny inch-long fish left over from the Ice Age and the kangaroo rat that never drank water. There were strange places, too, like a ghost town where an outlaw was once hanged, buried, dug up and then hanged again to oblige a newspaper reporter.

There were modern day outlaws here, too. Our entire ranger staff had a part in the investigation and arrest of the "Manson Family." And how could I forget the man with a serious proposal to turn all of Death Valley into a sewage lagoon "in order to solve and correct for all time the pollution problems of the Los Angeles Basin."

Los Angeles Basin

Now, from much greener pastures, I remember Death Valley as a land of sunshine and shadows and of vast distances and great silences. Ever since my last day there, it has never been completely out of my mind. I am thankful I did not turn back at Hell's Gate. For where else on earth could one enjoy all the benefits of hell without paying the price?

Spring, 1967: Don Carney in Death Valley, Tin Mt. 9,000 ft. in rear.

A Little Fellow Named "Charlie"

By **Don Carney**

Every national park has its own distinct personality with associated grandeur, seasonal moods and potential for real-life excitement and adventure. Perhaps none is so foreboding as Death Valley in summer when daily highs can go above 120 degrees for months on end. It is one of our nation's largest parks, with nearly 3.5 million acres spread out over a length of 150 miles. For the five permanent park rangers who were assigned there in the summer of 1969, the heat and isolation was an everyday test for all their physical and mental capabilities, including those of this writer, who had grown up in Rice Lake and felt like a duck out of water. We had to be mentally prepared to meet every situation and park visitors from the ordinary to the very bizarre, sometimes beyond all imagination. Like that of the old western sheriff, it was a chancy job

1969, Death Valley, Ladybird Johnson in front of a watchful park ranger Don Carney.

that made a man watchful and…a little lonely.

Just how bizarre could things get? We were soon to find out as we became aware of a bright-eyed little hippie who would now and then drive through and who talked about the end of the world and one of his idols, Adolph Hitler. Little did we know that he had a "family" or a following of 20-30 flower children (societal dropouts) who lived in an old miner's shack in terrible squalor near the park's southwestern border. The family was a loose collection of mostly young women and would change every few weeks as some left while other new ones were added.

During the late summer, we learned from media headlines that some horrendous murders had taken place only a little more than 100 miles to the south, in the Los Angeles complex. One of our more perceptive park rangers guessed that the little fellow with very long hair we knew only as "Charlie" may have been involved in these gruesome crimes, which became known as the Tate-LaBianca murders.

On September 19, 1969 everything seemed to come to a boiling head when we received an early morning call from our maintenance crew in the distant back country of the park, about 40 miles away. They reported that someone had set fire to our Michigan front-end loader during the night near what we called "The Racetrack." We jumped into our park pickup truck and reached the scene in about 45 minutes. We then followed the suspect's trail on dirt roads through Lost Burro Gap, Hidden Valley, Goldbelt and over Hunter Mountain. We were about 25 miles east of Lone Pine, California, when we came to a blacktop road and lost the trail. Later that day, we returned to the scene of the loader fire to look for evidence and found a used wide-stemmed book match that said "Northwoods." There was little doubt that this match had started the fire.

On October 12, accompanied by the California Highway Patrol, we raided the filthy little desert shack where we thought our main suspect may be hiding. After a brief search, we found him in a little storage cabinet under the bathroom sink. As we searched his all-buckskin outfit, we found a Northwoods matchbook in his pocket. He identified himself as Charles Manson and continually insisted he was actually Jesus Christ. He and other members of the family were immediately arrested and charged with arson, grand theft auto, receiving stolen property and possession of illegal firearms.

Charles Manson (center) and other members of the Manson Family were arrested on the Spahn Ranch in Chatsworth, California on August 16, 1969 for car theft. On October 12, 1969 he and several cult members were arrest at a prospectors ranch in Death Valley on suspicion of vandalism. The confessions of Susan Atkins, while held in detention on suspicion of murdering Gary Hinman during an unrelated incident, led detectives to realize that Manson and his followers were involved in the Tate/ LaBianca killings.

We took them to the Inyo County Courthouse at Independence, California, where a preliminary hearing was held soon after. Before a trial could be held, authorities from Los Angeles entered the case and family members were accused of murdering movie star Sharon Tate and four others as well as Leno and Rosemary LaBianca. We then began to realize that we were a part of a real-life drama that was stranger than fiction. It was so bizarre that when the Inyo County sheriff first heard an audio tape of what had happened, he threw it against the wall of his office in disbelief. No investigator was ever certain of how many homicides the family had committed, but stories of pure horror and terror emerged at every turn. None of us ever dreamed that this story would still be alive and in the news over 40 years later. For more details, read "Desert Shadows" by Death Valley National Park superintendent Bob Murphy.

From our present distance in time and space, maybe being in Death Valley for 5 years was not such a bad deal after all. Where else could you enjoy all the benefits of hell without paying the price?

Don Carney's earliest memories are of the mid-1930's when he lived at 1 S. Main Street above the Chronotype offices. He left Rice Lake in 1952 and spent most of his working years employed in national parks as a ranger, naturalist and historian. He retired in 1990.

E. Main Street, Rice Lake, Wisconsin

Scrip Kept City Going in Financial Crisis

By **Don Carney**

"If youth but knew and age were able, poverty would be a fable." So goes an old saying that comes to the fore in every financial crisis. Somehow our society has not been able to learn from and take advantage of the mistakes of previous generations.

It seems hard to believe that only one lifetime ago, in the early days of 1933, anyone with a $20 bill could walk into the First National Bank on Main Street and exchange it for a beautiful double eagle $20 gold coin. Both monetary units had equal value. That is, both would buy about 120 gallons of gasoline. It is even harder to believe that the meltdown value of the same gold coin will now buy nearly 500 gallons of gasoline while the same paper $20 dollar bill will buy less than 6 gallons. This is one measure of how weak and diluted our paper currency has become.

From the time our nation was formed in 1789 and up until 1971, we were on some form of gold standard. For most of that time, gold served as a form of collateral for a sound dollar with associated low taxes and steady prices. The standard was suspended during war emergencies and was weakened at intervals after creation of the Federal Reserve in 1914. During each suspension a great deal of new paper money was created, which laid the basis for future economic downturns. This included an authorization for a huge monetary increase in 1922 that put the groundwork in place for the Great Depression, first named by President Hoover in 1930.

6858

HOMESTAKE MINING COMPANY

INCORPORATED UNDER THE LAWS OF THE STATE OF CALIFORNIA NOV. 5th 1877.

This is to Certify that -- M. V. HAGGIN-- is the owner of ONE HUNDRED Shares of the Capital Stock par value Twelve and 50/100 Dollars each of the Homestake Mining Company transferable in person or by Attorney on the surrender of this Certificate duly endorsed. This Certificate is not valid until countersigned by the Transfer Agent and the Registrar.

In Witness Whereof the duly authorized officers of said Company have hereunto subscribed their names this day of JUL 26 1937

R. A. Clark SECRETARY. Edward H. Clark PRESIDENT.

As banks failed nationwide in the early 1930's, people turned to gold as a safe haven. This became a near panic in early 1933 when $20 million worth of our paper money was exchanged for gold coins. The most fortunate investors of that time were holding gold stocks, such as Homestake Mining, an established gold producer, which soared about 1,000% from 1930-1938 while paying huge dividends. There was so much excitement over gold stocks that one

little company called Gold Dust saw a large rise in its stock until investors learned that it only produced soap powder.

When President Roosevelt took office in March 1933, he immediately suspended all dollar redeem-ability for gold, and it soon became apparent that he had a definite plan in mind. He first declared a bank holiday, which lasted about 2 weeks. No checks could be written, and currency could not be withdrawn from any bank. **A Monopoly like scrip was allowed as a substitute, and Rice Lake was the very first city in Wisconsin to use it. The rules were that bank customers could withdraw, in scrip, up to 10% of what they had on deposit. The scrip had to be signed by Mayor J. H. Wallis and co-signed by trustees Herb Forbes and Guy Hill.** The bank closures were not as serious then as they would be now, since people did not trust banks and hoarded their money at home in jars, under rugs and in mattresses. **Some people had one or two gold coins, and pure silver coins were common in every day transactions.**

32nd President of the United States, Franklin D. Roosevelt Presidential Campaign, 1933.

Mr. Roosevelt also called for all gold held in private hands to be turned in at banks for dollars. Only coins with numismatic value were exempted from the requirement. **It was said to be unpatriotic for people to hold gold, but in spite of threats of large fines and long jail terms people everywhere pretty much ignored the May 1, 1933 deadline.** They actually tendered less than one-quarter of their gold and no prosecutions followed, at least to our knowledge. **The dollar was then devalued against gold so that it took $35 to buy an ounce**

instead of the previous $20.67. To put it another way, the price of gold rose to $35 an ounce and the enhanced gold value held by the U.S. Treasury was used by the Fed as backing to create more dollars. President Roosevelt used this new "wealth" to fund what became known as the New Deal.

By the middle and late 1930's, everyone was talking about the work programs of the Civilian Conservation Corps and the Works Progress Administration. At first, people were put to work by the city in wood cutting for fuel at 50 cents a cord. Other later projects had to do with rip-rapping the island and lakeshore, curb and gutter, refining the center boulevards, park and school work and so on. Through all-time record heat and cold, periodic dust storms swept over Rice Lake as our parents and

CCC Camp BR-73 Boise Project: Photo of CCC crew riprapping Boise Project main canal.

This park in Rice Lake, Wisconsin was named after the mother of the publisher of this book, Jon Larsen Shudlick.

grandparents struggled valiantly against all possible odds and adversaries.

Can we do as well as they did? This is a very serious question since we are immersed in far more debt than they ever were as well as very weak currencies worldwide, with two market crashes in a recent 10-year period. Is the Keynesian monetary system we are using a failure? Will gold and silver again play a role in a revitalized dollar? Will a great deal of effort and discipline bring us to new heights? We must all struggle with these and many other questions as we try to emerge from the economic turmoil we are in. Somehow we must finally disprove another old saying: The only thing we learn from history is that we learn nothing from it.

Artist Jason Seiler of Chicago is seen with his illustration of Pope Francis that appeared on the cover of Time magazine's Person of the Year issue. Trained to paint on canvas with oils and acrylics, Seiler used a 21-inch LCD display and digitally painted the pope's portrait. It took him more than 70 hours to complete.

Ex-Rice Laker Creates Time Feature Cover

By **Jon Larsen Shudlick**

I have found from past experience that the more important and busy a person is from whom you are requesting time and ideas, the more quickly you receive a response. Certainly this is the case with Jason Seiler, one of the world's most prominent caricaturists and recently appointed to do a series of paintings for the United States Postal Service (USPS). I was thrilled with Jason's prompt email response to the questions I asked him regarding his early years growing up in Rice Lake (Barron County) in northern Wisconsin.

When someone who has lived in your hometown becomes internationally successful it is a positive reflection on the whole community. This is the Jason Seiler story from his youth growing up in a small Mid-western town.

The Interview

Who first recognized your exceptional talent?

To be honest I am not sure how to answer that question? I have been drawing seriously my whole life. My dad was an art teacher in Rice Lake for many years. So, I grew up with an artist as a father and spent most of all my time drawing. Not sure if anyone recognized or discovered me? My parents always believed in me and what I wanted to do. I had a sense of what I wanted and then I worked really hard to get there.

Jason Seiler, self portrait, 2011.

What was the best part of your young life living in Campia and Rice Lake?

Campia was hands down my favorite home that I have ever lived in. We had a huge yard, lots of woods, and lived on the Red Cedar River. So in the summer time I spent most of my time catching frogs or crayfish, fishing etc. I have a younger brother who is 3½ years younger than me and we met two brothers that lived close

◀ *Cedar Side Walking Trail, Rice Lake, WI.*

by and became fast friends. Joey and Dan Weimert. We played all the time. One of my favorite memories was shooting bow and arrow. We had a hay bail that I would literally spend hours practicing. We first moved to Rice Lake when I was just about to start the 1st grade. I went to school at Jefferson for 3 years. I don't remember all that much, but I do remember our little red house that we rented. After 3 years, we moved out to Campia and I had to go to Brill public school for 4th and 5th grade. I wasn't too happy about that because I had to leave all my friends and go to a much, much smaller school. I didn't do well with a lot of the kids because I was into art and music and dressed accordingly. I don't think they understood me all that well. I got to go back to Rice Lake for 6th-9th grade. Because I had lost two years, everyone had made new friends and I had a hard time reconnecting. To be honest I was fine with that because all I wanted to do was draw anyway. I do remember a few friends to this day, Adam Vesper, Dave Durrand and my friend Joe Weimert. In between

9th and 10th grade, my dad took a job in Eau Claire and sadly I have never been back to Rice Lake since. But don't feel bad, I graduated High School in Eau Claire in 1996 and I haven't been back there since either.

Eau Claire, WI: Downtown Skyline from Water Street Bridge

Was living in an area with four distinct seasons helpful with your concept of colors, etc.?

Hahahah, no, but that is funny. I do miss Wisconsin quite a bit. My family lives in Laona Wisconsin now so I get to visit from time to time. Chicago in some ways is similar. I live a block from Lake Michigan, so it gets cold here for sure, but fall which is my favorite season is way to brief. I do think though that growing up in Northern Wisconsin helped in some ways because I was really interested in nature and would try to draw everything and anything that I could.

Belted Kingfisher perched by Eau Clair River bank.

What types of recreational outlets did you enjoy while there? (Hunting, fishing, etc.) How about now? (Do you jog, exercise, play chess, etc.)?

I spent most every weekend in the summer fishing and sometimes during the week if I was lucky. I love fishing! I remember catching 70 to 80 bluegill and crappie all in one day … and then my

Crappie

brother and I spending what seemed like hours cleaning them. It was fun though. I also did a lot of hunting but preferred fishing and still do to this day. As mentioned before I shot a lot of bow and arrow, but also road bike, played basketball, baseball, and football. We also used to play army in the woods which was always fun. These days for fun I draw and paint when I am not working on a deadline. I also like to play guitar and sing. I ride bike when I can and enjoy taking my dog Capone for walks. I have two daughters, Isabeau and Ava, and my wife Jacqueline who I love to spend time with … over all I am just a regular guy.

How many hours are you presently able to creatively utilize your talent daily or weekly? Do you need space after you complete a major project? How do you mellow?

I pretty much work all the time. Job to job. I try not to work nights or weekends. I mellow by drinking wine and watching fun shows. I don't need space, I always look forward to the next job. Some jobs are not as fun as others, and some are a blast.

Is there a particular caricature artist or any other person by whom you were influenced?

My dad isn't a caricaturist but he influenced me for sure. I am not really influenced by caricaturists, I have my own style and don't spend time really looking at the work of others. I have a lot of caricaturist friends who I respect but my influences are more fine artists, like Jenny Saville, and John Singer Sargent, Zorn etc. Early on when I was getting started with caricature, I liked the artists of MAD magazine, and then as I grew, I began to like more illustrator type caricaturists, like C.F. Payne, Roberto Parada, Philip Burke, Steve Brodner, and Sebastian Kruger.

“This magazine cover illustration of Pope Francis for Time was as challenging an assignment as it was a huge honor.”

JASON SEILER

Bio for United States Post Office!

From ***"It's Funny Because It's True"***

Posted by Seiler | jasonseilerillustration.blogspot.com

Jason Seiler grew up in Eau Claire, Wisconsin, where a simple teenage prank launched his artistic career. After getting caught drawing parodies of his high school history teacher, Seiler's principal gave him a job creating caricatures of other faculty members, and he never looked back. *(Publisher's note: After attending ninth grade in Rice Lake Jason's family moved to Eau Claire, Wisconsin just 60 miles southeast on Highway 53.)* In 1996, Seiler moved to Chicago and spent several years touring with bands as a guitarist and singer, torn between a life as an artist or as a musician. He ultimately chose art and went on to study fine art illustration at the American Academy of Art before becoming a full-time artist. Though he does not consider himself strictly a caricaturist, his paintings and illustrations often

include elements of caricature, used to exaggerate and create humor and depth in his subjects. His work, both humorous and serious, has been featured in numerous publications, including Rolling Stone, TIME, Der Spiegel, The New York Times, The Wall Street Journal, Business Week, MAD magazine, and The New Yorker. Seiler's client list has also included Disney, Universal Pictures, Penguin Group, Sony Image, and Tim Burton's Alice in Wonderland, for which he worked as a character designer. In 2010, Seiler won a silver award from the Society of Illustrators West for his portrait of Elvis Costello. For several years, Seiler has taught painting and drawing for the online art school Schoolism. Aside from drawing, he loves to skydive and dreams of one day cage diving with great white sharks. Until that day comes, he

Donald Trump - Utne Reader by Jason Seiler

2D - posted 25th February 2011

This was painted as a cover for The Utne Reader. The article title was "Burn the Rich". They wanted a Gulliver's travels type thing where Trump would be a giant ... they wanted him tied to the Trump Tower in New York. This is the second cover I've painted for them. Like most cover's that I've done, there's only a certain space available for the art, so you need to keep in mind that there will be text, a bar code, and the magazine title, and you have to design your idea around that. That is why this piece is open on the left side as the right side and bottom went off the side of the magazine. This piece was a lot of fun to work on. Besides the cover, I also had an interior piece due for the same article, giving me two weeks to complete both a cover and interior piece.

will spend his time not devoted to art with his two daughters, Isabeau and Ava. Seiler lives in the Andersonville neighborhood of Chicago. Celebrity Chefs (2014) is his first project for the U.S. Postal Service. I'm excited to say that it is official that I will be doing a series of paintings for the United States Postal Service! My official bio and pic have been approved! Let the painting begin!!!!

Steven Tyler for Adobe

My latest illustration for the Wall Street Journal accompanies an article about 30 year olds who have to live with their parents because of the current state of the economy.

Teacher/Student by David Antenne

I actually first learned of Jason Seiler through a website called "schoolism.com". In 2009 I was looking up a favorite cartoonist of mine named Mort Drucker, and happened upon a documentary about him produced by this website. I created an account with the site in order to purchase and view the streaming video. Thereafter I started receiving email updates from them highlighting different workshops and classes that the company holds.

David Antenne

In the early fall of 2013 I started thinking about developing my art skills some more, having taken a break from art school in order to pursue the things of the Lord. (I attended the Art Institutes International of MN as well as the Art Institute of Seattle, 2003-2005.) Regrettably, when an artist draws and paints without any feedback or helpful criticism, he tends to become stagnant in artistic growth. So, with that in mind, I decided to look into some instructional options and along the way checked out the class offerings on schoolism.com. I saw Jason's class "The Art of Caricature", and having loved caricatures ever since I was a small child (I copied a Ronald Reagan caricature from a MAD magazine when I was 4 or 5 years old), I quickly enrolled for the October 2013 semester.

His classes work like this: For every assignment the student receives a streaming video lecture through the website that Jason narrates while he paints or draws. For the homework, the students access downloadable files from their website account. These files include what Jason calls "citizens" (people he personally photographed, usually from his apartment building) along with some photo references of a celebrity like Anne Hathaway. The students are then assigned to sketch the citizens from varying angles, along with a final drawing or painting of the given celebrity as a caricature. The time frame for completion is usually 10 days. After submitting these drawings and/or paintings, the students later receive a downloadable critique video by Jason where he points out what's strong and also what lacks in the artwork. He does this while erasing and redrawing or drawing over the student's artwork. If requested by the student, Jason will send the critiqued drawing to a personal email address. I always requested it. I didn't think these classes were going to be so intense or advanced as they were, but learning always comes with challenges. I am very thankful that I was able to learn under a man who is at the top of his field in caricaturing. It is an education I can definitely build upon for years to come.

Hillary Clinton

Although I was his student for about two months, I didn't know Jason had lived in Wisconsin before let alone Rice Lake. Jason had sent his students an email telling us he was the one who painted the Pope for Time Magazine's "Person of The Year" cover. Then, just before Christmas, my father happened to show me an article published in the Catholic Herald of Superior discussing this particular cover of Time. He opened it up and said, "Hey Dave, the guy who painted the Pope for Time used to live in Rice Lake!" I answered by saying, "This guy is my art teacher!" Afterwards I emailed Jason and told him I too was from Rice Lake, and included a link to the Herald's web version of the article He responded back stating that he lived and attended school in Rice Lake from 3rd to 9th grade, also living in Campia during his school years here. In one of our exchanges I sent him a list of

Gene Wilder

middle school teachers I had and he responded by telling me he also had many of the same teachers. Although we both attended Rice Lake Middle School at the same time (1990-1992), Jason and I were not in the same grade together and, unfortunately, were never friends or even acquaintances. We were actually a year apart-Jason being a full grade ahead of me, so we never had any classes together or anything. He's probably in my old middle school yearbook somewhere.

Without a doubt, at a mere 35 years old, Jason is a Master Painter. I believe he paints near to a miracle. His paintings, even his caricatures, look like photographs. Folks should definitely check out his online portfolio from his website. It's incredible work. Jason is a very humble artist, which is extremely rare in a guy of his caliber. Jason is also a really humble instructor. He has a very down to earth tone to his lectures, as if you're sitting next to him in an easy chair. He doesn't talk down as he teaches. He also doesn't hand out complements or praise easily, so when he does, you know you've done something well.

Tyndale

STAND

"I would remind you that extremism in the defense of liberty is no vice! And let me remind you also that moderation in the pursuit of justice is no virtue!"

BARRY GOLDWATER

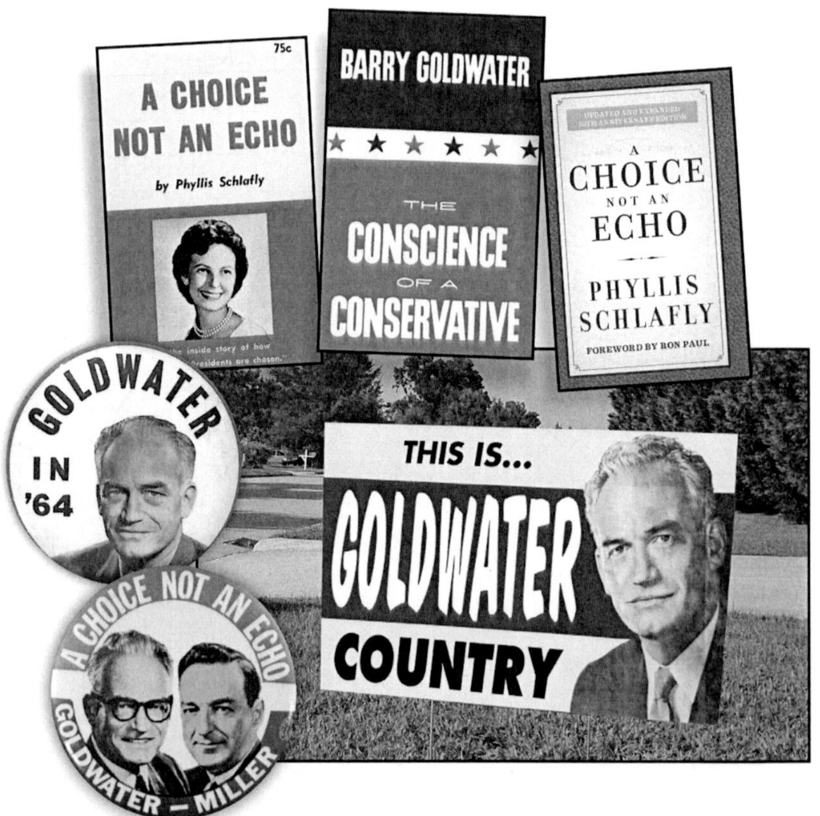

Sen. Rand Paul, R-Kentucky

RAND PAUL

Lonely Are The Brave

Republican Presidential Candidate Debate

Tuesday, December 15th, 2015
The Venetian in Las Vegas, Nevada

Republican presidential candidates *(L-R) Ohio Gov. John Kasich, Carly Fiorina, Sen. Marco Rubio (R-FL), Ben Carson, Donald Trump, Sen. Ted Cruz (R-TX), Jeb Bush, New Jersey Gov. Chris Christie and Sen. Rand Paul (R-KY) are introduced during the CNN presidential debate at The Venetian Las Vegas on December 15, 2015 in Las Vegas, Nevada. Thirteen Republican presidential candidates are participating in the fifth set of Republican presidential debates.* (PHOTO BY ETHAN MILLER/GETTY IMAGES)

PAUL: The question is, how do we keep America safe from terrorism? Trump says we ought to close that Internet thing. The question really is, what does he mean by that? Like they do in North Korea? Like they do in China?

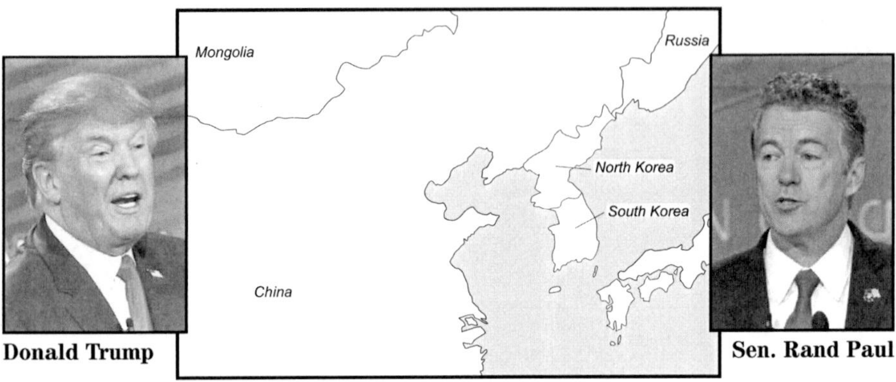

Donald Trump

Sen. Rand Paul

Rubio says we should collect all Americans' records all of the time. The Constitution says otherwise. I think they're both wrong. I think we defeat terrorism by showing them that we do not fear them. I think if we ban certain religions, if we censor the Internet, I think that at that point the terrorists will have won. Regime change hasn't won. Toppling secular dictators in the Middle East has only led to chaos and the rise of radical Islam. I think if we want to defeat terrorism, I think if we truly are sincere about defeating terrorism, we need to quit arming the allies of ISIS. If we want to defeat terrorism, the boots on the ground -- the boots on the ground need to be Arab boots on the ground.

Sen. Marco Rubio, R-FL – *Weakest of all candidates on immgration.*

As commander-in-chief, I will do whatever it takes to defend America. But

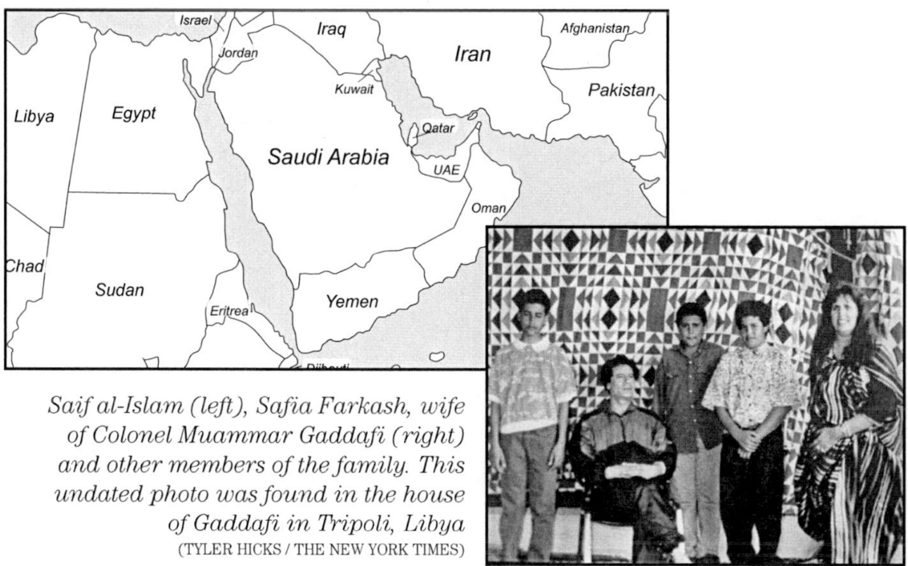

Saif al-Islam (left), Safia Farkash, wife of Colonel Muammar Gaddafi (right) and other members of the family. This undated photo was found in the house of Gaddafi in Tripoli, Libya
(TYLER HICKS / THE NEW YORK TIMES)

in defending America, we cannot lose what America stands for. Today is the Bill of Rights' anniversary. I hope we will remember that and cherish that in the fight on terrorism.

PAUL: You know, I think Marco gets it completely wrong. We are not any safer through the bulk collection of all Americans' records. In fact, I think we're less safe. We get so distracted by all of the information, we're not spending enough time getting specific immigration -- specific information on terrorists.

The other thing is, is the one thing that might have stopped San Bernardino, that might have stopped 9/11 would have been stricter controls on those who came here. And Marco has opposed at every point increased security -- border security for those who come to our country.

On his Gang of Eight bill, he would have liberalized immigration, but he did not -- and he steadfastly opposed any new border security requirements for refugees or students.

Last week, I introduced another bill saying we need more security, we need more scrutiny. Once again, Marco opposed this. So Marco can't have it both ways. He thinks he wants to be this, "Oh, I'm great and strong on national defense." But he's the

"Republocrats", Constitutional Traitors *who wrote the Comprehensive Immigration Reform Bill (CIR) aka Gang of Eight from left, are Jeff Flake, R-Ariz., Marco Rubio, R-Fla., Richard Durbin, D-Ill., John McCain, R-Ariz., Charles Schumer, D-N.Y., Robert Menendez, D-N.J., Lindsey Graham, R-S.C., and Michael Bennet, D-Colo.*

weakest of all the candidates on immigration. He is the one for an open border that is leaving us defenseless. If we want to defend the country, we have to defend against who's coming in, and Marco is -- has more of an allegiance to Chuck Schumer and to the liberals than he does to conservative policy.

PAUL: Marco still misunderstands the immigration issue. What I put forward was an amendment that would have temporarily halted immigration from high-risk terrorist countries, but would have started it up, but I wanted them to go through Global Entry, which is a program where we do background checks.

The thing is, is that every terrorist attack we've had since 9/11 has been legal immigration. Marco wants to expand that. I want more rules, more scrutiny, and to defend the country, you have to defend the border.

BASH: Senator Paul, Senator Paul, I want to go back to my initial question, which is you saying that ISIS grew stronger because of hawks in your party. And do you think your own party, the people who you're describing, are responsible for the rise of ISIS?

PAUL: I think that if you believe in regime change, you're mistaken. In 2013, we put 600 tons of weapons -- us, Saudi Arabia, and Qatar -- into the war against Assad. By pushing Assad back, we did create a safe space.

We had people coming to our Foreign Relations Committee and saying, "Oh, we need to arm the allies of Al Qaida." They are still saying this. It is a crazy notion. This is the biggest debate we should be having tonight is regime change a good idea; has it been a good idea.

Sen. Marco Rubio, R-Fla., center, worked with Sens. Charles Schumer, D-N.Y., and John McCain, R-Ariz., on a comprehensive immigration bill. (J. SCOTT APPLEWHITE, AP)

There are still people -- the majority on the stage, they want to topple Assad. And then there will be chaos, and I think ISIS will then be in charge of Syria.

BASH: Senator, we're going to talk about regime change in a bit.

BLITZER: Senator Paul, was getting rid of Saddam Hussein a pretty good deal?

PAUL: These are the fundamental questions of our time, these foreign policy questions, whether or not regime change is a good idea or a bad idea. I don't think because I think the regime change was a bad idea it means that Hussein was necessarily a good idea.

There is often variations of evil on both sides of the war. What we have to decide is whether or not regime change is a good idea. It's what the neoconservatives have wanted. It's what the vast majority of those on the stage want.

They still want regime change. They want it in Syria. They wanted it in Iraq. They want it in Libya. It has not worked.

Saddam Hussein's statue hauled down in Baghdad as his regime collapses, April 9, 2003

Out of regime change you get chaos. From the chaos you have seen repeatedly the rise of radical Islam. So we get this profession of, oh, my goodness, they want to do something about terrorism and yet they're the problem because they allow terrorism to arise out of that chaos.

BLITZER: Thank you.

HEWITT: Senator Paul, let me ask you, you heard Governor Kasich say Assad must go. Do you agree?

PAUL: No, I think it's a huge mistake. I think regime change in Syria, and this is what -- I've been saying this for several years now. In 2013 when we first went in, I said, you are going to give arms to the allies of al Qaida, to radical jihadists? That's crazy.

But the other thing I said is the great irony is you will be back fighting against your own weapons. Had Assad been bombed when he used chemical weapons two years ago, ISIS would be in charge of all of Syria now.

We have to have a more realistic foreign policy and not a utopian one where we say, oh, we're going to spread freedom and democracy, and everybody in the Middle East is going to love us. They are not going to love us.

BLITZER: Senator Paul -- Senator Paul, I want you to respond to what we just heard from Governor Christie. If there was a no-fly zone, you say that potentially could lead to World War III. Why?

PAUL: Well, I think if you're in favor of World War III, you have your candidate. You know, here's...

... the thing. My goodness, what we want in a leader is someone with judgment, not someone who is so reckless as to stand on the stage and say, "Yes, I'm jumping up and down; I'm going to shoot down Russian planes." Russia already flies in that airspace. It may not be something we're in love with the fact that they're there, but they were invited by Iraq and by Syria to fly in that airspace.

Well, I think if you're in favor of World War III, you have your candidate.

And so if we announce we're going to have a no-fly zone, and others have said this. Hillary Clinton is also for it. It is a recipe for disaster. It's a recipe for World War III. We need to confront Russia from a position of strength, but we don't need to confront Russia from a point of recklessness that would lead to war.

This is something -- this type of judgment, you know, it's having that kind of judgment; who you would appoint and how you're going to conduct affairs, that is incredibly important.

I mean, I think when we think about the judgment of someone who might want World War III, we might think about someone who might shut down a bridge because they don't like their friends; they don't want to -- you know, they want to (inaudible) a Democrat.

So I think we need to be very careful.

BLITZER: Senator Paul, you didn't answer the question about the 2,000 Syrian refugees who are already here in the United States. Will you send them back or let them stay?

PAUL: What my bill would do would be only for refugees going forward. So I haven't taken a position on sending anyone home. But I have taken the position that we have a lot of problems here in our country. And that one of the things that we do -- charity is about giving your own money. Charity isn't giving someone else's money. To put everyone in government housing and food stamps and bring them in from around the world I think is a mistake. To give of your own money, I've given to my church. My church has helped people that came from Bosnia. That's a good thing.

But we shouldn't have a program where we just say that we're going to take care of the world's refugees. Nobody in the Middle East is doing anything. Saudi Arabia, Qatar, Kuwait -- all the Gulf nations are doing nothing. They need to step up and take...

BLITZER: Now it's time for the closing statements from the candidates. Each one has 30 seconds.

Senator Paul.

"The greatest threat to our national security is our debt. We borrow a million dollars a minute." Sen. Rand Paul, R. Kentucky

PAUL: The greatest threat to our national security is our debt. We borrow a million dollars a minute. And whose fault is it? Well, frankly, it's both parties' fault. You have those on the right who clamor and say, oh, we will spend anything on the military, and those on the left who say the same for domestic welfare.

But what most Americans don't realize is there is an unholy alliance. They come together. There's a secret handshake. We spend more money on everything. And we are not stronger nation if we go further into debt. We are not projecting power from bankruptcy court.

To me, there is no greater threat than our debt. I'm the only fiscal conservative on the stage because I'm willing to hold the line on all spending. I hope you will consider me in the election. Thank you very much.

Secrets of the Federal Reserve

By **Eustace Mullins**

Questions and Answers

While lecturing in many countries, and appearing on radio and television programs as a guest, the author is frequently asked questions about the Federal Reserve System. The most frequently asked questions and the answers are as follows:

Q: What is the Federal Reserve System?

A: The Federal Reserve System is not Federal; it has no reserves; and it is not a system, but rather, a criminal syndicate. It is the product of criminal syndicalist activity of an international consortium of dynastic families comprising what the author terms "The World Order" (see "THE WORLD ORDER" and "THE CURSE OF CANAAN", both by Eustace Mullins). The Federal Reserve system is a central bank operating in the United States. Although the student will find no such definition of a central bank in the textbooks of any university, the author has defined a central bank as follows: It is the dominant financial power of the country which harbors it. It is entirely private-owned, although it seeks to give the appearance of a governmental institution. It has the right to print and issue money, the traditional prerogative of monarchs. It is set up to provide financing for wars. It functions as a money monopoly having total power over all the money and credit of the people.

Q: When Congress passed the Federal Reserve Act on December 23, 1913, did the Congressmen know that they were creating a central bank?

A: The members of the 63rd Congress had no knowledge of a central bank or of its monopolistic operations. Many of those who voted for the bill were duped; others were bribed; others were intimidated. The preface to the Federal Reserve Act reads "An Act to provide for the establishment of Federal reserve banks, to furnish an elastic currency, to afford means of rediscounting commercial papers, to establish a more effective supervision of banking in the United States, and for other purposes." The unspecified "other purposes" were to give international conspirators a monopoly of all the money and credit of the people of the United States; to finance World War I through this new central bank, to place American workers at the mercy of the Federal Reserve system's collection agency, the Internal Revenue Service, and to allow the monopolists to seize the assets of their competitors and put them out of business.

Q: Is the Federal Reserve system a government agency?

A: Even the present chairman of the House Banking Committee claims that the Federal Reserve is a government agency, and that it is not privately owned. The fact is that the government has never owned a single share of Federal Reserve Bank stock. This charade stems from the fact that the President of the United States appoints the Governors of the Federal Reserve Board, who are then confirmed by the Senate. The secret author of the Act, banker Paul Warburg, a representative of the Rothschild bank, coined the name "Federal" from thin air for the Act, which he wrote to achieve two of his pet aspirations, an "elastic currency", read (rubber check), and to facilitate trading in acceptances, international trade credits. Warburg was founder and president of the International Acceptance Corporation, and made billions in profits by trading in this commercial paper. Sec. 7 of the Federal Reserve Act provides "Federal reserve banks, including the capital and surplus therein, and income derived therefrom, shall be exempt from Federal, state and local taxation, except taxes on real estate." Government buildings do not pay real estate tax.

Q: Are our dollar bills, which carry the label "Federal Reserve notes" government money?
A: Federal Reserve notes are actually promissory notes, promises to pay, rather than what we traditionally consider money. They are interest bearing notes issued against interest bearing government bonds, paper issued with nothing but paper backing, which is known as fiat money, because it has only the fiat of the issuer to guarantee these notes. The Federal Reserve Act authorizes the issuance of these notes "for the purposes of making advances to Federal reserve banks... The said notes shall be obligations of the United States. They shall be redeemed in gold on demand at the Treasury Department of the United States in the District of Columbia." Tourists visiting the Bureau of Printing and Engraving on the Mall in Washington, D.C. view the printing of Federal Reserve notes at this governmental agency on contract from the Federal Reserve System for the nominal sum of .00260 each in units of 1,000, at the same price regardless of the denomination. These notes, printed for a private bank, then become liabilities and obligations of the United States government and are added to our present $4 trillion debt. The government had no debt when the Federal Reserve Act was passed in 1913.

Q: Who owns the stock of the Federal Reserve Banks?
A: The dynastic families of the ruling World Order,

internationalists who are loyal to no race, religion, or nation. They are families such as the Rothschilds, the Warburgs, the Schiffs, the Rockefellers, the Harrimans, the Morgans and others known as the elite, or "the big rich".

Q: Can I buy this stock?

A: No. The Federal Reserve Act stipulates that the stock of the Federal Reserve Banks cannot be bought or sold on any stock exchange. It is passed on by inheritance as the fortune of the "big rich". Almost half of the owners of Federal Reserve Bank stock are not Americans.

Q: Is the Internal Revenue Service a governmental agency?

A: Although listed as part of the Treasury Department, the IRS is actually a private collection agency for the Federal Reserve System. It originated as the Black Hand in mediaeval Italy, collectors of debt by force and extortion for the ruling Italian mob families. All personal income taxes collected by the IRS are required by law to be deposited in the nearest Federal Reserve Bank, under Sec. 15 of the Federal Reserve Act, "The moneys held in the general fund of the Treasury may be ....deposited in Federal reserve banks, which banks, when required by the Secretary of the Treasury, shall act as fiscal agents of the United States."

Q: Does the Federal Reserve Board control the daily price and quantity of money?

A: The Federal Reserve Board of Governors, meeting in private as the Federal Open Market Committee with presidents of the Federal Reserve Banks, controls all economic activity throughout the United States by issuing orders to buy government bonds on the open market, creating money out of nothing and causing inflationary pressure, or, conversely, by selling government bonds on the open market and extinguishing debt, creating deflationary pressure and causing the stock market to drop.

Q: Can Congress abolish the Federal Reserve System?

A: The last provision of the Federal Reserve Act of 1913, Sec. 30, states, "The right to amend, alter or repeal this Act is expressly reserved." This language means that Congress can at any time move to abolish the Federal Reserve System, or buy back the stock and make it part of the Treasury Department, or to altar the System as it sees fit. It has never done so.

Q: Are there many critics of the Federal Reserve beside yourself?

A: When I began my researches in 1948, the Fed was only thirty-four years old. It was never mentioned in the press. Today the Fed is discussed openly in the news section and the financial pages. There are bills in congress to have the Fed audited by the Government Accounting Office. Because of my exposé, it is no longer a sacred cow, although the Big Three candidates for President in 1992, Bush, Clinton and Perot, joined in a unanimous chorus during the debates that they were pledged not to touch the Fed.

Q: Have you suffered any personal consequences because of your exposé of the Fed?

A: I was fired from the staff of the Library of Congress after I published this exposé in 1952, the only person ever discharged from the staff for political reasons. When I sued, the court refused to hear the case. The entire German edition of this book was burned in 1955, the only book burned in Europe since the Second World War. I have endured continuous harassment by government agencies, as detailed in my books "A WRIT FOR MARTYRS" and "MY LIFE IN CHRIST". My family also suffered harassment. When I spoke recently in Wembley Arena in London, the press denounced me as "a sinister lunatic".

Q: Does the press always support the Fed?

A: There have been some encouraging defections in recent months. A front page story in the Wall Street Journal, Feb. 8, 1993, stated, "The current Fed structure is difficult to justify in a democracy. It's an oddly undemocratic institution. Its organization is so dated that there is only one Reserve bank west of the Rockies, and two in Missouri...Having a central bank with a monopoly over the issuance of the currency in a democratic society is a very difficult balancing act."

Publisher Jon Larsen Shudlick with mentor and friend Eustace Mullins. Mr. Mullins was designated the only authorized biographer of Ezra Pound by letter from him dated July 24, 1958. Four of Ezra Pound's protegés have previously been awarded the Nobel Prize for Literature, William Butler Yates, for his later poetry, James Joyce for "Ulysses", Ernest Hemingway for "The Sun Also Rises", and T.S. Elliot for "The Wasteland". Jon Larsen Shudlick produced three beautifully edited DVD's with Eustace Mullins; "Secrets of the Federal Reserve", "The New World Order", and "Murder by Injection", an expose of the Federal Drug Administration.

BOB BERTRAND
Tried and True Friend

By **Jon Larsen Shudlick**

Bob Bertrand, Justice Seeker, Patriot

Bob has personally delivered over one million pro-Constitution anti-lawyer brochures throughout Florida.

When you think of a million dollar man most of us relate to that idea of the "The Six-Million Dollar Man" portrayed by Lee Majors in the TV show from the mid 1970's.

However, let me tell you about my "million brochure" activist friend, Bob Bertrand. You see, Bob has personally handed out over a million brochures which he created and copied throughout his many years of protesting the tyranny of the oligarchy into which this country has morphed. Bob sometimes leaves his house after work at 6:00 or 7:00 in the evening dropping his flyers into bank depositories, business drop slots and handing them out to anyone he may come across including those all-night restaurant workers and their customers.

I have never known anyone more passionate about our Forefather's Constitution than my friend, Canadian born and educated, Bob Bertrand. Bob has been a successful businessman in his own right owning a motel and several condominiums in Miami Lakes, Florida. However, Bob isn't truly happy unless he is fighting the good fight to preserve our country's Constitutional values. I asked Bob recently, "Bob, how many courthouses do you think you and I together have picketed throughout the years?" He said, "Jon, probably 25 or 30." I know several times together we had been involved in trying to wake up the populous by marching, waving placards and shouting through bullhorns just so people would see and hear that there was someone alive out there who really cared. Some of those county seats involved were Palm Beach, Broward, Dade, Hendry, Glades, Collier, Lee, Leon (state capitol in Tallahassee) and others, even some federal and state buildings numerous times. Sometimes the marching and picketing events were during the day and sometimes at night.

Bob was with me when I gave The Great Speech before the American Bar Association at Lake Buena Vista, Florida in December of 1992. Bob even made thousands of copies of that speech and sent them out in mailers around the country. My friend, Bob Bertrand was also with me when I spoke before the Supreme Court of the state of Florida on Monday, April 5, 1993 in opposition to the Anti-Discrimination Proposal of the Florida Bar Anti-Discrimination hearing. Both of those speeches are in the Rice Lake Connection section of this book.

I also remember a significant event held at Bayfront Park in downtown Miami. It was on a Sunday afternoon at a Second Amendment rally where the organizers were not going to let me speak. After the last name on the program spoke I walked up the steps with Bob at my side and told the audience that the organizers had told me I could not speak that day at their event! I told the audience that this was a public location and I was going to speak. If they wanted to hear the real truth I was ready, willing and able to give it to them. I started the extemporaneous speech by repeating the oath of office that I took when I was drafted into the United States Army swearing my allegiance to the Constitution and that I would fight all enemies foreign and domestic. I explained to the large and growing crowd the only foreign enemies we have seem to be those which our foreign policies have created; and that by far the biggest challenge to freedom and liberty for our country and other like-minded people throughout the world is the domestic terror that is the end result of the many central banking systems throughout the world.

I also remember very fondly one night in Fort Lauderdale when Bob and I attended an alleged pro-Second Amendment meeting managed by a cadre of lawyers. Of course, they wanted to compromise our Second Amendment rights away by allowing registration of firearms. Bob and I could see the handwriting on the wall. It would be registration first, then licensing (permitting) of hand guns and finally confiscation. Bob and I were sitting in the front row and we started asking pertinent questions and eventually raising so much consternation that the left-wing organizers finally called it quits exiting the building in a huff. We stayed for almost an hour afterwards explaining that no government in the USA had any legal right to challenge any of the Bill of Rights to the Constitution of the United States of America, specifically for tonight the Second Amendment, the right to keep and bear arms. Well, that's why I say Bob is a tried and true friend because outside of his love for his three daughters, a good brouhaha is a strong passion for Bob Bertrand and in the thick of the fight he'll stand with you.

Bob Bertrand also believes whole heartedly in what Judge Catherine Crier is doing to change our legal system for the better. Her book titled, The Case Against Lawyers is one of Bob's favorites and has been promoted nationwide.

Bob's favorite new author.

I am a very lucky man. Many of the stories published in this book are authored by my personal friends and fellow patriots. I am so happy that I met Bob Bertrand at a pro-men's rights meeting over thirty years ago. His avid support for our Forefather's Constitution and those ideals of liberty and freedom which he stands for is truly an inspiration to me.

One of the shear joys in my life is reading emails or letters from my friends who love our patriotic Forefathers and their writings just as much as I do.

God bless America!

VERMIN

From **Paul Harvey's**
"The Rest of the Story"

If there is a stain on the record of our forefathers, a dark hour in the earliest history of the American colonies, it would be the hanging of the so-called "witches" at Salem.

But that was a pinpoint in place and time – a brief lapse into hysteria. For the most part, our seventeenth-century colonists were scrupulously fair, even in fear.

There was one group of people they feared with reason – a society, you might say, whose often insidious craft had claimed a multitude of victims, ever sine the Middle Ages in Europe.

One group of people, were hated and feared from Massachusetts Bay to Virginia. The magistrates would not burn them at the stake, although surely a great many of the colonists might have recommended such a solution. Our forefathers were baffled by them.

In the first place, where did they come from? Of all who sailed from England to Plymouth in 1620, not one of those two-legged vermin was aboard.

"Vermin." That's what the colonists called them. Parasites who fed on human misery, spreading sorrow and confusion wherever they went. "Destructive," they were called.

And still they were permitted coexistence with the colonists. For a while, anyway. Of course, there were colonial laws prohibiting the practice of their infamous craft. Somehow a way was always found around those laws.

In 1641, Massachusetts Bay colony took a novel approach to the problem. The governors attempted to starve those “devils” out of existence through economic exclusion. They were denied wages, and thereby it was hoped that they would perish.

Four years later, Virginia followed the example of Massachusetts Bay, and for a while it seemed that the dilemma had been resolved.

It had not. Somehow, the parasites managed to survive, and the mere nearness of them made the colonists’ skin crawl.

In 1658 in Virginia the final solution: Banishment. Exile. the “Treacherous Ones” were cast out of the colony. At last, after decades of enduring the psychological gloom, the sun came out and the birds sang and all was right with the world. And the elation continued for a generation.

I’m not sure why the Virginians eventually allowed the outcasts to return, but they did. In 1680, after twenty-two years, the despised ones were readmitted to the colony on the condition that they be subjected to the strictest surveillance.

How soon we forget!

For indeed, over the next half-century or so, the imposed restrictions were slowly, quietly swept away. And those whose treachery had been feared since the Middle Ages ultimately took their place in society.

You see, the “vermin” that once infested colonial America, the parasites who preyed on the misfortune of their neighbors until finally they were officially banished from Virginia, those dreaded, despised, outcast masters of confusion were lawyers.

Paul Harvey Aurandt (Sept. 4, 1918 – Feb. 28, 2009), better known as Paul Harvey, was a conservative American radio broadcaster for the ABC Radio Networks. He broadcast *News and Comment* on weekday mornings and mid-days, and at noon on Saturdays, as well as his famous *The Rest of the Story* segments. From the 1950s through the 1990s, Harvey’s programs reached as many as 24 million people a week. *Paul Harvey News* was carried on 1,200 radio stations, 400 Armed Forces Network stations and 300 newspapers.

DOWN DIXIE WAY

Notes of a Fed-Up Southerner

By **Fred Reed**
March 6, 2014

Coming up as I did a Southern boy, usually barefoot, lots of times with a cane pole and a string of bream I caught in Machodoc Creek, and other signs of higher civilization, I believe I could get tired of Northerners huffing and puffing about how moral they are. Ain't nothing like a damn Yankee for smarmy hypocrisy. They can spit it out in chunks like saw logs. A Yankee can't open his mouth without preaching about how everybody else ought to do something he won't do himself.

It's always the same thing, about how the South keeps blacks in poverty and has lynch mobs. (Actually, it's been at least three weeks since I was in a lynch mob.) To listen to these pious frauds, you'd think Northerners just loved black people and spent most of their time with them at the country club, talking the stock market. Why, how else *could* it be?

I couldn't lie so much if you gave me a bird dog and a buzz saw. It ain't in me. The worst schools in the country are in Mississippi, which doesn't have any money, and the second worst in Washington, DC, which has all our money. Yes, Washington, so virtuous it makes your teeth curl. How many white kids are in those schools? Uh-huh. It's you and him integrate, not us.

You've heard about white flight. In nearly about every city in the North white people streak for the suburbs so's not to be near black people, and then they talk about how bad Southerners are for doing the same thing. I guess talking moral is more fun than being it.

Fact is, you can see more social, comfortable integration in a catfish house in Louisiana than you can in probably all of Washington.

Now, sometimes I have to yield to the truth. I don't like to, but it's forced on me. Blacks do live miserable in Southern cities. It can't be denied. There's a shameful list of awful cities and it hurts me to write it: Newark, Trenton, Camden, Detroit, Flint, Chicago, and Gary. Pretty much the entire South.

Facts is, the South itself was always poor, dirt poor, pea-turkey poor, especially after 1861, and a lot of what it was and how it felt came out of that. Songs like *Ode to Billy Joe* to Yankees are funny, the kind of thing you'd expect from those hicks down there. But they tell how it was for a lot of folk. Red dirt hills where nothing much wanted to grow, and there was nothing much to do and sometimes nothing much to eat. It was ugly, Tobacco Road, and the North laughs it. Even in the mid-Fifties you saw—I saw—kids from the countryside of Alabama with their teeth black from decay, and in some regions school vacations came at cotton-picking and cotton-chopping time. You could easy find people living in fall-down shacks, white people too. Thank you, Mr. Lincoln.

Piety quiz: Everybody take out a sheet of paper. Who said the following: "I will say then that I am not, nor ever have been in favor of bringing about in anyway the social and political equality of the white and black races – that I am not nor ever have been in favor of making voters or jurors of negroes, nor of qualifying them to hold office, nor to intermarry with white people…." (1) Mahatma Ghandi (2) Mother Theresa (3) Tinker Belle or (4) Abraham Lincoln. Hint: It wasn't any of the first three.

Let me remind us that the South has generally had to bring to the North the benefits of culture. It figures. Industrial society is so full of stench and soot and misery and crowding that people can't even do a good job of being unhappy. That's why the great blues men like Mississippi John Hurt and Lightnin' Hopkins came out of Dixie. So did jazz, and country music, and Dixieland jazz, which is different, and bluegrass, and rock'n'roll thanks to Big Boy Crudup and Elvis. Yankees can play long-hair music pretty good, but they stole it from Europe.

The South, though. It was a different place, mostly kind of sad I guess if you looked close, but it could grow on you. Those hot, quiet cotton fields in the Delta, where time passed sweet and slow like sorghum syrup dripping on busted china, and it was so peaceful and the air so soft you figured maybe there was a God after all. There wasn't, though. At the time you could stand there and think that it would go on forever, that there was something comfortable and familiar that wouldn't turn into something else you didn't want. But it did. Nothing lovely can last when next door you have an infernal industrial smoke pit.

There was a wildness to the South, a sense that anything could happen. It didn't feel controlled. Maybe it wasn't obvious. People talked soft and slow like the Good Lord intended, instead of honking through their noses the way they do in Brooklyn, and they were polite and friendly. You didn't want to lean on them, though. That wasn't a good idea.

If you knew the place, it wasn't surprising the moonshine runners came from there, and later turned into NASCAR. Hopped-up flathead mill, tank of bust-head corn in the trunk, flying through the Tennessee night with the dam federals after them. Back then, like now, Washington didn't want people to drink what they wanted or smoke what they wanted. They was always sticking their long possum noses where they didn't belong. And not just in the South. They'd invade anybody they'd ever heard of. Mexico in 1846 and 1916, Spain in 1898, Europe in 1917, on through Iraq and Yemen, wherever that is, and Afghanistan and I don't know where all. Anything but mind their own business.

And now we got another Yankee president from Chicago messing with the whole country, turning America into Russia. That sort of thing never did set too well below Mason and Dixon's Line.

Piety quiz: Which of the following in the decades surrounding the Civil War said over and over that he wanted to send all the black folks to Africa? (1) Susan Anthony (2) Pallas Athena (3)

Sophia of Anhalt-Zerbst (4) Abraham Lincoln. Hint….

But enough about Washington, the world's central deposit of oleaginous purity. Let's talk about cars. Dixie was a car culture from when it first got the chance. It still is. I remember when, come summer, at umpty-dozen tracks the night howled and yowled and roared as muscle cars raced, taching high and sometimes blowing rods but things don't always turn out perfect. In the stands they drank beer out of paper cups and hollered for Jimmy Jack or Joe Bob to take the lead. It was their place in the world and they were doing what they liked with people they liked and there were no dam feds telling them they had to put catalytic converters on the race cars. Yet.

That was something the South always liked. Being left the hell alone.

On the weekends of races at Road Atlanta, from all over the South, from little towns like Farmville, Virginia, trailers and motor homes towing race cars streamed in. They'd set up and bring out the tool boxes and start prepping for the races the next day. Wives and girlfriends would help and everyone hollered greetings at new arrivals.

The wives and girlfriends were real women, and seemed to think being a woman was a good thing. Men thought it was a good thing, that's for sure. It was like there were two kinds of people, men and women, instead of just one. It's a novel concept, I reckon. But we liked it. And they were just nice. You could easy tell a Southern gal from a menopausing crocodile. Up North, you'd need a DNA test.

Anyway, half the crowd already knew each other and the others didn't have to because it was a common culture and if you had a race car, you were in.

Greasy-purity quiz: "I will say in addition to this that there is a physical difference between the white and black races which I believe will forever forbid the two races living together on terms of social and political equality. And inasmuch as they cannot so live, while they do remain together there must be the position of superior and inferior, and I, as much as any other man, am in favor of having the superior position assigned to the white race." (1) George Wallace (2) David Duke (3) Nathan Bedford Forrest (4) Abraham Lincoln

Uh-huh. The Great Emancipator. Himself. How I *do* love goodness.

The red field represents the Blood of Christ.
The white border represents the Protection of God.
The blue "X" represents the Christian Cross of Saint Andrew, the first Disciple of Christ Jesus and Patron Saint of Scotland.
The 13 stars represent the 13 Southern States of Secession.
Thus, the message in the Confederate Battle Flag is:
"Through the Blood of Christ,
with the Protection of God,
We, the Thirteen States,
are united in our Christian fight for liberty."

Fred Reed

Fred Reed is author of Nekkid in Austin: Drop Your Inner Child Down a Well, A Brass Pole in Bangkok: A Thing I Aspire to Be, Curmudgeing Through Paradise: Reports from a Fractal Dung Beetle, Au Phuc Dup and Nowhere to Go: The Only Really True Book About VietNam, and A Grand Adventure: Wisdom's Price-Along with Bits and Pieces about Mexico.

Warning From A Former Canadian Minister Of Defense by George D. Larson

No one less than a former Canadian Minister of Defense, Paul T. Hellyer, is speaking out in the strongest possible terms about the imminent danger facing Americans, Canadians, and all the other peoples of the West. In The Money Mafia: A World In Crisis,[1] he exposes and denounces the criminal cabal that is hellbent on imposing an Orwellian police state on the entire earth. And he has some chilling—absolutely shocking—news about a company in Portland, Oregan.

Years ago Gunderson Brothers was famous for building cruise ships such as The Mariposa. But of late they seem to have been led down a very different path, apparently enticed by the federal government into a very different—and highly sinister—line of work. Hellyer cites Phil Schneider, a government geologist and structural engineer:

> *"Recently, I knew someone who lived near where I live in Portland, Oregon. He worked at Gunderson Steel Fabrication, where they make railroad cars. Now, I knew this fellow for the better part of 30 years, and he was kind of a quiet type. He came to see me one day, excited, and he told me 'they're building prisoner cars.' He was nervous. Gunderson, he said, had a contract with the federal government to build 10,720 full length railroad cars, each with 143 pairs of shackles."* [2]

Hellyer adds:

> *"If I were an American I would certainly want to know if I was one of the more than a million and a half people on some secret list to be transported to a concentration camp somewhere!"* [3]

---

[1] Walterville, OR: Trine Day, 2014.

[2] Ibid., pp., 204-05. Also see p. 297, n. 13; pp. 296-97, n. 5; p. 199.

[3] Ibid., p. 205.

KNOWLEDGE IS POWER!!!

"Psychologists use the term 'Cognitive dissonance' to apply to the inability of one to accept the viability of evidence beyond that of which he/she has been pre-programmed to believe, regardless of how convincing that evidence might be. For instance, even after Magellan circumnavigated the world, the notion that the Earth was flat prevailed amongst the majority of the world's populace for decades following."

– ***Pat Shannan***
Everything They* Ever Told Me Was a Lie

"The only people who don't believe in the conspiracy theories of history are those many who have not studied them."

– ***Pat Shannan***

HOW DO WE LEARN MORE ABOUT CONSPIRACIES AND WHAT THE TRUTH REALLY IS?

We learn by reading one book or one newsletter at a time, by watching one documentary or one conspiracy DVD at a time, by visiting one website at a time, by listening to one conspiracy CD at a time and by becoming involved with other patriots in our community. The websites, emails, books and radio broadcasts listed below have been helpful in my search for the truth. One source of knowledge inevitably leads you to a variety of other sources and these are just a small sample of those which have been valuable to me.

WEBSITES and EMAILS

- www.scripturesforamerica.org Identity Christian, Biblical truth 307-742-7582
- www.zundelsite.org Email: irimland@zundelsite.org (opinions of Ingrid Zundel) 865-774-7756
- www.veteranstodaynetwork.com Email: gm@veteranstodaynetwork.com
- Subscribe to a free email newsletter *Restore Self Government* email: rsgleela@aol.com
- www.drudgereport.com for current news articles. He broke the Monica Lewinski/Bill Clinton story.
- www.stormfront.org News you won't get anyplace else; the Don and Derek Black show on AM radio
- www.gunowners.org Larry and Eric Pratt; no compromise on the Second Amendment since 1975, join now
- www.rommellaw.com Peter Jon Simpson; wordsmith superb 320-857-2400 – legal, health & financial consultations pursuant to strict Biblical principles
- www.popularliberty.com always up to date new Libertarian and national news

- www.krisannehall.com wonderful interview on our Forefathers' Constitution 386-466-4556
- www.shadowstats.com real statistics from several different perspectives
- www.infowars.com hard core truth (Alex Jones website) wonderfully controversial
- www.huffingtonpost.com/...worlds-best-countries_n_2205270.html List of the world's best countries to be born in for 2013 – Top 5: Switzerland, Australia, Norway, Sweden and Denmark – U.S. is 16th
- Pat Buchanan: www.buchanan.org first-class website, prolific writer of conservative causes
- Victor Thorn: Investigative reporter and former Assignment Editor for American Free Press and founder of WING TV Email: sisyphus1285@cs.com 814-272-4664 http://www.wingtv.net Beginning in2001, WING TV has focused on exposing the New World Order and all the conspiracies associated with it.
- Diane MacMillan: Email: diane@dunlookin.com weather modification conspiracy, fires floods and future starvation?
- 10 DVD's for mastering billiards, pool or golf: World Champion, Jimmy Reid 772-370-0311 Email: worldchampionjreid@gmail.com or jimmyreidpro@bellsouth.net best billiards and pool DVD's available on earth.
- Google: Rick Steves' Iran
- Christian Defense League, P.O. Box 9166, Mandeville, LA 70470 www.historycommons.org
- Google: Wesley Swift
- www.mikebrownsolutions.com uninhibited creativity
- www.brownslegalresearch.com
- www.leviticus11.com
- www.prisonplanet.com
- www.lewrockwell.com tons of information fresh daily
- www.libertycrier.com

- www.constitutionalguardian.com
- www.judicialaccountability.org
- www.disbarthefloridabar.com
- www.attorneysabovethelaw.com
- www.resist.com
- www.counterpunch.org 1 (800) 840-3683
- www.realityzone.com G. Edward Griffin website
- www.davidduke.com 985-626-7714
- www.libertyradio.com
- www.themoneymasters.com Email: moneymastersmail@aol.com Complete history of money
- www.dirtyspendingsecrets.com
- Google: Researching Criminal Zionism
- www.iamthewitness.com Type *interview with Harold Rosenthal* into the search bar
- www.ae911truth.org www.ae911truth.org/911investigator
- Dr. Adrian H. Krieg: a2zpublications.com Sign up for Dr. Krieg's free newsletter at http://eepurl.com/guoci
- Confederate Veteran: www.scv.org
- General Jubal A. Early Camp Post 556, Tampa, Florida www.tampascv.org Mike Herring, 813-681-6922, Commanding Officer – Join as a friend of Early Camp, Paul Elmore, PR., 813-841-7070
- Google: Kaminski: Hijacked by a Foreign Power
- Wes Templeton Public Speaker on the History of Money: Email: scotch@centurylink.net Wes can speak for an hour without notes, DVD available 941-575-7657.
- Bob Bertrand legal reformer: great interview 305-823-6076
- David Knight on www.prisonplanet.com great voice … best nightly news on the Internet or anyplace else

- Paul Joseph Watson on www.infowars.com (Alex Jones)
- www.againstcronycapitalism.org

BOOKS

- **The E-Myth Revisited** Why Most Small Businesses Don't Work and What to Do About It by Michael E. Gerber
- The Secret Empire (Introduction, Part I and Part II) by Cushman Cunningham … Best ever conspiracy books rsgleela@aol.com
- A Writ for Martyrs by Eustace Mullins … America's treasure – Eustace Mullins, 60 years of research, 5,000 years of history.
- Secrets of the Federal Reserve by Eustace Mullins
- The New World Order by Eustace Mullins
- Murder by Injection by Eustace Mullins
- Rape of Justice by Eustace Mullins – Books by Eustace Mullins available at *American Free Press*, 202-544-5977
- The Jews and Their Lies by Martin Luther
- Whores Galore by Pastor Peter J. Peters: 307-742-7582
- War Is A Racket by Major General Smedley D. Butler … an eye opener and free on the Internet
- The Trillion Dollar Meltdown by Charles R. Morris … He had the crystal ball.
- The Creature from Jekyll Island by G. Edward Griffin
- End the Fed by Ron Paul
- What Happened in Education? by David Barton … The communist takeover
- The American Dream/Nightmare – Obama's Plan by Dr. Adrian H. Krieg … My favorite reference book
- Our Political Systems by Dr. Adrian H. Krieg … www.a2zpublications.com

- July 4th 2016 The Last Independence Day by Dr. Adrian H. Krieg
- Oz in the New Millennium by Dr. Adrian H. Krieg
- Everything They*Ever Told Me Was a Lie (Volume One) by Pat Shannan … This book will knock your socks off.
- Brown's Lawsuit Cookbook by Michael Halsey Brown … www.brownslegalresearch.com
- Strength of Sampson by Michael H. Brown … leviticus11.com
- Criminal Defendant's Bible 2016 vol. 1 Pre Trial www.brownslegalresearch.com
- Sex, Money and Power The Bible Tells You How by Michael Halsey Brown
- Bloody Iron Practical Knife Fighting by Michael Halsey Brown
- Attorneys Above the Law by Dennis Schuelke www.attorneysabovethelaw.com
- New World Order Assassins by Victor Thorn
- Made in Israel: 9-11 by Victor Thorn
- "Reality" Bomb by Victor Thorn
- The Talmud Unmasked by Father I. B. Pranitis
- Father Coughlin Answers His Critics by Father Coughlin … The most honest man of his time
- Behind Communism by Frank L. Britton
- DemoCRIPS and ReBLOODlicans by Jesse Ventura … He's been there and done that.
- American Conspiracies by Jesse Ventura with Dick Russell
- 63 Documents the Government Doesn't Want You to Read by Jesse Ventura with Dick Russell
- The Man Who Knew Too Much by Dick Russell
- On the Trail of the Kennedy Assassins by Dick Russell
- Mary's Mosaic by Peter Janney … Full of truth and guts … THE **CIA** KILLED **JFK** (Insider's epiphany)

- Live Rent Free Guaranteed by Jim Anderson shud21@comcast.net
- Male Liberation and Sex Equality by Frank Bertels 239-218-4028
- The Lincoln Elementary Dream Team by Jon Larsen Shudlick … "I think it could be scored right up there with Tom Brokaw's *The Greatest Generation.* It has a lot of wonderful subliminal messages. God Bless, Foster." 239-218-4028
- It's Dangerous to Be Right When the Government Is Wrong by Judge Andrew P. Napolitano … The greatest speaker I have seen since George Wallace
- Theodore and Woodrow by Judge Andrew P. Napolitano
- More Guns Less Crime by John R. Lott, Jr.
- Involuntary Separation Corporate Downsizing Gone *Fatally* Wrong by Rick Lacey 239-849-1467 Email: rplacey@hotmail.com
- A Pretext for War by James Bamford
- Body of Secrets by James Bamford
- The Shadow Factory by James Bamford
- The Puzzle Palace by James Bamford
- Vigilantes of Christendom by Richard Kelly Hoskins
- Final Judgment by Michael Collins Piper
- The Protocols of the Meetings of the Learned Elders of Zion The *Protocols* purports to document the minutes of a late 19th century meeting of Jewish leaders discussing their goal of global Jewish hegemony by subverting the morals of the Gentiles, and by controlling the press and the world's economies.
- The Talmud
- The Synagogue of Satan by Andrew Carrington Hitchcock

- Peace Not Apartheid by President Jimmy Carter
- No Cash? No Problem! How to get what you want in business and life, without using cash by Dave Wagenvoord and Ali Pervez www.nocashnoproblem.net 727-424-4991
- Bush Family Dynasty by Roger Stone
- A Choice Not an Echo by Phyllis Schlafly (on Barry Goldwater)
- Federal Reserve Update 2015 Global Tyranny Betrayal of the 99% Majority by Dr. A.H. Krieg
- Back to Basics on JFK by George D. Larson, Ph.D. History
- Crimes of the Educators by Samuel Blumenfeld & Alex Newman (Every schoolboard member, parent and teacher should be required to read this most important book).
- The Great Deformation: The Corruption of Capitalism in America by David Stockman
- Classified Woman – The Sibel Edmonds Story: A Memoir by Sibel Edmonds (American Whistleblower)

PUBLICATIONS

- *American Free Press* www.americanfreepress.net 1-888-699-NEWS (6397)
- *The Nationalist Times* www.anu.org Don Wassall, editor 702-851-5861
- *The Truth At Last* Dr. Ed Fields, P.O. Box 1211, Marietta, GA 30061 770-422-1180
- *The David Duke Report* Representative Dr. David Duke, Box 188, Mandeville, LA 70401, www.davidduke.com 985-626-7714
- ***Power*** (Personal Opinions of Ingrid Zundel) Ingrid Zundel, 3152 Parkway, 13-109, Pigeon forge, TN, 37863, 865-774-7756 www.zundelsite.org

OTHER

- North Carolina, Council of Conservative Citizens, A.J. Barker, 555 Centenary Road, Clemmons, North Carolina, 27012
- Email: cofcceditor@gmail.com
- Citadel Intl. Gun Shop & Indoor Shooting Range www.citadelinternational.net
- Email: citadelinternational@comcast.net
- Jonas E. Alexis – Columnist Hardcore Truth
- Kenneth O'Keefe – Anti War Activist

MOVIES

- ***Lawrence of Arabia*** 1962 Starring Peter O'Toole
- ***Tora! Tora! Tora!*** 1970
- ***Executive Action*** 1973 Starring Burt Lancaster. An absolute must see film. The start of a clear alternative to the bogus Warren Report.
- ***JFK*** 1991 Oliver Stone, director
- ***Mr. Death: The Rise and Fall of Fred A. Leuchter, Jr.***
- ***9/11: Explosive Evidence – Experts Speak Out*** Architects and Engineers for 911 Truth www.ae911truth.org

I have available for my personal use over 100 secretaries at a moment's notice. You may use them all **free of charge**. Just call the reference line at your local public library.

KNOWLEDGE *IS* POWER!

THE POWER OF ONE!!